USING LITERATURE

IN THE MIDDLE GRADES:

A THEMATIC APPROACH

Using Literature

In The Middle Grades:

A Thematic Approach

Joy F. Moss

Christopher-Gordon Publishers, Inc.
Norwood, MA

CREDITS

Christopher-Gordon Publishers, Inc.
480 Washington Street
Norwood, MA 02062

Printed in the United States of America

10 9 8 7 6 5 4 3 2 1   99 98 97 96 95 94

ISBN: 0-926842-38-2

DEDICATION

To Arthur, our children, and grandchildren, and

to teachers who bring literature into the lives of children.

ACKNOWLEDGMENTS

I would like to express my appreciation to the children, teachers, and librarians who have explored the world of literature with me over the years and whose questions inspired me to write this book.

I would like to extend special thanks to Hiram Howard for his encouragement and support from the very beginning and to Susan Folan for her responsive and thoughtful involvement in this project.

I also want to thank the reviewers, Rebecca Bowers Sipe, Dianne Monson, and Kathleen Dudden Andrasick, whose comments and suggestions helped me rethink and revise the manuscript, and Pat Ames for her excellent secretarial assistance and her interest in the unfolding text.

Finally, I want to express my gratitude to my husband, Arthur, for his wisdom, understanding, and love.

TABLE OF CONTENTS

DEVELOPING A
LITERATURE PROGRAM
WITH THEMATIC UNITS

This book is about literary experiences in middle-grade classrooms and the use of a thematic approach to build a literature program as an integral part of the curriculum. Each chapter features a literature unit which is organized around a topic, genre, literary theme, or narrative element and which integrates content with language arts. Over twenty years ago I developed an instructional model called a Focus Unit, to provide a framework for literary experiences for my own students (see pages 13-15). I have been using and building on this model ever since, and it has been adopted and adapted by many other teachers in a wide variety of classroom settings. Each Focus Unit, developed around a central focus, is designed to provide opportunities for students to read extensively as well as intensively; to experience stories and poems and to reflect on these personal experiences; to learn new ways to expand and deepen their reading experiences and their responses to literary texts; to explore authors' craft as a basis for studying content, reflecting on reader response, and creating their own literary texts; to make connections between diverse literary texts and between fiction and life; and to respond to literature in the social community of the classroom or in solitary reflection through written response (see Moss, 1984, 1990). The literature program as a whole is made up of a series of these Focus Units developed throughout the school year to meet student needs, to respond to their interests, and to realize teacher goals and objectives. The plan for the Focus Unit featured in each chapter can be modified for use by individual teachers with the whole class, small groups, or for independent study in grades 4 through 8.

This book is also about teachers as readers. My work with classroom teachers in inservice courses and collaborative studies in numerous and diverse school districts during the past twenty years has convinced me that the only way teachers can provide rich literary experiences for their students is to engage in rich literary experiences themselves. Teachers who are active readers and students of literature are prepared to expose their students to a wide variety of literature and to help them become active readers and students of literature, too.

Susan Lehr concludes her book *The Child's Developing Sense of Theme: Responses to Literature* (1991) with her own thoughts about teachers as readers and students of literature:

> I would like to suggest that, as we thoughtfully choose our books and questions and watch children leap into new territory, new ways of knowing and structuring their worlds, we be unafraid to grow with them... As we set out to stretch children in their responses to the literature that we share, let's make sure that we have signed on as well (p. 167).

I have included Lehr's concluding comment in this opening segment to highlight an underlying thesis for this book: Teachers who read literature and view it as important in their own lives are prepared to bring literature into the lives of those they teach; in the process of teaching literature they draw from this literary background, and along with their students, they become involved in experiencing literary texts and engaging in inquiry and discovery and intellectual stretching.

This book is for those who are or who plan to be teachers of middle-grade students. It is intended as an invitation to become involved in the literary experiences outlined in the Focus Units presented here and to use the bibliographies as suggestions for personal reading. It is an invitation for teachers to experiment with thematic units in their own classrooms, to create new literary experiences in collaboration with their own students, and to "grow with" their students by experiencing literature along with them.

Basic Assumptions

This literature program, built around a series of Focus Units, is based on a set of assumptions about literacy and literary experiences and learning in the classroom:

1. Students have opportunities to read, listen to, discuss, and write about a wide variety of literary selections.

2. As readers, students generate meaning by bringing their own knowledge and experience to written texts.

3. Students have opportunities to learn about themselves and others as they engage in transactions with texts.

4. Students have opportunities to learn about literary texts and how writers create meaning through texts.

5. Open-ended questions which stretch the mind and imagination, invite divergent thinking, and suggest ways to extend reading experiences and study texts and authors' craft are introduced by the teacher and used as teaching tools. Student-initiated questions are used as learning tools and the basis for constructing meaning during reading and writing.

6. Reading and writing are taught together as complementary processes of meaning-making. Reading and dialogue provide a context for student writing; writing enables students to discover, clarify, and extend their understanding of what they read.

7. Students have opportunities to share their individual responses to texts within the social context of the classroom community.

8. The literature program is initiated by the teacher, but the content and form of the literary/literacy learning experiences evolve out of a collaboration between the teacher and students who explore literature together.

9. Thematic teaching provides opportunities for cumulative learning and the discovery of connections between diverse literary texts.

10. Teachers are active readers who enjoy exploring literature and are able to draw from their own literary background to provide rich literary experiences for their students.

11. The ultimate goal of the literature program is to enable students to discover that reading and writing can be personally satisfying and enjoyable and that literature addresses their own needs and concerns and questions. If the literature program is successful, it will provide the basis for forming life-long reading and writing habits.

Exposure To Literature

In order for middle-grade students to experience and explore literature, they need exposure to the diverse genres found in traditional and modern literature and to a wide variety of teacher-selected and self-selected books. In her book *The Child's Developing Sense of Theme* (1991), Susan Lehr reviews the findings of two studies of the relationship between exposure to literature and reading effectiveness (Stanovich, 1986; Nagy and Anderson, 1985) which suggest that high exposure to literature gives readers access to new vocabulary, meaning structures, and ideas. Reporting on her own research in this area (Lehr, 1988), she comments:

> I found that the children with a higher exposure to literature were able to discuss themes for books at more abstract and generalized levels of meaning than were their less well-read counterparts (Lehr, 1991, p. 13).

Thematic units offer a context in which students are exposed to a wide variety of genres, authors, themes, and topics, and are given opportunities for in-depth literary study. Each Focus Unit described in this book includes a bibliography of thematically-related titles that serve as the literary core of the unit. Many of the books in this literary core or "Focus Unit Collection" are housed in the classroom throughout the Focus Unit experience. Others can be found in the school library or local public libraries. These books are discussed in whole-class meetings, in small dialogue groups, and in informal conversations. Students are invited to exchange ideas about their independent reading experiences and to recommend titles to their peers. The books in the classroom are displayed on a special shelf or table to call attention to the Focus Unit Collection and to allow easy access and frequent browsing. In this context of exposure, study, sharing, and availability, students have opportunities to read widely and deeply, to experience and reflect on literary selections as individuals, and to respond to literature in social contexts.

Reading Literature

This brings us to the second assumption underlying the literature program suggested in this book: Students bring their own knowledge and experience to a text to generate meaning. This reading strategy can be developed through cumulative experiences with literature.

For over twenty years, reading researchers have been examining the act of reading and how readers comprehend and respond to texts. Generalizations that have emerged from this reading research emphasize the active role of readers in generating meaning and contribute to our understanding of the way one reads literature.

One of the most important insights about the act of reading is the impact of prior knowledge on comprehension. According to Frank Smith, "The meaning that readers comprehend from text is always relative to what they already know and to what they want to know" (1988, p. 154). The prior knowledge a reader brings to a text is organized. Smith refers to this organized knowledge or cognitive structure as "the theory of the world in our heads" and explains that "...the system of knowledge in our heads is organized into an intricate and internally consistent working model of the world, built up through our interactions with the world and integrated into a coherent whole" (1988, p. 7). This theory of the world enables us to predict as we read. "Prediction means asking questions, and comprehension means being able to get some of the questions answered... There is a *flow* to comprehension, with new questions constantly being generated from the answers that are sought" (Smith, 1988, p. 19). Comprehension depends on the nature of the questions a reader generates. In the context of the Focus Unit, students are given opportunities to expand and change their "theory of the world" and to develop questioning strategies to guide the reading/thinking process as they encounter literary texts.

Louise Rosenblatt's transactional theory of reading has served as a beacon for researchers and educators who have explored, in the years since her early work (1983 [1938]), various aspects of readers' response to literature.

> Reading is a transaction, a two-way process, involving a reader and a text at a particular time under particular circumstances. I use John Dewey's term, transaction, to emphasize the contribution of both reader and text. The words in their particular pattern stir up elements of memory, activate areas of consciousness. The reader, bringing past experience of language and of the world to the task, sets up tentative notions of a subject, of some framework into which to fit the ideas as the words unfurl (Rosenblatt, 1982, p. 7).

Rosenblatt distinguishes between reading for information and reading for experience. She uses the term "efferent" to refer to the stance or "mental set" of the reader who "focusses on accumulating what is to be carried away at the end of the reading" (1982, p. 7). If the reader chooses an "aesthetic" stance, "his attention will shift inward, will center on what is being created *during* the actual reading" (p. 7). Aesthetic readers enter into the story and become a part of it. It is a personal and emotional experience during which the reader creates his/her own story out of personal memories, literary experiences, linguistic background, and feelings, beliefs, and expectations.

Judith Langer also distinguishes between reading literature and reading to gain information (1992):

> A literary orientation is one of exploration — where uncertainty is a normal part of response and newfound understandings provoke still other possibilities. Readers contemplate feelings, intentions, and implications, using their knowledge of human possibility to go beyond the meanings imparted in the text and fill out their understandings. In this way, readers explore possibilities on two levels: in terms of their momentary understandings, and in terms of their changing sense of the unfolding whole.
>
> In contrast, when the purpose of reading is primarily to gain information (as is generally the case when reading expository prose, for example), readers' orientation can be characterized as *maintaining a point of reference* (Langer, 1992, p. 37).

In the context of the Focus Unit, students record their experiences as aesthetic readers in literary journals and share these experiences in dialogue or conversation with others. As individual readers verbalize their feelings and ideas about a literary text in a group setting, students discover that a single text stimulates diverse responses and that the experiences of other readers may open up new meanings for them.

The Focus Unit experience provides opportunities for the wide reading necessary to build a background of prior knowledge. The more one reads, the more knowledge about language, literature, and the human experience one has to bring to transactions with new texts. The Focus Unit is designed as a cumulative experience in which students read a series of related texts and search for connections between them. "Learning and understanding are processes of making connections. We are able to understand what we read only because of the connections we make between the current book and our past experiences, which include books we have read or written" (Harste, Short, and Burke, 1988, p. 358). In the context of the Focus Unit, reading one text serves as a preparation for reading subsequent texts; students are invited to discover that their own literary histories play a central role in each new literary experience, including rereading books read in the past.

Learning About Oneself and Others

Literature is about life. "By its very organizing properties literature has the power to shape and give coherence to human experience" (Huck, Helper, Hickman, 1993, p. 12). Literary transactions enable readers to enter into the lives of others, to live through their experiences, to see the world through their eyes. In the process, readers have opportunities to gain insights about human experience and to learn about feelings and motivation and relationships.

Literary transactions can also trigger associations from readers' own experiences and inner lives. Reflecting on aspects of their own lives, readers can learn about themselves. Louise Rosenblatt remarks that

> For years I have extolled the potentialities of literature for aiding us to understand ourselves and others, for widening our horizons to include temperaments and cultures different from our own, for helping us to clarify our conflicts in values, for illuminating our world... Precisely because every aesthetic reading of a text is a unique creation, woven out of the inner life and thought of the reader, the literary work of art can be a rich source of insight and truth (Rosenblatt, 1982, p. 21).

Learning About Literature

The Focus Units described in the following chapters are designed to highlight specific literary genres, elements, devices, and structures of written texts to help students discover the special knowledge authors use to create meaning and to help them learn the language used in the study of literature.[1] Knowledge of literary genre and elements and authors' craft can enrich literary experiences and provide a basis for studying text content and how writers use literary techniques to manipulate reader response.

Thematic units can be incorporated into a cumulative sequence to form a literature program that, as a whole, provides opportunities for students to:

1. Experience a wide variety of literary material over the course of the school year;

2. Learn about basic structures or forms of oral and written discourse: narration, description, exposition, and argumentation;

3. Explore literary genres: traditional literature; modern fantasy; contemporary realistic fiction; historical realism; biography; poetry; and informational books;

4. Discover narrative elements and the relationships between these elements: setting, character, conflict or problem, plot (sequence of events or attempts to solve problems, solutions, or resolution), theme or message, viewpoint, style, and tone.

By building up this background of literary knowledge, students are empowered as readers and writers. Through the study of literature they learn about the tools authors use to create meaning so that they, in turn, can use these tools to generate meaning as they read and in their own writing. In an article entitled, "Reading Like a Writer" (1984), Frank Smith explains that one learns to write by reading like a writer, that the knowledge writers require resides in texts, so reading like a writer helps the student build a background of writer's knowledge (Smith, pp. 52-53). Readers use their knowledge of writers' craft to generate meaning and to respond to literary texts. The quality of the reading experience depends, in part, on the literary knowledge the reader is able to bring to the process of reading literary texts.

Questions

Questions shape the reading experience and are generated in the process of reading. According to Frank Smith, comprehension of a text is related to what a reader knows and wants to know; comprehension means asking questions and getting answers (Smith, 1988, p. 154). Judith Langer notes: "Teachers who support literary understanding assume that after completing a piece, readers come away with questions as well as understandings, and that responding to literature *involves* the raising of questions. Thus, teachers continually invite students' questions, in many contexts" (Langer, 1992, p. 44). Reader-generated questions serve as catalysts for examining the ambiguity and complexity inherent in a given literary text and for exploring the multiple perspectives, interpretations, and possibilities offered by the text.

Teacher-initiated questions are used to stimulate higher-level transactions and written and oral responses to literature. Teachers use questions as teaching tools: to suggest ways for students to think about their own experiences as readers; to call attention to literary elements, genres, and authors' craft; to invite students to search for connections between diverse texts and between literary texts and life. Open-ended questions stimulate divergent, creative, hypothetical thinking; exploration of possibilities as a text unfolds; multiple interpretations of single texts; and synthesis of multiple texts. Teacher-initiated questions are invitations to talk and write about literature: to share personal responses to reading experiences, to analyze literary texts, to view a text from different perspectives, and to develop and defend interpretive and evaluative statements.

The ultimate goal of teacher-initiated questions is to enable students to initiate their own questions. Student-initiated questions are used as learning tools to guide their own literary transactions and explorations. In the process of learning about literature and ways to think about literary texts, students are encouraged to formulate questions to enrich the nature of their literary experience and response. In the context of the Focus Unit experience, students collaborate with the teacher and peers to generate questions used to enhance learning. In the process, they learn to generate their own questions in order to gain independence as thinkers and learners.

Reading-Writing Connections

The literature program evolves in a classroom in which reading and writing are viewed as complementary processes of meaning construction and are combined in the curriculum to enable students to use reading and writing to achieve deeper understandings through reflection and critical thinking. Literature has the potential for bringing out what is in the minds of readers. As they respond to a literary selection in a group discussion or in writing, students can verbalize their memories and associations, and their feelings, thoughts, and ideas that have been triggered by listening to or reading that selection. As they move from personal response to critical response, they use discussion or writing to reflect on their own ideas and those expressed by the author or by classmates. Students reread segments of the literary text, or what they have written in response to it, to consider different perspectives and interpretations and to answer questions they have initiated to generate meanings.

Rereading and rewriting that have been generated by reflection and new questions lead to rethinking possible meanings. It is during this rethinking stage of the meaning-making process that students often discover new perspectives or gain new insights about themselves, about others, and about literary texts and authors' craft. Eventually, through rereading and rewriting and ongoing interchanges with peers and the teacher, students can begin to consider the text in terms of the larger context of contemporary social issues or historical events or significant truths about the human experience.

Several studies have focussed on the use of journal writing as a vehicle for exploring reader response to literature (Tashlik, 1987; Crowhurst and Kooy, 1986; Atwell, 1987; Oberlin and Shugarman, 1989). Joanne Golden and Elaine Handloff analyzed the journal writing of students in a fifth grade class who were encouraged to record their own unique reactions to the books they read in an independent reading program: "to express their feelings and opinions, to look for ties to their own lives, and to think about how the author's style of writing affected their responses to the book. They were also encouraged to use examples from the literature to illustrate a point or support an opinion" (Golden, 1993, p. 177-178). Golden and Handloff concluded from their findings that "the journal provided a valuable means of engaging children in literary response" (p. 183) and enabling teachers to observe and learn about reader response during and after literary transactions.

In the context of the Focus Unit experience, literary journals are used as vehicles for reader response, for integrating reading and writing, and for teachers to learn about their students as readers and writers. In addition to journal writing, students are invited to write stories and poems, description, exposition, and argumentation and to experiment with literary language and different genres to extend their literary experiences and opportunities for thoughtful and creative response.

Sharing Literary Experiences

The study of literature develops in a social context, in a "community of readers" (Hepler and Hickman, 1982), in which children share their reading experiences with others and talk about their thoughts, feelings, associations, and questions in a supportive environment. Time for whole class discussions, small-group dialogues, teacher-student conferences, and informal peer interactions is built into the schedule. In informal interactions students exchange personal responses, explore meanings together, and recommend books to each other. Small groups may be formed by students who want to discuss a particular book or author or genre they have selected to read. These small groups are not unlike the adult book clubs that have emerged across the country in recent years, established by groups of friends interested in sharing reading experiences on an informal basis. Other small groups are formed to discuss books selected from the Focus Unit Collection. Shared reading experiences or sessions with the whole class are scheduled to allow a cumulative dialogue about the series of related texts selected for the Focus Unit. The content of some of these discussions is determined by the students. Other discussions are guided by the teacher who initiates questions designed to invite personal responses to literary texts and to focus on literary elements, genres, and authors' craft and connections between diverse selections in the series and between the literary selections and the lives of the students.

In this social context, in which students exchange personal responses, interpretations, and insights about literary texts, they have an opportunity to see that readers respond to texts in different ways. Students are invited "to see these differences as indications of the uniqueness of each reader and as opportunities to learn something about others" (Probst, 1992, p. 66). Examples of similarities and differences in personal responses to texts can be used as the focus of class discussion. These discussions are designed to reinforce the notion that meaning is generated by the reader transacting with a text and "may lead students to see the text, themselves, and one another more clearly" (Probst, p. 67).

Time is also set aside to allow students to record responses to reading experiences in personal literature journals. These journals may take the form of dialogue-journals in which the teacher responds to student entries in the journal and invites the student to engage in a written interchange (see Staton 1980, 1989; Bode, 1989; Atwell, 1987). Thus, an ongoing written conversation about books, thoughts, and feelings is established and the connections between reading and writing are reinforced. Some students may choose to carry on a written dialogue in a journal with a peer-partner. This form of the journal is one option for using journals as part of the social context of the literature program. Another possibility is to use the literary journal as a springboard for oral dialogue: Students are invited to read aloud a particular segment from their journal (a question, discovery, insight, connection, interpretation, etc.) to generate discussion in a small dialogue group or a large-group meeting. This option highlights the connections between oral and written language, and it can be especially helpful for students who are reluctant to make spontaneous contributions to group discussions.

Teacher-Student Collaboration

The Focus Unit experience evolves out of a collaborative interaction between students and the teacher. They experience and explore literature together in shared reading experiences that involve the in-depth study of single texts and comparative analysis of multiple texts in a cumulative dialogue in which shared texts are discussed in relation to the literature selected by individual students for independent reading. The teacher introduces questions during the shared reading experience to help students learn ways to think about literature, to explore possibilities, and to engage in authentic discussions about literature. The goal is to help students become independent thinkers who formulate their own questions to guide their response to literature and who develop their own unique understandings and interpretations and participate in collaborative meaning-making with their teacher and peers. Small dialogue groups are established to provide opportunities for students to initiate their own literary discussions with limited input from the teacher who joins each group for brief visits. Thus, students learn to work together to explore literature and build meanings and understandings.

Students are given opportunities to work with the teacher and their peers to plan activities and projects, to select material for group and independent study, and to formulate questions to guide this literary study. Within the literature program, assigned or guided reading and writing experiences are balanced with free choice in reading and writing. Students are encouraged to pursue their own interests as readers and writers. In addition, they are introduced to diverse authors, topics, and genres to expand their experience as readers, and they are invited to experiment with diverse literary forms and techniques and to use literature as a rich context and springboard for writing to expand their experience as writers.

Thematic Teaching: Developing Focus Units

Each chapter in this book describes a plan for a Focus Unit in which literary experiences are organized around a topic or literary theme or genre or narrative element. These thematic units are designed to provide opportunities for students to engage in aesthetic reading and to verbalize, in personal journals or dialogue, their responses to the text. The units also feature interactions between readers and texts involving interpretation and a study of what authors do to create literary texts. Each unit is a cumulative experience in which students read, listen, write, and talk to generate meaning.

In the context of each Focus Unit, teachers and students explore a series of related literary texts. This cumulative learning experience has both depth and breadth: they engage in in-depth analyses of single texts and search for connections among multiple texts representing a variety of genres, authors, styles, and viewpoints and offering many possibilities for interpretation and study. The cumulative study of thematically related literary texts through reading, dialogue, and writing enables students to build their literary background, to deepen their understanding of a particular theme, topic, or genre; to discover connections between literature and life; and to develop insights about human experience.

The literature used as the core of some of these Focus Units was selected in response to student concerns and interests. For example, the unit featuring friendship stories (Chapter 2) was developed in response to student preoccupation with peer relationships. The literature collection for this unit includes titles identified by the teacher as well as titles suggested by students. The literature collections developed for the other units also represent teacher and student input. The focus for the unit in Chapter 5 was selected because of the general popularity of family stories among many generations of young readers. The unit, "On Their Own," described in Chapter 8, was also created in response to evidence of the general popularity of "survival tales" among middle-grade readers. Both collections include familiar titles as well as new ones. Each unit is designed to introduce students to books they might not discover on their own and to set the stage for a comparative analysis of a wide variety of stories with a common theme.

The literature that is the core of other units presented in this book was selected in response to curricular considerations and to achieve specific instructional goals. For example, the unit described in Chapter 7 was initially conceptualized as a plan to enrich a social studies unit about World War II with historical fiction. As the plan evolved, the unit took the form of an integrated social-studies-literature program in which fiction and non-fiction were used as complementary sources for learning about historical events and the human lives shaped by those events. At the same time, this unit was designed to help students learn about historical fiction as a literary genre.

The unit "Between Two Worlds," in Chapter 9, was developed as part of a broader curricular goal to provide students with opportunities to form a multicultural perspective. In addition, this unit represents a response to the special concerns of students who are, themselves, "between two worlds."

The selection of the focus of and the literary material for any given unit is determined by a number of factors, such as student interests and concerns, curricular considerations, instructional goals, current issues, and the developmental and social needs and experiential level of a particular group of students. Each chapter in this book begins with the rationale for the focus of a given unit; together, these chapters suggest a few of the many possibilities for creating thematic literature units. Since each teacher is unique and works with very different groups of individual students each year, only he or she can decide on the nature and sequence of literature units to develop with a particular group in a given school year.

Focus Units are built around age-appropriate, meaningful, and relevant reading materials to foster personal involvement and the discovery of connections between literature and life. Each unit is planned to provide literary experiences that will enable students to develop and practice strategies for reading literature and engaging in literary analysis to enrich the meaning-making process and the nature of reader response. Questions are used as a valuable tool to guide the study of literature and to stimulate critical and creative thinking. Teacher-initiated questions are used to introduce literary concepts and forms and to develop an awareness and appreciation of authors' craft as well as to suggest ways to interact with texts to generate meaning. The goal is for students to generate their own questions to guide their transactions with literary texts and to stimulate richer reading-thinking experiences. To this end, students are encouraged to formulate their own questions. For example, entries in their personal journals can be introduced with a question. Key ideas and issues that emerge during group discussions of literary selections can be turned into questions to guide subsequent interactions with texts. Most of the lists of questions included in each chapter represent a combination of teacher and student input.

Most of the units are introduced in a whole-group session in which students are invited to share personal knowledge and thoughts about the topic. In subsequent sessions the teacher reads aloud at least one of the books in the collection of literature selected for the unit. In this way, the whole class has at least one shared reading experience to complement and enrich their individualized reading experiences. The teacher uses this shared experience to explore literature with students, to demonstrate ways to experience and study literary texts, and to set the stage for individualized literary experiences, for dialogue in small literary study groups or in informal conversations, for written responses in personal journals, and to extend reading experiences into other forms of creative expression.

The Focus Units in this book are structured around literary experiences that address issues of importance to students and are designed to stretch their minds and imaginations. Students are challenged to reach beyond the boundaries of their own lives to think about ideas, issues, and events that affect the larger community.

Teachers and Students

The last two assumptions on which the literature program is based relate to teachers and students as readers and students of literature. Teachers who are active readers and enjoy exploring literature are prepared to help their students discover the joys of reading literature and develop life-long reading and writing habits.

The Focus Units in this book are *not* intended to serve as recipes for teaching literature. Rather, they are intended as invitations to those who plan to be or who are teachers to become students of literature and to think about possibilities for creating literature programs in their own classrooms.

I hope that the explorations of specific literary selections and the connections between diverse literary texts featured in each chapter will spark new ideas for sharing familiar texts and will generate interest in unfamiliar titles. I hope that readers of this book will be inspired to explore literature in their own lives and to bring literature into the lives of their students and help them develop life-long habits of reading, writing, thinking, and talking about literature. This is the ultimate goal of the literature program.

To reach this goal, students need opportunities to discover that reading and writing can be personally satisfying and enjoyable and that literature addresses their own needs, concerns, and questions. Learning to read is an ongoing, cumulative process that begins in early childhood and continues through adulthood. Readers whose literary histories are filled with memorable books that trigger personal and meaningful response are often the ones who continue to engage in literary experiences throughout their lives. The Focus Units described in this book are presented as invitations to teachers and students to engage in aesthetic reading experiences, to explore literary content and craft, to discover connections between diverse literary selections and between literature and life, and to enjoy these encounters with literature as shared experiences.

THE FOCUS UNIT EXPERIENCE:
An Overview of Basic Components

I.   SELECTING THE UNIFYING THEME OR FOCUS

The focus of each unit is selected in response to student concerns and interests, curricular considerations, instructional goals, current issues, and the learning needs and experience of the students who will be involved in the Focus Unit experience.

II.   STUDYING LITERATURE AS A CUMULATIVE EXPERIENCE

Students explore a series of thematically related texts and search for connections between them as they engage in reading, listening, dialogue, and writing. Reading one text serves as preparation for reading subsequent texts; readers draw from their literary histories to generate meaning in each new literary experience. The Focus Unit experience is a cumulative one that involves in-depth analyses of single texts and comparative analyses of multiple texts representing a wide variety of themes and topics and literary elements and genres. This cumulative experience serves as a context in which students can expand their literary knowledge base and develop the habit of reading each new text in light of previous ones.

III.   THE FOCUS UNIT COLLECTION

The literary core of the unit or the "Focus Unit Collection" includes a wide variety of related texts selected by the teacher in conjunction with his/her students. This Collection can be housed in the classroom throughout the Focus Unit experience to allow easy access and frequent browsing. The Collections used in the Focus Units described in this book provide exposure to traditional literature, modern fantasy, contemporary and historical realism, poetry, biography, and informational books.

IV.   THE SHARED READING EXPERIENCE

Each Focus Unit includes a series of whole-class sessions in which the teacher reads aloud one or more books in the Collection and invites students to engage in a dialogue about the shared text. This *shared reading experience* serves as preparation for individual, self-selected reading experiences, written responses in literary journals, and student-lead dialogue groups. In the cumulative dialogue, students exchange personal responses to the shared text and collaborate with the teacher to analyze the unfolding text and identify connections with other literary texts or life experiences. As they explore shared texts, students are encouraged to formulate and defend opinions, viewpoints, and interpretations. The teacher introduces questions to teach and guide literary analysis; to develop an awareness and appreciation of authors' craft; to encourage reflection about reader response and the significance of literary connections; and to stimulate critical and creative thinking.

V.   INDEPENDENT READING

Students are expected to select from the Focus Unit Collection one or more books to read independently. The number of self-selected texts students are required to read is determined by the teacher. Some Focus Unit Collections are organized into two or more categories, and students may be asked to select one title from each category.

VI.   LITERARY JOURNALS

Students record their responses to the shared text as it is read aloud in the whole-class sessions and to self-selected texts as they read these independently. The entries in these journals include personal feelings and opinions; understandings, insights, interpretations, and questions; predictions and revisions of assumptions; connections to other literary texts and between literature and life; and responses to teacher- and student-initiated questions.

Because students respond to a text during and after reading or listening to it, the literary journal becomes a "running record" of reader response and meaning-making and serves as a vehicle for teachers to learn about their students as readers and writers.

The literary journal takes the form of a dialogue-journal when the teacher responds to student entries and invites the student to enter into a written conversation.

VII.   DIALOGUE GROUPS

Small dialogue groups are formed by students who select from the Focus Unit Collection the same title, books by a single author, or books with a common theme. Members of each group share and discuss their independent reading choices in terms of narrative elements and genre, authors' craft, and literary connections. They record insights and discoveries and formulate questions to challenge subsequent readers of these books. Entries in literary journals can be used to initiate dialogue in these small student-centered groups. The dialogue serves as a context for connecting self-selected texts read independently and the shared text(s) read to the whole class and for extending the cumulative dialogue begun in the shared reading experience.

VIII.   QUESTIONS

Teacher-initiated questions are used as *teaching tools* to demonstrate ways to interact with literary texts, to explore content through narrative analysis, to examine authors' craft, and to identify the connections between diverse texts and between literature and life. Teacher-initiated questions are used to stimulate critical and creative thinking as students respond to literary texts in group dialogue and in writing. The ultimate goal of teacher-initiated questions is for students to generate their own questions as they engage in reading and writing and responding to literary texts.

Student-initiated questions are used as *learning tools* to guide their own literary transactions and explorations. Throughout the Focus Unit experience, students are encouraged to formulate their own questions to enrich the nature of their experiences with literature and to enhance the quality of their oral and written responses to these experiences.

IX. READING-WRITING CONNECTIONS

In addition to their "running records" of reader response in the Literary Journals, students engage in a variety of other writing projects that provide them with opportunities to use different forms of discourse (narration, description, exposition, and argumentation) to extend literary experiences; to experiment with different literary genres (traditional literature, modern fantasy, contemporary or historical realism, biography, poetry, or informational books); and to use their growing knowledge of narrative elements and writers' craft to create literary texts. Questions formulated by teachers and students can be used as springboards for writing about literature or about their own lives. Some writing projects are designed to encourage students to use reading as a starting point for reflecting on their own feelings and experiences, to learn about themselves and about others. Other writing experiences involve the exploration of interrelations between selected fiction and non-fiction, between authors and their works, and between authors' craft and reader response. Most Focus Unit plans include writing projects that invite students to draw from the literary experiences of a given unit to create original narratives or poems.

X. EXTENDING LITERARY EXPERIENCES: OTHER PROJECTS

Throughout the Focus Unit experience, the exploration of literary texts suggests opportunities and possibilities for drama, role play, dance, storytelling, and art activities. Students engage in library and community research to study the background of an historical novel or the social and political issues addressed in a contemporary novel; to learn about authors and illustrators; and to tap community resources to explore areas of interest triggered by literary experiences.

XI. SYNTHESIS

In the course of the Focus Unit experience, students move from personal transactions with literary texts to individual and shared responses to and analysis of single texts to comparative analysis of multiple texts. By the end of this cumulative experience, they are ready to work toward a synthesis of ideas derived from their study of the literary texts selected for this Focus Unit. One or more concluding sessions are scheduled for the whole class to participate in an overview of what they have learned from their literary explorations: discoveries, insights and understandings, concepts, connections, and knowledge. This overview sets the stage for students to move beyond single texts in order to consider the Focus Unit Collection as a whole and to formulate larger ideas and insights about literature and life.

Some teachers may prefer to have their students work independently on the analysis-to-synthesis process as a written assignment *prior* to the whole-class dialogue in the concluding sessions. This would allow students to do their own thinking and to bring a written record of their ideas to the class discussion. This would also provide teachers with a record of student thinking and learning for purposes of individual assessment.

References

Atwell, Nancie. (1987). *In the Middle: Writing, Reading, and Learning With Adolescents.* Portsmouth, NH: Boynton/Cook.

Bode, Barbara. (1987). "Dialogue Journal Writing." *The Reading Teacher* (42), 568-571.

Crowhurst, M. and M. Kooy. (1986). "The Use of Response Journals in Teaching the Novel." *Reading-Canada-Lecture, 3,* 256-266.

Golden, Joanne, and Elaine Handloff. (1993). "Responding to Literature Through Journal Writing." In *Journeying,* edited by Kathleen Holland et al. Portsmouth, NH: Heinemann.

Harste, Jerome, Kathy Short and Carolyn Burke. (1988). *Creating Classrooms for Authors: The Reading-Writing Connection.* Portsmouth, NH: Heinemann.

Hepler, Susan, and Janet Hickman. (1982). " 'The Book Was Okay. I Love You' —Social Aspects of Response to Literature." *Theory into Practice* 21, 278-283.

Holland, Kathleen, Rachael Hungerford, and Shirley Ernst, editors. (1993). *Journeying: Children Responding to Literature.* Portsmouth, NH: Heinemann.

Huck, Charlotte, Susan Hepler, and Janet Hickman. (1993). *Children's Literature in the Elementary School* (5th edition). Fort Worth, Tx: Harcourt Brace Jovanovich.

Langer, Judith, editor. (1992). *Literature Instruction: A Focus on Student Response.* Urbana, IL: NCTE.

Lehr, Susan. (1991). *The Child's Developing Sense of Theme: Responses to Literature.* NY: Teachers College Press.

Lehr, Susan. (1988). "Classroom Research Explores the Child's Construction of Meaning." *Reading Research Quarterly, 23,* 337-357.

Moss, Joy F.(1990). *Focus on Literature: A Context for Literacy Learning.* Katonah, NY: Richard C. Owen, Publishers.

Moss, Joy F. (1984). *Focus Units in Literature: A Handbook for Elementary School Teachers.* Urbana, IL: NCTE.

Nagy, W. and R. Anderson. (1984). "How Many Words Are There In Printed School English?" *Reading Research Quarterly, 19,* 304-330.

Oberlin, Kelly, and Sherrie Shugarman. (1989). "Implementing the Reading Workshop with Middle Grade LD Students." *Journal of Reading, 32,* 682-687.

Probst, Robert. (1992). "Five Kinds of Literary Knowing." In *Literature Instruction,* edited by Judith Langer. Urbana, IL: NCTE.

Rosenblatt, Louise. (1938, 1983). *Literature as Exploration.* 4th edition. NY: MLA.

Rosenblatt, Louise. (1982). "The Literary Transaction: Evocation and Response." *Theory into Practice, 21(4),* Autumn, OSU College of Education, Columbus, Ohio [reprinted in *Journeying: Children Responding to Literature* edited by Kathleen Holland, et al., Heinemann, 1993, pp. 6-23].

Rosenblatt, Louise. (1978). *The Reader, The Text, and The Poem.* Carbondale, IL: Southern Illinois University Press.

Smith, Frank. (1984). "Reading Like a Writer," in *Composing and Comprehending,* Julie Jensen, ed. Eric. NCRE.

Smith, Frank. (1988). *Understanding Reading: A Psycholinguistic Analysis of Reading and Learning to Read.* 4th edition. Hillsdale, NJ: Lawrence Erlbaum Associates.

Stanovich, K. (1986). "Matthew Effects in Reading: Some Consequences in the Acquisition of Literacy." *Reading Research Quarterly*, 21, 360-406.

Staton, Jana. (1989). "An Introduction to Dialogue Journal Communication." In *Dialogue Journal Communication*, edited by Staton et al. Norwood, NJ: Ablex.

Staton, Jana. (1980). "Writing and Counseling: Using a Dialogue Journal." *Language Arts*. Vol. 75, no. 5, May, 514-518.

Tashlik, Phyllis. (1987). "I Hear Voices: The Text, the Journal and Me." In *The Journal Book*, edited by Toby Fulwiler. Portsmouth, NH: Boynton/Cook.

Foot Note:

1. Rebecca Lukens' *A Critical Handbook of Children's Literature*, (1990), Glenview, IL: Scott Foresman, offers an excellent overview of literary genres and elements.

2

FRIENDSHIP STORIES

"The only way to have a friend is to be one."
— Ralph Waldo Emerson

Friendship is a vital component of childhood, adolescence, and adulthood. The search for friendship is likely to be a recurring theme in one's life. The desire to make contact with others is part of the human experience. Although friendships are not always easy to establish and sustain, they have the potential to enrich our lives and teach us to live in a social world. The bond of friendship serves as a context for learning to identify with others and to see the world through their eyes, and also for self-exploration and personal growth. A friendship characterized by mutual respect and acceptance allows one to engage in authentic interaction with another individual.

For the young child, friends are generally the first link with the world outside the immediate or extended family. By the middle grades, friendship has become a key preoccupation. The search for friendship is often intertwined with the search for identity and social status.

The meaning of friendship is explored in many novels written for middle grade readers. The popularity of these novels reflects the middle graders' special interest in the problems of establishing and sustaining friendships. As one seventh grader commented, "I always look for books about kids my age. I like to see how they work things out with other kids — like with a best friend or getting in with the right group — the popular kids."

The Friendship Focus Unit

Novels that portray friendship can be used as the core of a Focus Unit that invites middle graders to engage in literary analysis and, in the process, to explore the meaning of friendship, factors that foster friendship and those that can threaten or destroy a relationship. On a personal level, students are encouraged to respond subjectively to the stories, to bring their own emotional and social histories to the texts, and to generate new understandings about themselves as well as others. After their personal transaction with each literary text, students reflect on their personal experiences within the story world and then step outside the story to focus on literary elements and authors' craft. In the course of this Focus Unit experience, students examine settings, characters, conflicts, and themes, and identify examples of literary devices, such as foreshadowing, that have been used by the authors of these friendship novels. This study of literary craft serves as a context for exploring content and searching for connections between the related texts selected for this Focus Unit.

Shared Reading Experiences

A central feature of the Focus Unit is the series of shared reading experiences, in which the teacher reads aloud one of the novels selected for this unit and invites the students to enter into a dialogue. This is a cumulative dialogue that serves as a social context for exchanging personal responses to the shared text and for a collaborative literary analysis of this text and its connections to related texts selected for this unit. As teachers and students respond to the unfolding text, key questions and understandings are recorded on a chart to set the stage for three additional activities that are central to the Focus Unit experience: *independent reading,* writing in *literary journals,* and student-initiated discussion in small *dialogue groups.*

Independent Reading

A collection of "friendship novels" is placed on display in the classroom, and the students are invited to select one or more of these novels for independent reading. The number of books required by the teacher will depend on the grade level, time factors, and the reading ability of individual students. The collection is located near a bulletin board so that student-generated "best seller" or "recommended" lists can be posted alongside written responses and art work inspired by the books in the collection. Students are encouraged to add to the collection as they discover additional novels with the friendship theme.

Literary Journals

Students are given notebooks for recording their responses to the novel being read aloud in the shared reading sessions and those selected for independent reading. The entries in these literary journals include personal responses, understandings, or questions as well as responses to teacher-initiated questions or those generated in the small dialogue groups.

Students are encouraged to record their responses *in the process of interacting* with a text as well as after they have finished reading the story. Whether as independent readers or as listeners in the group sessions, they are invited to respond to the story as it unfolds, to jot down questions, comments, feelings, predictions, connections to other books or personal experiences, or revisions of initial assumptions about a particular character or the nature of the story as a whole.

Judith Langer, Professor of Education at the State University of New York at Albany, uses the term "envisionment" (Langer, 1990, p. 812) in her discussion of a process approach to reading that focusses on student thinking in reading. According to Langer, "envisionment" refers to "the understanding a reader has about a text — what the reader understands at a particular point in time, the questions she has, as well as hunches about how the piece will unfold. Envisionments develop as the reading progresses. Some information is no longer important, some is added, and some is changed. What readers come away with at the end of the reading, I call the final envisionment. This includes what they understand, what they don't, and the questions they still have. The final envisionment is also subject to change with time, as a result of conversations with others, the reading of other works, or pondering and reflection" (p. 812).

In this view, students engage in meaning-making through an envisionment-building process as the story unfolds and after it comes to an end. The literary journal provides a vehicle for recording points in the process of building an understanding of a text during and after reading or listening to it. It can serve as a "running record" of reader response and calls attention to the notion of reading as a fluid process of meaning-making.

Small Dialogue Groups

When two or more students select the same book for independent reading, they are invited to discuss it in a small dialogue group. In order to facilitate the formation of these informal groupings, students record their independent reading choices on a list near the collection display. Multiple paper-back copies of the most popular titles are included in the collection. Some groups are formed by students reading books by the same author. The dialogue in these small groups is initiated by the students, although each group is expected to formulate questions about the particular book or books they are discussing as well as general questions which could apply to most of the friendship novels. The specific questions are recorded on a 5 x 8 index card and placed inside the book to challenge subsequent readers. The general questions are recorded for use in the shared reading sessions. In the process, students learn the art of asking significant questions, an art which is central to the learning process.

The First Shared Reading Session

The Focus Unit built around the theme of friendship begins with the students' ideas and experience. They are asked to respond to the question:

What does the word "friendship" mean to you?

As students and teacher share their thoughts, feelings, and personal experiences, the teacher records recurring words or phrases that suggest key issues about building and sustaining friendships. The key issues embedded in this general discussion about the meaning of friendship are formulated into a series of statements which are, in turn, transformed into questions. The following questions, generated by this discussion, provide a framework for a study of the nature of friendship in the novels selected for this unit:

1. What is the meaning of friendship?
2. What holds a friendship together?
3. What kinds of problems can pull friends apart?
4. What are the benefits of friendship?
5. What is most important in being a friend?

After students and their teacher discuss friendship in their own lives and generate relevant questions to guide their study of friendship novels, students are introduced to the friendship novel collection and the basic expectations for independent reading, writing in literary journals, and forming small dialogue groups. The teacher briefly describes a number of books in the collection to assist the selection process that begins at the end of this initial session. Students are invited to talk about novels they have already read. Often, more students decide to read a particular book than there are copies in the collection. In this case, they may decide to select another one or arrange to share the available copy (or copies), or locate that title in the school library or public library. Near the collection is a list of all the titles so that each student can record his/her name in the space next to the title selected. When the selection process is completed, the list is consulted so that the dialogue groups can be formed. Students who select a title or author not chosen by others are guided by the teacher to join a group whose book is similar in theme, plot, characters, setting, or author. Finally, after a schedule is set up to allow time for independent reading and for meeting in the dialogue groups, students are given the notebooks to be used as literary journals.

The Second Shared Reading Session

In this session, the teacher introduces the novel selected from the friendship-novel collection to be read aloud. The choice of a novel to share with the whole group depends on the nature of the group in question: their experiential and literary background, their interests and needs. In the course of the school year, the teacher can select novels that feature both male and female protagonists as well as characters who reflect the ethnic and racial diversity of the classroom. Read-aloud novels are selected for their literary merit as well as their potential for providing enjoyment and for stretching the minds and imaginations and touching the hearts of middle-grade students. Older novels which have been given enthusiastic reviews by middle-grade readers over the years are also considered in the process of selecting books to share with the whole class as part of the Focus Unit experience. The novel selected as the shared text to introduce the Focus Unit described in this chapter is Katherine Paterson's *Bridge to Terabithia* (1977),[1] a story about an isolated rural community where Jess Aarons and a newcomer, Leslie Burke, build a special friendship and a secret kingdom in the woods which they name Terabithia. It is here that Jess, guided by Leslie, discovers worlds of imagination, learning, and language, and embarks on a journey of self-discovery and maturation.

Before reading aloud the first chapters of the novel, the teacher asks the class to examine the covers of the original hardcover edition of the book and subsequent paperback editions. Several students notice that the hardcover and 1978 paperback feature characters who could be either male or female, while the 1987 paperback shows two characters who are clearly identified as male and female and look older. Others observe that the 1978 paperback cover states that this is "The story of a special friendship between a boy and girl." They also note that the first paperback edition (1978) shows "two kids back in the woods who look older than the two kids in front" and that the cover of the 1987 paperback "just has two kids — about 13 or 14 years old. The boy is staring into space but he's probably listening to the girl reading the book opened in front of her on the rock." They attempt to explain these differences and use the information on the covers to make predictions about the story. For example, one student comments: "It's probably going to be a regular friendship between a boy and a girl — not a romantic boyfriend-girlfriend kind. They're younger. In this picture [hardcover edition] it's like the boy-girl difference isn't important." Another comment is that "Even in the picture of the older kids, it doesn't look romantic. Probably the publisher put a picture of older kids on the cover to get older kids to read it. When I first saw the picture on the hardcover, they looked awful young and I didn't think I'd like it. But then this one [the 1987, Harper edition] is better."

The first three chapters are read aloud in this session to introduce the setting, the central characters, and the initiating event. Students are asked to share what they learn about the rural community which is the setting and about Jess and Leslie, the central characters. They are encouraged to use their own knowledge of school life as a lens for viewing the classroom and playground scenes and to comment on the significance of such details as the clothes worn by Leslie on the first day of school, the yogurt she brings for lunch, the gender separation on the playground, the boys' race — which Leslie wins — and Jess' internal response on page 28: "Lord, the girl had no notion of what you did and didn't do."

In the discussion generated by these questions, personal experiences as students and as readers of fiction enrich responses. Because of firsthand knowledge of the school world, students are able to grasp the peer dynamics and the unstated rules inherent in the school culture.

The initiating event that sets the plot into motion is identified by some as the arrival of the newcomer and by others as the race on the playground. Some who predict that Jess and Leslie will eventually become friends suggest that the starting point for the friendship is the moment Jess forces Gary Fulcher to let Leslie run in the race. Students are asked to support their statements with evidence from the text. Throughout the cumulative dialogue generated in the context of the shared reading experiences, students share their own responses, predictions, interpretations, and insights about literary texts and, in the process, discover that readers experience a shared text in different ways.

Miss Edmunds, the music teacher introduced in Chapter 2, is identified as an important character because she's the only one who seems to recognize and appreciate Jess' artistic talent. She reminds some students of special teachers or other adults who understood and appreciated them as unique individuals.

The Third and Fourth Shared Reading Sessions

In the next two sessions, Chapters 4, 5, and 6 are read aloud and discussed. In Chapter 4, a new character, Janice Avery, a seventh grader, is introduced, and Jess changes his mind about Leslie. For a composition assignment, Leslie describes her favorite hobby, scuba diving; Jess' response reveals his own deep-seated fears (p. 64). It is also in Chapter 4 that Leslie and Jess create Terabithia, a secret land where Jess is introduced into a world of literary language and fantasy, a world of imagination and possibility.

By Chapter 5, May Belle, Jess' younger sister, plays a significant role in the relationship between Jess and Leslie. In this chapter they collaborate on a complex plan designed to avenge the theft of May Belle's special treat by Janice Avery. In Chapter 6 the Christmas preparations and the gift exchanges provide further insights about the family dynamics in Jess' home and about the nature of the relationship between Jess and Leslie.

By the third session, most students are reading independently another friendship novel selected from the collection and are ready to incorporate initial responses into the discussions of *Bridge to Terabithia*. For example, they discover connections between Terabithia, the fantasy world created by Leslie and Jess, and the "imagining games" that are central to the friendships formed in novels such as *Afternoon of the Elves* (Lisle, 1989); *The Egypt Game* (Snyder, 1967); *The Changeling* (Snyder, 1970); *The Village by the Sea* (Fox, 1988); *Next-Door Neighbors* (Ellis, 1990); *Daphne's Book* (Hahn, 1983), and *The Refugee Summer* (Fenton, 1982).

A student reading *The Egypt Game* comments: "I like stories with secret worlds like this one and where the kids change when they're in it." Another student reading *The Egypt Game* notes that the love of reading shared by the two central characters is the catalyst for building a friendship and for the "imagination games" which become the focus of the plot. In contrast, in *The Bridge to Terabithia*, only Leslie has read widely, and it is she who introduces the world of literature to Jess, initiates the magic, and serves as mentor for Jess.

Students reading *Daphne's Book, The Afternoon of the Elves,* and *The Village by the Sea* contrast the miniature worlds constructed in these novels with the life-size worlds created in *The Egypt Game* and *Bridge to Terabithia*. They discover a common thread which ties these books together: In each story those who are drawn together in friendship are from very different backgrounds. This discovery sets the stage for a closer look at the different backgrounds that have shaped the lives of Jess and Leslie.

In classrooms where multiple copies of *Bridge to Terabithia* are available, students are invited to reread the first six chapters in search of clues about these differences and to review the entries in their journals for relevant information. The differences identified in these chapters are listed on a wall chart; additional items are recorded as new information is revealed in subsequent chapters. Students are encouraged to read aloud specific passages in the text that provide evidence for entries on the list such as "language"; "relationship to parents"; "religion"; "work"; "family income"; "rural-urban"; "self-confidence"; "experience"; "books in the home"; "TV." Each item represents a significant difference between the families of Jess and Leslie or their personalities. For example, in Jess' family, work is viewed as necessary for survival while Leslie's family sees work as a form of pleasure or recreation. For Jess' family, religion is a matter of dogma; for Leslie's family, religion seems to offer an intellectual experience. Jess' family's financial insecurity is sharply contrasted with the financial security enjoyed in Leslie's family. The restricted language of Jess' family provides a contrast with the rich language of Leslie's family.

The Fifth and Sixth Shared Reading Sessions

As Chapters 7, 8, and 9 are read aloud, students are encouraged to continue to jot down ideas in their literary journals: any new insights or revisions of initial impressions or predictions; evidence of foreshadowing; questions raised by new information in the text; or items that can be added to the list of differences between Jess and Leslie. The process of meaning-making is recursive in nature: as the story unfolds and new information is brought to light, students rethink earlier responses, revise initial impressions, and apply relevant personal knowledge and experience to create new understandings.

Entries in the literary journals can be introduced into the cumulative dialogue generated in the Shared Reading Sessions. For example, a student reads his response to Chapter 7: "It tells more about Leslie and how she really wants her dad to pay attention to her, and Jess is sort of jealous of Bill [Leslie's father] but Leslie doesn't seem to *see* it." Another student reads from her journal: "Jess is more sensitive about people's feelings" and refers to the scene in Chapter 7 that centers around Janice Avery and Jess' sense of responsibility and sensitivity toward someone in pain. "Leslie is learning a lot of things from Jess — like caring about people and helping people in trouble." This student adds that because Leslie learns more about Janice as a person, she can begin "to feel sorry for her instead of just seeing her as a bully." Almost all students have had experiences with people who earn the label "bully," and many have read stories or seen movies in which the antagonist is a bully. These personal and literary experiences enrich the discussion generated by this brief but significant scene in which understanding and compassion results from a willingness to reach beneath the surface to discover what might be behind the overt behavior of another person.

In Chapter 8, when Leslie attends the Easter service with Jess' family and shares her thoughts about the story of Jesus with Jess and May Belle, she unleashes in them powerful emotions about the Bible, God, and death. The interchange at the end of this chapter highlights the gulf between the two families in terms of beliefs and perspective (p. 85). In response to this scene, students share their own personal beliefs as a way to build a deeper understanding of these central characters as they struggle to bridge the gulf between them.

Chapter 9 illuminates Jess' deep inner fears in contrast to Leslie's self-confidence and apparent lack of concern about potential danger. Students who have copies of *Bridge to Terabithia* are asked to find evidence of Jess' inner turmoil in this chapter. Selected lines in the text are reread to generate an exploration of Jess' struggle with himself and the polarities in the personalities of Jess and Leslie.

The Seventh Shared Reading Session

The final four chapters of *Bridge to Terabithia* are best read as a unit to allow students to live through them and experience their full emotional impact.

In Chapter 10, Jess continues to struggle with his deep anxieties and sense of dread and his conflicting desires to avoid danger and to confront it. His thoughts move from "I'll just grab that old terror by the shoulders and shake the daylights out of it" to "Leslie, I don't want to go over there today" (p. 96). This inner dialogue is interrupted by a call from his favorite teacher, Miss Edmunds, who invites him to drive down to Washington to go to the Smithsonian and the National Gallery. As Jess experiences the joy of his first trip to Washington and his first visit to an art gallery, he has fleeting thoughts of Leslie and his failure to have the invitation extended to her as well. On the trip home, the sun is finally shining again, and Jess thinks that "this one perfect day of his life was worth anything he had to pay" (p. 101). His joy is shattered when Brenda breaks the news that Leslie is dead.

The title of Chapter 11 is "No!" — a natural response to the news of a loved one's death. Denial is followed by guilt. "It had been so dumb of him not to ask if Leslie could go — *I'm really sorry Leslie*" (p. 106). "His stomach felt suddenly cold. It had something to do with — the reason he had not remembered to ask if Leslie could go with them to Washington today... *I was scared to come to Terabithia this morning*" (p. 107).

The scene at breakfast reveals Jess' attempt to push away the terrible truth as he concentrates on eating his pancakes — until his father says, "Your friend Leslie is dead, Jesse. You need to understand that" (p. 110).

In Chapter 12, Jess' denial and guilt turn to anger when Leslie's father talks of cremation. He is forced to face the fact that he will never see his best friend again.

> That meant Leslie was gone... She went and died just when he needed her the most. She went and left him... she had left him stranded there... Alone (p. 114).

Angry tears begin to flow when he leaves Leslie's house and continue to flow as he grabs the paper and paints Leslie had given him for Christmas and throws them into the dirty brown water of the stream. It is his father who comforts Jess in his agony of anger and sorrow. When Jess reveals his secret fear that Leslie could go to Hell, his father reassures him, responding with understanding and gentleness.

In Chapter 13 — the final chapter, entitled "Building the Bridge" — Jess begins to travel the road to recovery. He resumes his chores and returns to the creek, crossing to Terabithia where he makes a funeral wreath for Leslie, the queen of Terabithia. Using the words he knows Leslie would have liked, he creates the magic of the sacred grove: "Father, into Thy hands I commend her spirit" (p. 120).

The next stage of the healing process is portrayed in the final scene as Jess completes the construction of a bridge into Terabithia and leads May Belle across so that she can become the new queen of Terabithia.

The seventh session concludes with the final moving lines of the novel. After living through the events and emotional upheavals of the last four chapters, students need time for reflection and to let the story as a whole unfold in their minds. When they come together for the next group session, they will be invited to share their personal responses to the last chapters and then to interpret the novel as a whole.

The Eighth Shared Reading Session

In preparation for this and a subsequent session, students are asked (1) to review the running responses recorded in their journals as the text unfolded; (2) to be ready to share questions, insights, interpretations, and observations related to any part of the text that might contribute to an understanding of the whole text; and (3) to record on a 3 x 5 card what they consider to be of most importance about the story or what they think the story is really about. By writing their ideas on a card, they formulate their thoughts independently prior to participation in dialogue with others.

Group discussion and analysis of a text "opens up the text in ways that individual readers would not have seen" (Hansbury, 1988, p. 106). In the context of such discussion, students learn about others' experiences with the text, that there are many valid ways to interpret a given text, and that different readers construct different meanings in response to the same text.

The question **"How did the last four chapters make you feel?"** is used to initiate the discussion in Session Eight. Responses generally reveal strong emotional identification with the central character and an active involvement in the events. One student's comments expressed the feelings of many of her classmates:

> At first I just couldn't believe that Leslie had died. I was *sure* it was a mistake, and I kept waiting to find out she was really okay. Then I got mad at the author for making her die. It just wasn't fair!

Another comment reflects the way readers live through a text:

> I just kept wishing Jess did ask Leslie to go on the trip. Then she'd be alive! I wanted to be able to go back in time so Jess could ask her to come along!

Emotional responses are unleashed at the thought of May Belle replacing Leslie as the queen of Terabithia. Puzzlement and shock are expressed in response to Jess' behavior:

How could he just sit there and eat all those pancakes?

Why did he hit May Belle?

How come he threw away the paints?

After ample opportunity is provided for sharing immediate impressions, feelings, and questions evoked by the text, students are invited to respond with possible explanations and interpretations of the events. This allows students to move beyond initial meaning generation, to step back and rethink what is troubling about the text in light of personal knowledge and experience. For example, a student who had experienced the death of a classmate explains that his own reaction had been much like Jess'. He describes the feelings of disbelief, denial, guilt, and anger he experienced before finally accepting the death and living with the loss. After similar insights and experiences are shared, scenes in the text that had originally been a source of confusion or shock are reread and begin to make more sense. One comment reflects this new understanding:

> I get it. It's like if he ate all the pancakes, everything would be *normal* and Leslie wouldn't be dead. He couldn't make his mind believe she's really dead. So his dad has to say it again to *make* him understand.

A student familiar with *A Taste of Blackberries* [2] explains that the central character in this story struggles with the same kinds of feelings that Jess had in his response to the sudden death of his best friend, Jamie. He adds: "Now I can understand that book better — especially when he thinks if he *doesn't* eat, then everything would be okay again and Jamie wouldn't be dead. He was playing that 'if game.' "

Discussion of the nature of Jess' response to Leslie's death prompts some students to question the sudden intrusion of death in a story about friendship. Student comments suggest different ways to think about the story:

> It's about life — and in real life people die.

> In some books you know someone's going to die like in *A Summer to Die*,[3] but here it's too sudden and you're not ready.

> It's easier if it's an older person like in *Mama's Going to Buy You a Mockingbird*.[4]

> It's hard because you really get to *know* Leslie instead of just being someone in the background you don't really care about.

The Ninth Shared Reading Session

This session begins with the interpretation of details in retrospect. Students are asked to reflect on passages or details in the first part of the text which may take on new meaning after further information is revealed. This retrospective interpretation prompts some students to discover that the author "gives us a lot of warning signals." They note that the last lines of Chapter 7 (p. 77); Chapter 8 (p. 85); and Chapter 9 (p. 93) foreshadow the tragic event that is the focus of the last four chapters. Others observe that the author introduces Mrs. Myers and Miss Edmunds as background characters in the first part of the story and moves them into the foreground in key scenes later in the story.

Details such as Jess' fear of dark water (p. 33) and dark places (p. 39) and Leslie's hobby, scuba diving — which reveals her apparent lack of fear of the danger of such a sport — take on added significance when viewed in light of subsequent events leading up to the time of the accident. Some students engage in speculation: "*If* Leslie had not been such a fearless person, she might not have tried to cross the creek when it was so high. *If* Jess had been able to tell her he was afraid, she might have stayed back with him."

In retrospect, the chapter titles also take on new meaning. For example, students see that the title of Chapter 11, "No!" emphasizes Jess' initial denial of Leslie's death. In Chapter 12, "Stranded" suggests his sense of loss and his conflicting feelings of anger (p. 114).

The next step is to look at the story as a whole. Students are invited to share their written responses to the questions, **"What do you think the story is really about?"** or **"What do you consider to be of most importance about the story?"**

Their responses reflect different perspectives, personal experiences, priorities, and preoccupations of individual students, again demonstrating the diversity of reader response to a given text. For some, the novel is really about friendship; for some, it's about Jess' growth toward maturity; for some, it's about death; for others, it's about the struggle to overcome deep fears; for others, what's most important is the parent-child relationship; others see Terabithia as the most important part of the story. Any one of these themes could be used as a starting point for exploring ways in which all the others are woven together with it to create one richly textured meaning. Since *Bridge to Terabithia* is being used to introduce a unit on friendship, this theme is chosen as the starting point for discussion and the context for considering other themes the students identify. The five questions about friendship generated during the introductory session for this literature unit are reviewed at this point and used to guide the discussion of this theme (see p. 22).

A review of the list of differences between the two central characters and their families sets the stage for exploring the way family relationships, values, and life style appear to shape the characters, Jess and Leslie, and, in turn, the way the differences between them influence the evolution of their friendship. Because of her worldliness and rich cultural experiences, Leslie is well suited to serve as mentor to Jess and to guide his journey into a world of imagination and learning. Under her tutelage, Jess expands his world, discovers his inner resources, and begins to develop a sense of his own potential as an individual. Together, they create Terabithia as a refuge from the pressures of the outside world, a secret place which represents to them a world of possibility. Leslie inspires Jess to move toward maturity and to build an inner strength which enables him to cope with her unexpected death and to carry on without her.

Students read aloud selected passages in the final chapter that focus on the meaning of this friendship for Jess, the meaning of Terabithia, and Leslie's legacy. Students identify key lines that illuminate the role of Leslie's friendship and Terabithia in Jess' life:

...Terabithia was like a castle where you came to be knighted. After you stayed for a while and grew strong you had to move on... It was up to him to pay back the world in beauty and caring what Leslie had loaned him in vision and strength (p. 126).

They find lines which point to Jess' growing ability to confront his fears and to take control of them in the scene with May Belle after Jess rescues her from the tree bridge.

Everybody gets scared sometimes, May Belle... It's like the smarter you are, the more things scare you (p. 123).

One student's response to this rescue scene underlines Jess' new understanding of the relationship between fear and courage: "He *knew* the danger, and he was really afraid but he did it [rescued May Belle] anyway. *That* is what takes courage."

The final scene in the novel (pp. 127-128) is read again to initiate a dialogue about Leslie's legacy. Students recognize that Jess wants to ensure that Leslie's legacy is passed on, that May Belle will be given a chance to grow and develop her imaginative powers in Terabithia and, in this way, honor Leslie's life and gift to the world. Jess builds the bridge into Terabithia as an act of love for May Belle, to ensure her safe passage into this secret kingdom.

And when he finished, he put flowers in her hair and led her across the bridge — the great bridge into Terabithia... (p. 128).

The Tenth Shared Reading Session

In this session, the teacher shares with the class two selections from Katherine Paterson's *Gates of Excellence.*[5] The first is the chapter entitled "Yes, But Is It True?" (pp. 56-64), in which Ms. Paterson shares the autobiographical origins of *Bridge to Terabithia.* The second is from her Newbery Medal Acceptance for *Bridge to Terabithia* (pp. 112-115), in which she presents an eloquent explication of the bridge.

Independent Reading and Writing

While *Bridge to Terabithia* is being read and discussed in a series of shared reading sessions over an extended period of at least two to three weeks, students are engaged in reading, discussing, and writing about the friendship books they've chosen to read independently. The small dialogue groups generate questions which can be used to guide response to "friendship novels." Questions from each group are collated and copied for every student. Students are asked to select two or more of the questions on this list to use as "starters" for writing about one of the novels they have chosen to read independently. They are invited to share these written responses with other dialogue groups studying different novels. As a result of this interchange, many students are motivated to read additional books that have been discussed and recommended by classmates.

Student-generated questions are listed below:

1. What do the friends in this book have in common? What bonds hold them together?
2. What is special about the friendship?
3. In what ways are the friends different?
4. In what ways are the friends similar?
5. What problems do the friends have? How do they handle the problems?
6. How do the central characters change and grow? What do they learn?
7. Was the friendship beneficial for one or both of the friends? Explain.
8. Was one of the friends a "leader"? Explain.
9. What is the conflict in the story?
10. Who is the narrator? Explain how this is important for the story.
11. Compare this story with *Bridge to Terabithia* or other stories about friendship in terms of setting, characters, plot, theme, style, viewpoint.
12. Compare novels in terms of the nature of the external forces or problems that threaten the friendships.
13. What special literary techniques, devices, or forms are used by the author to write this story?
14. How does peer pressure influence the friendship in this story? How does peer pressure influence your choice of friends?
15. Does this story remind you of your own experiences or of people you know? Explain.
16. Which characters do you like best? Why? Which characters do you like least? Why? Which characters seem most real to you? Why?
17. Which characters seem to have the same kinds of problems that you have or used to have?
18. Does this story help you understand yourself or other people better? Explain.

Some questions are selected as a framework for writing because of their relevance to a specific book. Other questions are relevant to all the friendship novels. The first question can be used by any student to introduce the central characters and the bonds between them. For example, in stories such as *Bridge to Terabithia, Daphne's Book, The Egypt Game, Afternoon of the Elves,* and *The Changeling,* characters share a common interest in imagining games and fantasy building.

In *Libby on Wednesday,* (Snyder, 1990), creative writing draws a group of very diverse individuals together as friends. In *They're All Named Wildfire*

(Springer, 1989), the common bond is a love of horses; in *The Moves Make the Man* (Brooks, 1984), it's basketball; and in *The Facts and Fictions of Minna Pratt* (MacLachlan, 1988), it's music. In some stories, the bond of friendship is shaped by a common history or a shared experience which draws two individuals together into a close relationship. For example, in stories such as *Kate* (Little, 1971); *The Devil in Vienna* (Orgel, 1978); *Friedrich* (Richter, 1970); *Friends First* (McDonnell, 1990); and *The Changeling* (Snyder, 1970), friendships evolve from a shared childhood. In *A Friend Like That* (Slote, 1988), Robby and Beth are drawn together, in part, because they have both experienced the trauma of a break in the family circle. Robby's mother has died; Beth's parents are divorced. In *Silver* (Mazer, 1988), a bond of friendship is formed when a young girl shares with another the terrible secret of sexual abuse that she has carried inside for too long.

In *Fast Sam, Cool Clyde, and Stuff* (Myers, 1975), a twelve-year-old boy becomes part of a friendship group which provides mutual support, caring, and protection. When members of this group have problems at home, at school, or on the street, they know they are not alone. They share a common experience of living in Harlem and struggling to survive amidst drugs and violence and the degradation of racism. They help each other keep hope alive in a world which makes this a daily challenge.

The second question is relevant for all the novels, but is generally selected by those writing about a friendship they consider unusual. For example, in *The Eternal Spring of Mr. Ito* (Garrigue, 1985), a young British evacuee to Canada during World War II develops a close friendship with Mr. Ito, an elderly Japanese-Canadian gardener. In *The Whipping Boy* (Fleischman, 1986), a Prince develops a friendship with his whipping boy. In *Across the Creek* (Smith, 1989), the central character develops a friendship with a young girl he thinks is the spirit of his dead mother as a child. *The Princess in the Pigpen* (Thomas, 1989) is a time-travel novel in which a 17th-century English girl, a duke's daughter, develops a friendship with a farmer's daughter in Iowa in 1988. *Everywhere* (Brooks, 1990) reveals the special relationship between a ten-year-old boy and his beloved grandfather. *After the Rain* (Mazer, 1987) is a portrait of two very independent individuals, fifteen-year-old Rachel and her grandfather. They develop a very close bond, and she stays with him as he struggles with cancer and right up to the very end.

Hoops (Myers, 1981), set in Harlem, is the story of seventeen-year-old Lonnie Jackson and his friendship with Cal, an older man, a wino, who had once gained fame and fortune as a basketball player, but had been kicked out of the National Basketball Association because of his involvement with gamblers. Now he's coaching Lonnie's team for a city-wide basketball tournament. Cal knows that Lonnie has the potential to be a pro-basketball player; he shares with Lonnie his own life, as a warning about giving into pressures that can ruin him.

Questions 3 and 4 can be used in conjunction with other questions. For example, identification of the differences between two characters may serve as the context for a discussion of problems they encounter within their friendship (see question 5) or for exploring external forces such as prejudice and ethnic or racial tensions that threaten their relationship (see question 12).

The fifth question is used to explore books in which religious, racial, or ethnic differences represent significant obstacles, such as in *Autumn Street*

(Lowry, 1980); *The Devil in Vienna* (Orgel, 1978); *Friedrich* (Richter, 1970); *They're All Named Wildfire* (Springer, 1989); *The Eternal Spring of Mr. Ito* (Garrigue, 1985); *Circle of Fire* (Hooks, 1982); *Words by Heart* (Sebestyen, 1979); *Waiting for the Rain* (Gordon, 1987); *Several Kinds of Silence* (Singer, 1988); and *Ludie's Song* (Herlihy, 1988).

Question 6 can be used in the analysis of all the friendship novels. Most of the central characters grow and change as they gain new insights about themselves and others. Like David in *Friends till the End* (Strasser, 1981), many central characters learn to take control of their own lives rather than allow peer pressure to define what is important in life. Like Adam in *The Secret Language of the SB* (Scarboro, 1987) and Blaze in *Words of Stone* (Henkes, 1992), some of these dynamic characters move beyond their preoccupation with their inner worlds to reach out to others and enrich and expand their own lives. Like Jenny in *They're All Named Wildfire* (Springer, 1989) and Marty in *Ludie's Song* (Herlihy, 1988), some of the central characters lose their childhood innocence as they discover the racial prejudice and hatred hidden beneath the surface among people they've known all their lives and when they witness the cruelty and violence directed against innocent human beings. Jenny and Marty each demonstrate their growth as individuals as they take a courageous stand against bigotry and ignorance and acts of violence in their community.

Although most of the central characters grow and change as they gain new understandings and insights about themselves and others and learn to cope with new challenges and to take control of their lives, there are some who resist change. For example, in *Waiting for the Rain* (Gordon, 1987), Frikkie, a white boy in South Africa, does not like anything in his own world to change: "...why couldn't things just go on the way they've always been?" (p. 210). He does not look beyond his own world or consider what apartheid means to members of the Black community. He simply does not bother to think about how it must feel to be treated as an inferior being. He is trapped in his own narrow vision and unquestioning acceptance of the status quo. Thus, Frikkie is an interesting subject for discussion because he is *not* a dynamic character.

Question 7 focusses on the benefits of friendship. *The Gift Giver* (Hansen, 1980) is about a group of middle grade friends who live on 163rd Street in the Bronx and become acquainted with a new boy, Amir, who moves onto their block and gives them a gift of friendship which changes each of them. Amir is a thoughtful observer of the people around him and responds to their needs and helps them develop their strengths. Amir and Doris, the narrator, become close friends, and he helps her gain the self-confidence to grow as a unique individual instead of simply following the crowd. At one point in the narrative Amir shares with Doris the words of an elderly man with whom he had developed a relationship during one of his numerous placements in a foster home: "He said kindness always comes back to you. He told me I'd been a blessing to him. He called me the little gift-giver" (p. 86).

The ninth question focusses on conflict. In some of the stories, the conflict is in the friendship and is related to significant differences between the two friends (see question 3). For example, in *One Friend to Another* (Feuer, 1987), Nicole and Rhonda, both seventh graders, have very different ideas about the meaning of friendship. Nicole defines friendship in terms of mutual trust, respect, and loyalty. Rhonda defines friendship only in terms of her own needs and goals. She *uses* Nicole to maintain her academic status in the honors program, where she does not belong, and in the end, betrays Nicole, who discovers, too late, Rhonda's cruelty and deceit. For Nicole, this friendship is detrimental instead of beneficial.

In response to question 11, several novels are compared to *Bridge to Terabithia* because the friendship featured is between a boy and a girl who are not involved in a romantic relationship: *A Friend Like That* (Slote, 1988); *Whose Side Are You On?* (Moore, 1988); *The Goats* (Cole, 1987); *Randall's Wall* (Fenner, 1991); *The Facts and Fictions of Minna Pratt* (MacLachlan, 1988); *Arthur, for the Very First Time* (MacLachlan, 1980), *Mariposa Blues* (Koertge, 1991), and *Blue Heron* (Avi, 1992).

Other Bells for Us to Ring (Cormier, 1990) is the story of 11-year-old Darcy Webster, whose father has been transferred to an Army camp in Massachusetts during the Second World War. Darcy feels like an outsider in her new French-Canadian neighborhood, but her world changes when she meets Kathleen Mary O'Hara. Because her own family is Unitarian, Darcy is fascinated with Kathleen's stories about Catholicism. Kathleen is the leader in the friendship that develops between them (see question 8) and, like the central characters in *Bridge to Terabithia*, she and Darcy have very different family backgrounds. Darcy is an only child of loving parents; Kathleen is part of a large family controlled by an alcoholic, physically abusive father. Like Jess in *Bridge to Terabithia*, Darcy suffers the loss of her best friend when Kathleen is killed by a car as she tries to escape from her drunken father. In the final scene of the novel, Darcy is holding the doll Kathleen Mary had bought for her:

> I stood there in the bedroom holding my childhood in my hands. When my father called to me, I said good-bye to that lost childhood and went into the living room to open my Christmas gifts (p. 136).

Question 12 invites students to engage in a comparative analysis if they have read at least two novels which feature friendships threatened by external issues and obstacles, such as religious, racial, and ethnic differences. *Several Kinds of Silence* (Singer, 1988) portrays the growth of a relationship between Franny Yeager and Japanese-American Ren Tanazaki. Franny cannot tell her family about Ren because her father, who works for an auto parts plant, hates the Japanese and sees them as a threat to his job security.

In *The Eternal Spring of Mr. Ito* (Garrigue, 1985), Sara Warren is separated from her special friend, Mr. Ito, a Japanese-Canadian, when he and his family are sent to the camps in the mountains following the Japanese attack on Pearl Harbor. Sara continues to keep in touch with Mr. Ito and his family, but her contacts with them must be kept secret. Mr. Ito will always be a part of Sara's life, even after his death.

Friedrich (Richter, 1970) and *The Devil in Vienna* (Orgel, 1978) are historical novels set in Europe during World War II. *Friedrich* is the story of a friendship between two boys, a Jew and a non-Jew. *The Devil in Vienna* is the story of a friendship between a Jewish girl and the daughter of a Nazi. In each novel, Nazi terror threatens the friendship and makes it dangerous to maintain the relationship. Like Sara and Mr. Ito, the central characters in these two novels struggle to transcend the fear and hatred surrounding them in order to sustain the bonds of friendship between them.

Racial tensions set the stage for a number of novels about interracial friendships. *They're All Named Wildfire* (Springer, 1989), set in a small town in rural Pennsylvania, is the story of Jenny and Shanterey, who are drawn together in friendship when they discover they both love horses and collect model horses. But Shanterey is African-American and the people in this rural town have racist attitudes and treat blacks with suspicion and hatred. Jenny is forced to choose between her friendship with Shanterey and the acceptance of her peers. When she finally chooses to maintain her friendship with Shanterey, Jenny discovers what it is like to be a victim of ignorance and hate, to be isolated and harassed. She learns of the cruelty and violence hidden beneath the surface of people she had known all her life.

Ludie's Song (Herlihy, 1988), set in rural Georgia in the 1950s, is the story of thirteen-year-old Marty who develops a secret, forbidden friendship with Ludie, an African-American girl. Marty, like Jenny, becomes a victim of the hatred, ignorance, and violence in this small town when she refuses to give up her friendship with Ludie.

The narrator of *Circle of Fire* (Hooks, 1982) is eleven-year-old Harrison Hawkins, whose two best friends are African-American. The setting is North Carolina in 1936 and the violence of the Ku Klux Klan is a constant threat to the black community. Now that he is almost twelve, Harrison is pressured to give up his childhood friends. Now he must choose between maintaining this friendship and giving in to the powerful social forces bent on separating them.

In *Waiting for the Rain* (Gordon, 1987), a childhood friendship between a white boy and a black boy in South Africa is challenged by the realities of apartheid. The lines that separate them become more clear as they mature and enter separate, conflicting worlds. At the end of the book, they discover that remnants of that friendship still remain inside them: "What had been before between the two of them had proved to be stronger than what was going on now between the whites and the blacks" (p. 207).

Question 13 calls attention to authors' craft. For example, *Waiting for the Rain* is told from two separate and conflicting viewpoints: Frikkie, a white boy who will one day inherit the family's land, and his childhood friend, Tengo, a black boy whose family works for Frikkie's uncle. The reader sees the realities of apartheid through the eyes of Frikkie, who wants his life to remain the same, and through the eyes of Tengo, who seeks an education and fights for human rights in order to change life for himself and his people.

In *Taking the Ferry Home* (Conrad, 1988), the story of the friendship between Ali and Simone is told through first-person accounts by each of them in alternating chapters. The reader learns the secrets that each girl carries inside but cannot share with the other.

In her book, *After the Rain*, Norma Fox Mazer uses third-person, present-tense narration in which the narrator, as an outside observer, tells the story as it unfolds. Students are invited to discuss these authors' use of viewpoint to shape each story and the effect of the viewpoint on reader response (see question

10). They are also invited to experiment with different viewpoints in their own narrative writing.

The Juniper Game (Jordan, 1991) is the story of a friendship which grows between fourteen-year-old Juniper and her classmate Dylan as they experiment with telepathy and find themselves travelling into the past together. This is an unusual friendship novel because a contemporary realistic story is embedded in a time-travel fantasy.

In addition to focussing on the author's craft, students can compare these novels with *Bridge to Terabithia* in terms of the nature of the relationships in each novel (see questions 8 and 11). For example, Juniper, like Leslie, is the leader in the initial stages of the friendship. It is Juniper who controls the relationship in the beginning and leads Dylan into the time-travel exeprience. However, as in *Bridge to Terabithia*, the relationship between Juniper and Dylan becomes more balanced as their friendship matures. They develop a bond based on mutual respect and trust, and each demonstrates a deep sensitivity to the other's feelings and needs.

In Pam Conrad's *Taking the Ferry Home*, two sixteen-year-old girls from very different social classes spend the summer together on a resort island. Simone is rich and beautiful and lives like a princess in a magnificent mansion. Ali's father has rented for the summer a small cottage owned by Simone's family. It is Simone who decides to befriend Ali, and she maintains control of the relationship. Unlike the friendships portrayed in *Bridge to Terabithia* and *The Juniper Game,* this one never evolves into a deeper relationship based on mutual trust and respect. The reader is given a glimpse into Simone's private world, to which Ali has no access: Simone sits alone in her beautiful room with her tarot cards and whispers, "Will I ever learn to be a good friend?" (p. 158).

Question 14 is especially relevant to particular stories. For example, in *The Fastest Friend in the West* (Grove, 1990), Lori's brief friendship with a homeless girl is a source of conflict: "Two things were swirling around inside me — pity for Vern, and embarrassment at the fact that people were already starting to think I was her friend" (p. 41). *Daphne's Book, The Changeling,* and *Afternoon of the Elves* are also about friendships between conventional characters and social isolates (or outcasts). In each story, peer pressures toward conformity and the need to be accepted by the peer group, especially the "popular group," conflict with the desire to participate in a meaningful friendship with someone who is "different" and whose difference is not tolerated by the larger peer group.

A seventh grader recognizes the social dynamics and peer pressure portrayed in *Daphne's Book:* "Kids *do* ignore someone who's different. Even if she wears the right clothes but not the right way, she's *different*. The way it works is if a popular kid associates with someone like Daphne, it's okay. It wouldn't hurt her reputation. But if you're not popular, then it *would* matter, and the other kids wouldn't like you. That's why Jessica was so worried when the teacher assigns her to work with Daphne on the writing project. If a popular, sophisticated girl like Michelle (a character in the novel) got assigned to Daphne, they never would get to be friends or get involved in a secret world together. Michelle was too sophisticated and Daphne would sense her contempt. Daphne would *never* open up to someone like Michelle."

The narrator of *Friends till the End* (Strasser, 1981) is a high school senior who is too busy with his own life to give any time to the new boy, Howie Jamison. However, when Howie is hospitalized with leukemia, David visits him, and they gradually develop a close friendship. At first, David's friends refuse to accept his commitment to Howie. David resists peer pressure to conform to the comfortable way of life of his social group and develops a growing awareness of what is really important in his life and the values which guide his choices as an individual.

In *Cal Cameron by Day, Spider-Man by Night* (Cannon, 1988), Cal, a popular high school junior, learns a great deal about himself and his friends as he struggles to understand the role of peer pressure in shaping relationships and behavior. Cal tells his story in a first-person narrative in which he is a participant and an observer. His running commentary about his observations reveal the insights he develops with experience. For example, on the first day of school, Cal observes that "The first day of school is just a big fashion show... The fact is, though, if you want to be accepted at our school, you have to look 'right,' no matter what that 'right' is. The look... changes all the time. The thing is to stay up with the changes. It's death if you don't" (p. 16). Cal realizes that he cares too much about being accepted and doing what others expect him to do. For example, when he develops a friendship with the new girl, Marti, he keeps their relationship a secret because "...Marti does not fit in at school" (p.59). By the end of the novel, Cal is ready to shape his own life without reference to the pressures and expectations of peers and family. He wants to define himself as an individual instead of allowing others to do it for him.

In *Fool's Gold* (Snyder, 1993), fourteen-year-old Rudy also confronts peer pressures and fears of rejection and, like Cal, studies the people around him to understand why they behave as they do. At the same time, Rudy embarks on a journey of self-discovery, searching for the origins of the phobia which has begun to take control of his life.

Moving Beyond the Texts: Reading-Writing Connections

Another writing project in this Focus Unit invites students to move beyond the novels and to use their reading as a catalyst for reflecting on their own experience. Suggestions for initiating this writing are listed below:

1. Write about a special person in your life.

2. Write a personality profile of someone who is similar to a character in a friendship novel. (e.g., a bully? a leader? a shy person? a loner?)

3. Write about a friendship in your own life. Bonds? Obstacles? Problems? Compromises? Benefits?

4. Select a book which seems to reflect or express your own experience or feelings. Write about the connection between the story world and your own world.

For the final writing project, students compose an original story about friendship. A class meeting is scheduled to prepare for this writing project: representatives from the dialogue groups share their literary analyses of the novels they had discussed and identify the different types of friendships found in these novels. This survey of the friendships described in these self-selected novels is used to generate a list of questions which students can consult as they become involved in the composing process and think about the characters who will live in their stories:

1. Are your main characters the same age or is one older or younger than the other?
2. Are they the same or different gender?
3. Are there racial, ethnic, or religious differences?
4. What do they have in common?
5. What obstacles, problems, or conflicts affect the friendship?
6. Do the characters grow or change?
7. What are the benefits of the friendship?
8. What are the negative consequences of the friendship?

The completed stories are typed and bound into individual booklets, shared in the small dialogue groups, and then placed in the friendship novel collection for others to select for independent reading.

The Concluding Session for the Friendship Focus Unit

The focus of this session is on the meaning of friendship. A review of students' original statements about friendship that were recorded in the introductory session is followed by an interchange in which students share new insights and perspectives about friendship acquired in the process of reading, discussing, and writing about friendship novels, engaging in literary analysis, making connections between related literary texts and between literature and life, and composing their own friendship stories. Students move from personal transactions with literary texts to shared explorations of literary craft, content, and connections between related texts toward a synthesis of ideas and the formulation of richer, expanded notions of the nature of friendship and conditions for establishing and sustaining friendships.

Social interactions which evolve in the course of the Focus Unit experience can provide a context for building friendships in the classroom community. As students share personal experiences with and responses to friendship novels and collaborate to generate meaning in the social context of the shared reading experiences and small dialogue groups, they have opportunities to learn more about each other and to discover common bonds which might well serve as a basis for establishing new friendships.

References

Hansbury, Patricia.(1988). "Readers Making Meaning: From Response to Interpretation," in *Literature in the Classroom — Readers, Texts and Contexts,* edited by Ben F. Nelms. Urbana, IL: NCTE.

Langer, Judith. (1990). "Understanding Literature." *Language Arts,* Vol. 67, 812-816.

Bibliography: Friendship Stories

Armstrong, Jennifer. (1992). *Steal Away.* New York: Orchard.

Asher, Sandy. (1982). *Just Like Jenny.* New York: Delacorte.

Avi. (1992). *Blue Heron.* New York: Macmillan.

Bawden, Nina. (1979). *The Robbers.* New York: Lothrop Lee & Shepard.

Beatty, Patricia. (1989). *Sarah and Me and the Lady from the Sea.* New York: Morrow Jr. Books.

Bond, Nancy. (1984). *A Place to Come Back To.* New York: Atheneum.

Boyd, Candy Dawson. (1985). *Forever Friends.* New York: Viking Penguin.

Bridgers, Sue Ellen. (1993). *Keeping Christina.* New York: Harper Collins.

Brooks, Bruce. (1990). *Everywhere.* New York: Harper and Row.

Brooks, Bruce. (1984). *The Moves Make the Man.* New York: Harper & Row.

Byars, Betsy. (1985). *Cracker Jackson.* New York: Viking.

Byars, Betsy. (1981). *The Cybil War.* New York: Viking.

Cannon, A.E. (1988). *Cal Cameron by Day, Spider-Man by Night.* New York: Delacorte.

Carrick, Carol. (1979). *Some Friend!* Boston: Houghton Mifflin.

Chang, Heidi. (1988). *Elaine, Mary Lewis and the Frogs.* New York: Crown.

Cleary, Beverly. (1952). *Henry and Beezus.* New York: Morrow.

Cole, Brock. (1987). *The Goats.* Farrar, New York: Straus & Giroux.

Conrad, Pam. (1988). *Taking the Ferry Home.* New York: Harper & Row.

Cormier, Robert. (1990). *Other Bells for Us To Ring.* New York: Delacorte.

Danziger, Paula. (1987). *Remember Me To Harold Square.* New York: Delacorte.

Deuker, Carl. (1993). *Heart of a Champion.* Boston: Joy St./Little, Brown.

Ellis, Sarah. (1990). *Next Door Neighbors.* New York: Margaret K. McElderry Books.

Fenner, Carol. (1991). *Randall's Wall.* New York: McElderry.

Fenton, Edward. (1982). *The Refugee Summer.* New York: Delacorte Press.

Feuer, Elizabeth. (1987). *One Friend to Another.* New York: Farrar, Straus & Giroux.

Fleischman, Sid. (1986). *The Whipping Boy.* New York: Greenwillow.

Fox, Paula. (1987). *Lily and the Lost Boy.* New York: Dell.

Fox, Paula. (1988). *The Village by the Sea.* New York: Dell.

Garrigue, Sheila. (1978). *Between Friends.* Scarsdale, NY: Bradbury.

Garrigue, Sheila. (1985). *The Eternal Spring of Mr. Ito.* Scarsdale, NY: Bradbury Press.

Geller, Mark. (1990). *The Strange Case of the Reluctant Partners.* New York: HarperCollins.

Gilson, Jamie. (1988). *Double Dog Dare.* New York: Lothrop Lee and Shepard.

Gordon, Sheila. (1987). *Waiting for the Rain.* New York: Orchard Books.

Greene, Bette. (1974). *Philip Hall Likes Me, I Reckon Maybe.* New York: Dial.

Grove, Vicki. (1990). *The Fastest Friend in the West.* New York: Putnam.

Hahn, Mary Downing. (1983). *Daphne's Book.* New York: Clarion Books.

Hamilton, Virginia. (1971). *The Planet of Junior Brown.* New York: MacMillan.

Hamilton, Virginia. (1987). *A White Romance.* New York: Harcourt Brace Jovanovich.

Hansen, Joyce. (1980). *The Gift-Giver.* Boston: Houghton Mifflin.

Havill, Juanita. (1991). *Leona and Ike.* New York: Crown.

Henkes, Kevin. (1992). *Words of Stone.* New York: Greenwillow.

Herlihy, Dirlie. (1988). *Ludie's Song.* New York: Puffin.

Hines, Anna . (1985). *Cassie Bowen Takes Witch Lessons.* New York: E.P. Dutton.

Hooks, William. (1982). *Circle of Fire.* New York: Atheneum.

Jordan, Sherryl. (1991). *The Juniper Game.* New York: Scholastic.

Keeton, Elizabeth. (1985). *Second-Best Friend.* New York: Atheneum.

Koertge, Ron. (1991). *Mariposa Blues.* Boston: Little Brown.

Konigsburg, E.L. (1975 [1967]). *Jennifer, Hecate, Macbeth, William McKinley and Me, Elizabeth.* New York: Atheneum.

Lisle, Janet Taylor. (1989). *Afternoon of the Elves.* New York: Orchard/Watts.

Little, Jean. (1971). *Kate.* New York: Harper & Row.

Lowry, Lois. (1980). *Autumn Street.* New York: Dell Pub. Co.

Lowry, Lois. (1989). *Number the Stars.* Boston: Houghton-Mifflin.

Lowry, Lois. (1987). *Rabble Starky.* Boston: Houghton-Mifflin.

MacLachlan, Patricia. (1988). *The Facts and Fictions of Minna Pratt.* New York: Harper & Row.

MacLachlan, Patricia. (1980). *Arthur, for the Very First Time.* New York: Harper & Row.

McDonnell, Christine. (1990). *Friends First.* New York: Viking.

Mazer, Norma Fox. (1987). *After the Rain.* New York: Morrow.

Mazer, Norma Fox. (1988). *Silver.* Wm. New York: Morrow.

Mills, Claudia. (1991). *Hannah On Her Way.* New York: Macmillan.

Mohr, Nicholasa. (1986). *Going Home.* (Sequel to Felita, 1979) New York: Dial.

Monson, A.M. (1992). *The Deer Stand.* New York: Lothrop.

Moore, Emily. (1988). *Whose Side Are You On?* New York: Farrar, Straus & Giroux.

Myers, Walter Dean. (1975). *Fast Sam, Cool Clyde, and Stuff.* New York: Viking Penguin.

Myers, Walter Dean. (1981). *Hoops.* New York: Delacorte.

Myers, Walter Dean. (1990). *The Mouse Rap.* New York: Harper & Row.

Norris, Gunilla. (1973). *The Friendship Hedge.* New York: E.P. Dutton.

Orgel, Doris. (1978). *The Devil in Vienna.* New York: Dial.

Paterson, Katherine. (1977). *Bridge to Terabithia.* New York: Harper & Row.

Peck, Richard. (1987). *Princess Ashley.* New York: Delacorte.

Peck, Richard. (1985). *Remembering the Good Times.* New York: Delacorte.

Peck, Robert Newton. (1974). *Soup.* (series) New York: Alfred Knopf.

Radin, Ruth Yaffe. (1986). *Tac's Island.* New York: Macmillan.

Richter, Hans. (1970). *Friedrich.* New York: Holt.

Rochman, Hazel, and Darlene Z. McCampbell, selectors. (1993). *Who Do You Think You Are?: Stories of Friends and Enemies.* Boston: Little, Brown.

Sachs, Marilyn. (1978). *A Secret Friend.* New York: Doubleday.

Savin, Marcia. (1992). *The Moon Bridge.* New York: Scholastic.

Scarboro, Elizabeth. (1990). *The Secret Language of the SB.* New York: Viking.

Sebestyen, Ouida. (1979). *Words by Heart.* Boston: Little, Brown.

Shannon, Jacqueline. (1992). *I Hate My Hero.* New York: Simon and Schuster.

Singer, Marilyn. (1986). *Lizzie Silver of Sherwood Forest.* New York: Harper & Row.

Singer, Marilyn. (1988). *Several Kinds of Silence.* New York: Harper and Row.

Slote, Alfred. (1988). *A Friend Like That.* Philadelphia: Lippincott.

Smith, Doris Buchanan. (1991). *The Pennywhistle Tree.* New York: Putnam.

Smith, Marya. (1989). *Across the Creek.* Boston: Little Brown.

Snyder, Zilpha. (1970). *The Changeling.* New York: Atheneum.

Snyder, Zilpha. (1993). *Fool's Gold.* New York: Delacorte.

Snyder, Zilpha. (1967). *The Egypt Game.* New York: Atheneum.

Snyder, Zilpha. (1990). *Libby on Wednesday.* New York: Delacorte Press.

Speare, Elizabeth. (1983). *The Sign of the Beaver.* Boston: Houghton Mifflin.

Springer, Nancy. (1989). *They're All Named Wildfire.* New York: Atheneum.

Stolz, Mary. (1978). *Cider Days.* New York: Harper & Row.

Stolz, Mary.(1977). *Ferris Wheel.* New York: Harper & Row.

Stolz, Mary. (1965). *The Noonday Friends.* New York: Harper & Row.

Strasser, Todd. (1981). *Friends Till the End.* New York: Delacorte.

Taylor, Mildred. (1987). *The Friendship.* New York: Dial.

Thomas, Jane Resh. (1989). *The Princess in the Pigpen.* New York: Clarion Books.

Whelan, Gloria. (1987). *Next Spring an Oriole.* New York: Random House.

Wilson, Nancy Hope. (1992). *Bringing Nettie Back.* New York: Macmillan.

Zeieur, Joan. (1993). *Stick Boy.* New York: Atheneum.

Foot Notes:

1. In informal discussions with middle grade students over the years, I have heard many spontaneous, positive comments about the book, *Bridge to Terabithia*. In an undergraduate course on children's literature which I teach at the University of Rochester, this title by Katherine Paterson is one of the few novels most of the students remember hearing and/or reading, and rereading, as middle grade students.
2. Doris Buchanan Smith. (1973). *A Taste of Blackberries.* New York: Crowell.
3. Lois Lowry. (1977). *A Summer to Die.* Boston: Houghton Mifflin.
4. Jean Little. (1984). *Mama's Going to Buy You a Mockingbird.* New York: Viking.
5. Katherine Paterson. (1981). *Gates of Excellence.* New York: E.P. Dutton.

Modern Fairy Tales and Traditional Literature: Revisions and Retellings

This chapter is about the content of modern fairy tales, the craft of modern writers, and the connections between these new tales and traditional literature, our literary heritage.

In his book *From Two to Five,* Kornei Chukovsky (1925, 1963), a children's poet and student of language and literature, explores the language, thought processes, and imagination of preschool children. His chapter on "The Sense of Nonsense Verse" (pp. 89-113) is a product of his study of that genre of children's folk rhymes which he calls "topsy-turvies." "By making a study of them I sought to prove... that even such deliberate deviations from the realities of life strengthen in children their sense of the real..." (Chukovsky, p. xvi).

In that chapter he addresses the question: "Why is it that so many typical children's rhymes, approved by millions of youngsters in the course of many centuries, cultivate with such persistence the obvious violation of reality?" (p. 95). For generations children have enjoyed folk literature in which nonsense is generated by the deliberate incorrect juxtaposition of familiar objects, the reversal of the strict order of things and events, and the interchange of the functions of objects. He cites examples of folk verse in which the motif of horse riding is distorted so that riders travel on geese, goats, beavers, and tiny beetles. Chukovsky emphasizes "that to be able to respond to these playful rhymes the child must have a knowledge of the real order of things... If he does not know, for example, that there is ice only in cold weather, he will not respond to the English verse,

> Three children sliding on the ice
>
> Upon a summer's day (p. 95).

He adds that "all such nonsense verses are regarded by children precisely as nonsense" (p. 95).

Chukovsky discovered the key to children's enjoyment of the incongruous, the absurd, and the distortion of normal ties between objects and their functions the day his two-year-old daughter created her first joke: "'Oggie-meow!' (p. 97). The key is *play*. "No sooner does [the child] master some idea than he is only too eager to make it his toy" (p. 98). As the child engages in this mental play he reveals and confirms his mastery of concepts of the world around him. He can only play with truths that he has mastered.

> When we notice that a child has started to play with some newly acquired component of understanding, we may definitely conclude that he has become full master of this item of understanding; only those ideas can become toys for him whose proper relation to reality is firmly known to him (p. 103).

All children search for order in their world and engage in a timeless quest to understand the real interrelations of ideas and things. "Topsy-turvies" clarify and strengthen the child's grasp of reality. In addition, the "topsy-turvies" develop in children a sense of humor. "No other kind of nonsense verse brings the child so close to the basic elements of humor" (p. 104). Thus, Chukovsky highlights in this special chapter the educational value of topsy-turvies as "wholesome mental nourishment" for young children (p. 105).

Literary Play in the Middle Grades

As children mature, they continue to enjoy the humor derived from playing with concepts and information they have accumulated over the years. They are amused by jokes that depend on word play for humor and by publications such as *Mad* magazine in which satire is used to play with realities of the media and society. *The Phantom Tollbooth*[1] appeals to young readers who delight in language play, and *Alice in Wonderland*[2] continues to provide amusement to each new generation by turning reality "topsy-turvy."

The Focus Unit featured in this chapter is designed to provide "wholesome mental nourishment" for middle-grade students through an exploration of modern fairy tales and traditional literature. In this Focus Unit experience, students are exposed to a wide variety of modern fairy tales and invited to discover their common roots in traditional literature and the craft of modern writers who draw from these old oral tales, handed down through the generations, to create new tales for modern audiences.

Playing with traditional literature is one technique modern writers use to create humor. They play with familiar plot patterns, motifs, character types, settings, and themes found in traditional folk and fairy tales, myths, legends, and fables. They generate humor with surprising twists, reversals, rearrangements, and contemporary touches. They engage in "literary play" to create spoofs, parodies, and satires. Some modern writers transform traditional tales to make statements about contemporary social and political issues, to promote rethinking of traditional ideas, and to generate new perspectives. These transformed tales may be light and humorous, or more serious in tone. Other writers draw from traditional patterns found in old folk and fairy tales to create original stories with contemporary psychological insights and social attitudes. Alison Lurie's anthology, *The Oxford Book of Modern Fairy Tales* (1993) includes a wide variety of modern fairy tales written by forty well-known authors over the past 150 years. This book can serve as an excellent resource for teachers and students in planning and implementing this Focus Unit experience.

Following Chukovsky's notion of "the sense of nonsense," it is clear that for readers to enjoy the literary play or to grasp the new meanings in modern fairy tales, they must have prior knowledge of the traditional plots, characters, themes, motifs, genres, or specific tales that modern writers use as sources for their new tales. Students who do not have this literary background are given opportunities to read relevant selections from traditional literature as preparation for reading the modern fairy tales featured in this Focus Unit. Students are also encouraged to return to familiar old tales to search for connections with these new ones.

Introducing Modern Fairy Tales

In the initial shared reading session, the teacher introduces two examples of modern fairy tales and invites students to identify their roots and the literary and artistic techniques which reflect the craft of authors and illustrators. In her book, *Snow White in New York*, Fiona French uses "art deco" style to illustrate this modern retelling of the Snow White story which is set in New York City during the 1920s or 1930s. Snow White's stepmother is "Queen of the Underworld," and she likes to see herself in the *New York Mirror*. When she reads about Snow White in the *Mirror*, the jealous stepmother plots to get rid of her. The plot is foiled when the bodyguard leaves Snow White alone in the dark city streets instead of shooting her. Fortunately, seven jazz-men take her into their night club, where she sings and attracts the attention of a handsome newspaper reporter. When Snow White's success as a singer is reported in the Mirror, her stepmother tries again to get rid of her with a poisoned cherry in a cocktail. Fortunately, Snow White wakes up in the glass coffin; she marries the reporter, and the stepmother is arrested by the police.

After this brief picture book is shared with the students, they are asked to compare it with the traditional story of Snow White. Several copies of Grimm's *Snow White and the Seven Dwarfs*, illustrated by Nancy Ekholm Burkert (1972), are available to refresh their memories about specific details in the traditional story. Students identify connections between this modern fairy tale and the traditional tale recorded by the Grimm Brothers. They also identify the changes made by the author/artist who created this modern tale. The teacher introduces the students to the term "parody" to call attention to the literary device used by the author to create humor and to contribute to their growing store of language used in literary analysis.

The True Story of the Three Little Pigs by A. Wolf (Scieszka, 1989) — another illustrated, modern revision of a traditional tale — is read aloud to introduce an example of a "viewpoint revision." In this humorous tale, Alexander T. Wolf presents his own version of what happened when he encountered the three pigs. In discussing this story as told by the villain, students identify elements of the traditional story and changes made by the author. They also identify literary devices such as the shift in viewpoint and the use of flashback to create this new tale. When Alexander T. Wolf introduces himself in the opening pages, the illustrations reveal his prisoner's garb. Then he tells his *own* version of the story of his encounters with the Three Little Pigs and the events that lead to his arrest. On the final page, he is shown behind bars and with a long white beard.

The students are given time to examine the illustrations in these picture books and invited to share their thoughts about each artist's style. They are also asked to identify details in the illustrations that extend the text and contribute to the humor in each story.

After this introductory shared reading session, students are invited to choose two or more of the revised tales in the Focus Unit collection (see Bibliography) to read and examine on their own or with a partner. Students are asked to identify and record in their literary journals connections between the modern revisions and traditional tales, changes made by the author/artist, and specific literary devices used to create these modern fairy tales. In addition, students are asked to write about the nature of each tale they've selected to read independently. Is it a humorous tale reflecting the author's lighthearted tone? Is it a more serious work prompting sober reflection about social or political issues? Is it a contemporary response to traditional literary themes? Is it a revision of a fable? a myth? a folktale? Later, students will have opportunities to share what they've discovered about these tales in group sessions and to create their own modern fairy tales.

A survey of the types of literary selections included in the Focus Unit collection is presented below to suggest the variety of modern revisions and retellings available for middle-grade students to enjoy and to learn about modern fairy tales, their roots in traditional literature, and the literary devices used by modern writers to create these tales.

Fable Revisions

Students who have an understanding of the form and content of traditional fables are ready to enjoy Florence Heide's *Fables You Shouldn't Pay Attention To* (1978). One young reader of these humorous parodies referred to them as "topsy-turvy fables." In each fable, traditional lessons are reversed so that carelessness, selfishness, and dishonesty are rewarded. Humor is grounded in expectations about virtues rewarded and vices punished, and in surprise endings associated with the violation of convention.

Another way to explore fable revisions is to compare a traditional fable with its modern counterpart. For example, many students are familiar with Leo Lionni's *Frederick* (1967), a picture book for young readers. A comparison of this modern fable with Aesop's "The Grasshopper and the Ant" reveals philosophical differences. Frederick did not collect grain with the other mice in preparation for winter, but these hard-working mice tolerated his uniqueness. They learned to appreciate his special contributions as an artist whose poetry provided them with food for the mind and spirit and imagination during the long, dark winter. They learned that "man does not live by bread alone." Their good-natured acceptance of individual differences represents a sharp contrast to the harsh justice and work ethic pronounced by Aesop's Ant.

The Hare's Race by Hans Baumann (1976) is a modern revision of Aesop's "The Hare and the Tortoise." Humor is generated by the contemporary touches as well as the surprise ending. When mole wins the race with hare, the reader expects the other animals to cheer him and to acknowledge that, as the winner, he has confirmed the notion that "slow and steady wins the race." However, the others laugh at him and hare has the last word:

> Of course you were first. Only tell me, what did you get out of it? You scratched and scraped, but I really had some fun! (unpaged).

One student commented that he preferred this modern revision and added that it reminded him of his gym teacher: "He always says it's more important to have a good time than to always worry about winning."

These modern fables feature two literary techniques: the use of contemporary settings and revised lessons. The element of surprise used by the writers to generate humor is based on their assumptions about readers' expectations concerning the nature of traditional fables. Once these techniques are identified by the students, they can use them to create their own revisions of traditional fables.

Fairy Tale Revisions

A Frog Prince, written and illustrated by Alix Berenzy (1989) is a modern revision of the familiar Grimm's tale "The Frog Prince." The author notes that when she read the Grimm's tale, her sympathies were with the frog instead of the spoiled princess. "And I couldn't help but wonder what the ideal story would be from the frog's point of view" (Jacket flap). So, Berenzy created a quest tale in which the frog, rejected by the princess after his retrieval of her golden ball and his offer of love, sets out on a journey in search of "a true princess, of a different mind." Like other brave and honorable heroes of traditional folk and fairy tales, the frog encounters danger, overcomes obstacles, provides help to those in need, is rewarded for his kindness, and finally reaches his destination. He climbs to the very top of the tower in the great castle in another kingdom. There he discovers the one he had been seeking: "In the bed, fast asleep, was the most beautiful princess the Frog could ever have imagined" (unpaged). On turning the page, the reader, too, sees the princess: a green frog sleeping in an elegant bed chamber. Of course, they are married and reign together in peace as Frog King and Queen.

Students who are not familiar with Grimm's classic story of "The Frog Prince" should read it before reading Berenzy's beautifully illustrated revision. For this purpose, it is useful to have available in the classroom *The Complete Grimm's Fairy Tales* (Pantheon, 1944, 1972), as well as some single illustrated editions such as Rachel Isadora's *The Princess and the Frog* (1989). Students are invited to compare Berenzy's tale with the traditional tale, to identify the nature of this revision, and to search for the connections between this modern fairy tale and the "quest tales" found in traditional literature.

Berenzy's revision invites the students to rethink the old fairy tale and, further, to assume a "what if...?" frame of mind as a starting point for composing their own modern fairy tales. In his book *From Communication to Curriculum,* Douglas Barnes suggests that "teachers should deliberately encourage and support their pupils in developing an open and hypothetical style of learning" (1975, p. 52). By approaching traditional tales with a "what if...?" frame of mind, professional writers and student writers engage in this open and hypothetical style of learning.

The Frog Prince Continued (Scieszka and Johnson, 1991) offers one answer to the question, "What if the story continued *after* the happily ever after ending?" This new story is told from the viewpoint of the Frog Prince, and the reader soon learns that he is not at all happy as a prince. He sets off on a quest to find a witch who will be able to change him back into a frog. Along the way, he encounters a number of witches from other fairy tales but eventually devises his own solution — one that pleases both the Prince and the Princess and surprises the reader. Steve Johnson's paintings contribute significantly to Scieszka's text, and students are encouraged to search for details in each picture that extend the humor and meaning of the story.

In *The Telling of the Tale: Five Stories* (1990) William Brooke uses a "what if..." frame of mind to recreate "Sleeping Beauty," "Cinderella," "Paul Bunyan," "John Henry," and "Jack and the Beanstalk." He poses such questions as "What if Cinderella didn't want to try on the slipper?" or "What if Paul Bunyan met up with Johnny Appleseed?" In his second volume, *Untold Tales* (1992), Brooke recreates fairy-tale characters and their stories to produce humor and to raise questions about "happily ever after."

Bruce Coville's *Jennifer Murdley's Toad* (1992) offers an answer to the question: "What happened to the toads that tumbled out of the mouth of the unkind girl in Perrault's tale of 'Diamonds and Toads'?" This novel is about contemporary middle grade students, but its theme is as old as the tale woven into it. *The Classic Fairy Tales* by Iona and Peter Opie (1974)[3] includes the first English translation of this tale as well as introductory comments about the basic theme found in hundreds of variants.

The True Story of the Three Little Pigs by A. Wolf (1989) was created by the author/artist collaboration of Jon Scieszka and Lane Smith. This team also produced *The Stinky Cheese Man and Other Fairly Stupid Tales* (1992), a collection of spoofs of traditional fairy tales. Along with literary play, the experienced reader will find irony, parody, running gags, social commentary, and literary criticism, and will discover that this author/artist team plays with the conventions of a book from cover to cover.

The Boardwalk Princess (Levine, 1993), set in Brooklyn at the turn of the century, is based on the Grimm's tale, "Brother and Sister." Since most students are not familiar with this traditional transformation tale, they can read it in *The Complete Grimm's Fairy Tales* before examining Levine's modernized, illustrated version.

James Marshall's humorous retelling of *Goldilocks and the Three Bears* (1988), *Hansel and Gretel* (1990), *The Three Little Pigs* (1989), *and Red Riding Hood* (1987) adds new life to each of these familiar, old tales. A new interpretation of each tale is found in the interdependent text and illustrations. Students are encouraged to read traditional retellings of each tale and to study the artistic interpretations of those who have illustrated these stories.

Other experimental tales with humorous illustrations are: *The Principal's New Clothes* (Calmenson, 1989), an updated revision of Andersen's story of the vain emperor; *Sydney Rella and the Glass Sneaker* (Myers, 1985), about the neglected youngest brother who longs to be on the football team; *The One and Only Robin Hood* (Gray, 1987), in which the author uses a question-and-answer format to recreate and weave together legendary characters and familiar nursery rhymes; and *Jack the Giant-Killer: Jack's First and Finest Adventures Retold in Verse as Well as Other Useful Information about Giants* (de Regniers, 1987).

Feminist Fairy Tales

In his book *Don't Bet on the Prince: Contemporary Feminist Fairy Tales in North America and England* (1986), Jack Zipes examines feminist fairy tales:

> Created out of dissatisfaction with the dominant male discourse of traditional fairy tales and with those social values and institutions which have provided the framework for sexist prescriptions, the feminist fairy tale conceives a different view of the world and speaks in a voice that has been customarily silenced (xi).

Zipes cites a number of examples of experiments with the traditional fairy tale, new tales and rewritten tales, and notes that these "...contemporary feminist fairy tales have drawn upon a rich tradition of feminist tales or tales with strong women which may not be widely known but have nevertheless provided models and the impetus ...to challenge the dominant male discourse" (p. 13).

The Practical Princess and Other Liberating Fairy Tales (Williams, 1978) is a collection of feminist fairy tales. Williams creates new tales in which the traditional passive princesses are replaced by active, intelligent, resourceful, independent, humane female characters. Princess Bedelia slays a dragon; Petronella rescues a prince, but discovers he's not worth the trouble. These heroines take control of their lives and make choices about their destinies.

One student, speculating about Jay Williams' reasons for writing these tales, wrote in her literary journal:

> He realized that women aren't always needing to be rescued and men aren't always brave. He wanted to show that women are brave and strong, too. Maybe he had a sister like Petronella!

Another student wrote:

> I think the author [Jay Williams] probably thought it wasn't fair to always have princesses sitting around being helpless and silly and waiting for a prince to give them a life! He knew that women can be doctors, and engineers, and Supreme Court justices! He wanted to show how things have changed and to talk about equal rights for women, so he used a modern fairy tale to do it.

The Last of the Dragons (E. Nesbitt, 1980 [1925]) portrays a resourceful young woman who challenges the tyranny of her father, the King of Cornwall, and manages to work with an unconventional prince to resolve the problem of the dragon and to move toward a more humane society.

In *The King's Equal* by Katherine Paterson (1992), a dying king proclaims that his self-centered son cannot wear the crown of the kingdom until he marries a woman who equals him in beauty, intelligence, and wealth. The arrogant prince believes this is impossible, until he finds someone who is far better than he.

Other contemporary writers have created feminist tales by rearranging well-known tales. For example, "Princess Dahli" (Lee, 1973, pp. 95-111) is a revision of the popular Walt Disney version of "Cinderella" that features a passive female as the central character. Princess Dahli rebels against her rich relatives and, when she sneaks into the ball, discovers that the Prince is fat and greedy. She chooses to marry his poor cousin whose character is more to her liking. "Princess Dahli" and the other tales in Lee's collection, *Princess Hynchatti and Some Other Surprises*, tell of princes and princesses who engage in traditional quests, of virtue rewarded and greed and cruelty punished, of weddings and happy endings. But traditional motifs, characters, and plot lines have been rearranged to produce unconventional and surprising tales.

In John Gardner's *Gudgekin the Thistle Girl* (1976), another Cinderella revision, Gudgekin refuses to be humiliated by the prince and teaches him to respect her integrity. *Moon Ribbon* (1976), Jane Yolen's revision of the Cinderella tale, challenges the patriarchal view of the world. *Sleeping Ugly* (Yolen, 1981) and *The Forest Princess* (Herman, 1974) are revisions of "Sleeping Beauty" and "Rapunzel."

Clever Polly and the Stupid Wolf (Storr, 1955; 1979) is a collection of parodies of nursery tales in which Polly outwits the wolf who plans to eat her. William H. Hooks' *The Three Little Pigs and the Fox* (1989) is an Appalachian version of the classic tale. In this regional interpretation, the youngest piglet is a girl named Hamlet who is intelligent and resourceful and manages to outwit the fox and free her brothers from captivity in the fox's den.

In her collection of transformed fairy tales, *The Door in the Hedge* (1981), Robin McKinley portrays self-confident and courageous young women who dare to oppose tyranny and seek alternatives to oppression. It is interesting to compare McKinley's "The Princess and the Frog" (pp. 79-103) with Berenzy's *A Frog Prince*, Scieszka's *The Frog Prince Continued*, and William Brooke's "A Prince in the Throat," in *Untold Tales* (Brooke, 1992).

Contemporary feminist fairy tales are also found in *Stories for Free Children* (Pogrebin, 1982) and *Free to Be... You and Me* (Hart, et al. 1974). For example, Jeanne Desy's "The Princess Who Stood on Her Own Two Feet" (Pogrebin, pp. 43-46) is about a tall, competent young woman who rejects the prince who humiliates her and finds someone who accepts her for who she is. Desy introduces humor into the tale in her parody of the male quest for power.

Jane Yolen's "The White Seal Maid" in *The Hundredth Dove* (1980, pp. 29-37), provides a response to Andersen's modern fairy tale, "The Little Mermaid." Yolen's heroine is not submissive and pliant, but in control of her life. She is portrayed as a caring and nurturing woman who chooses to return to the sea rather than live in a male-dominated world. Indeed, she *uses* Merdock the fisherman to help her save the seal people.

These feminist fairy tales reflect the different ways contemporary writers have responded to traditional tales and have invited readers to rethink conservative views of gender and power. Some of these writers use humorous characters and comic reversals to send their message. Others create narratives of a more serious and dramatic nature.

The Focus Unit Collection:
Rediscovering Picture Books and Folklore

Many of the books included in the Focus Unit collection are picture books. This genre can be used effectively with middle-grade students to teach literary analysis: picture books are short enough to be read and analyzed in single sessions, and students can identify literary elements and techniques with relative ease. A number of the picture books included in the collection can only be fully appreciated by students who have matured intellectually and emotionally beyond the age of the usual picture book audience. Often, these books are rejected by older readers because of their picture book format and their association with childhood. In the context of this Focus Unit, picture books that feature sophisticated humor, themes, plot, illustrations, and literary devices and which, in some cases, explore serious subjects are introduced to middle-grade students who would probably not discover them on their own. In addition to offering enjoyable reading experiences and a context for literary learning, picture books expose students to the work of gifted artists. As students explore the interdependence of text and illustration in picture books, they can discover techniques artists use to create meaning. The picture book promotes aesthetic enjoyment as well as artistic awareness.

This Focus Unit also functions as an invitation for middle-grade students to discover or rediscover traditional literature. According to the results of André Favat's study of children's reading interests, "...children's interest in fairy tales emerges at a prereading age and gradually rises to a peak of interest between the approximate ages of 6 and 8, and then gradually declines to a point of non-interest by the ages of 10 or 11...Concurrent with this decline in interest in the fairy tale, there is an emergence of interest in stories of reality" (Favat, 1977, pp 4-5).

As a teacher, I have observed children's reading choices for many years and have seen this shift in interest as children move into the middle grades and show a preference for realistic stories and informational books. Although I have observed only a very few middle-grade students select folklore on their own for independent reading, I have found many students who have enjoyed the folklore introduced in the literature program and some who returned to this genre on their own to choose material for independent reading. In the context of the Focus Unit presented in this chapter, students are introduced to traditional literature along with the work of writers who draw from these old stories to create modern fantasy. Many students enjoy the intellectual challenge of studying the connections between traditional and modern tales and exploring universal themes and structures, recurring patterns and motifs, rich language patterns, and the art of storytellers as well as the artists who illustrate many of these stories. Some students discover or rediscover the pleasures of folklore and add this genre to their private list of reading interests that guides their reading choices.

A variety of collections and single illustrated editions of diverse folktales, fairy tales, fables, myths, and legends should be available in the classroom so that students can discover, rediscover, and enjoy traditional literature and, in the process, build the literary background necessary to make sense of modern literature.

Short stories, novels, and poetry inspired by traditional literature and intended for a mature audience can also be incorporated into this Focus Unit to meet the needs of students who are ready for more challenging and complex literary experiences. A survey of some of these titles is included at the end of this chapter, following a description of reading-writing experiences which are woven into the Focus Unit plan for exploring modern revisions and retellings of traditional tales.

Reading - Dialogue - Writing Connections

After students examine stories from the collection and record their findings in their literary journals, they are invited to share their experiences in small dialogue groups or in a whole-group session. Students engage in a collaborative analysis of authors' craft and record the results of their analysis on a wall chart in the classroom. For example, they discover techniques used to produce humor; changes in viewpoint and setting; examples of social and political commentary; the use of illustration to offer a new perspective or interpretation of an old tale; and the use of "what if...?" or "What happened next?" questions to generate a revision.

The analysis and review of these stories in small or large dialogue groups prepare the students to write their own modern fairy tales. Each student chooses a familiar and favorite traditional tale and thinks of a new angle or perspective for retelling it. Suggestions such as the following, derived from the results of their literary analysis, are recorded on a second wall chart for those students who need help getting started:

1. Retell the tale from the viewpoint of the villain.

2. Let the central character tell his or her story in a first-person narrative.

3. Retell the story from the viewpoint of a minor character.

4. Use a contemporary setting as the context for retelling the story.

5. Create an illustrated retelling in which the pictures suggest a contemporary setting and a new interpretation of the old story.

6. Intertwine other familiar folktale characters into the plot line.

7. Rearrange or reverse traditional motifs, plot lines, and character interactions to generate humor.

8. Use the "what if...?" framework to create a new story.

9. Create personal histories for key characters and incorporate these into a revised tale.

10. Create a sequel to tell a story beyond its happy-ever-after ending.

11. Retell the story in verse form.

12. Use a question-answer format.

13. Revise a fable to teach a new lesson.

14. Re-create the story as a front page news item. Include interviews with witnesses of the events.

15. Re-create the story as it might be told by the central character to his/her grandchildren.

16. Re-create the story as it might be told by the central character to his/her psychiatrist.

17. Create a feminist revision.

18. Create a revision which makes a statement about contemporary social or political issues.

A student who had read *A Frog Prince* by Alix Berenzy (1989) and had identified with the author's comment that her sympathies were with the frog in the Grimm's tale, decided to retell "Rumpelstiltskin" from the viewpoint of the gnome. This student-author introduced her story with an "Author's Note":

> I never did think it was fair that Rumpelstiltskin gets destroyed in the end even though he did everything he promised to do and the girl didn't keep *her* promise. It doesn't make sense that he was the *helper* and wasn't appreciated for helping her. So my story has a happy ending for Rumpelstiltskin.

Another student transformed "The Tortoise and the Hare" from a simple fable into a long, complex narrative with a contemporary setting and well-developed characters whose extended dialogues reflected the language patterns of the student's own peer culture. In this story, Jack Hare challenges Paul Tortoise to compete in the decathlon in the Animal Olympics. Paul decides to do the best he can and spends the next two weeks working out at the Health Club to prepare for the ten events in the decathlon. But Jack does not train for this contest. "Jack was an up-beat, in-shape hare... who was very conceited... He was so sure of himself that he sent out invitations for his victory celebration party... He even invited Paul just to rub it in." This made Paul more determined than ever to work hard and win. In the end, of course, he does manage to win, but only barely. He had the greatest difficulty with the javelin and discus throws but did *very* well in the swimming event!

Since many of the stories written and illustrated by students for this "literary revision" project can be enjoyed at different levels, the students are invited to share their stories with peers as well as younger children in the school. An important by-product of this unit is the establishment of cross-grade interactions in which middle-grade students share their writing with young children, giving them an opportunity to enjoy the stories as well as the attention of older students.

Reading, examining, and writing revisions of traditional tales provide students with opportunities to engage in divergent and hypothetical thinking; to experiment with language ideas and literary conventions; to engage in literary analysis; and to discover connections between traditional and modern literature. The purpose of the "literary revision" project is to reinforce students' understanding of the modern fairy tale and the literary techniques and sources writers use to create these tales.

Challenges for Mature Readers

The Focus Unit described in this chapter is designed to expose students to the work of contemporary writers who draw from the oral tradition to create new stories and to introduce students to the craft of these writers as well as the artists who collaborate with them in retelling, revising, or reworking these old tales. Picture-books and collections of short stories are used as the core of the reading-dialogue-writing experiences reviewed above. For older students these experiences can serve as preparation for reading longer and/or more sophisticated and complex stories, novels, and poetry written by contemporary writers who draw from traditional literature to create fantasy and even realism. Students are encouraged to identify the traditional tales that are retold, woven into, or alluded to in a particular narrative and to reread these old tales in order to enrich their encounters with these modern fairy tales.

Jane Yolen's *Briar Rose* (1992) is included in the Fairy Tale series edited by Terri Windling. The novels in this series are based on traditional fairy tales. In her introduction, Windling discusses fairy tales and modern writers:

> The wealth of material from myth and folklore at the disposal of the storyteller (or modern fantasy novelist) has been described as a giant cauldron of soup into which each generation throws new bits of fancy and history, new imaginings, new ideas, to simmer along with the old. The storyteller is the cook who serves up the common ingredients in his or her own individual way, to suit the tastes of a new audience (Yolen, 1992 pp. 10-11).

In Jane Yolen's novel, the German tale, "Briar Rose" or "The Sleeping Beauty in the Wood" is retold as a contemporary story of a Holocaust survivor. Before her beloved grandmother dies, Rebecca Berlin promises her that she will find for her the "castle in the sleeping woods" (p. 25). All through her childhood, Rebecca had listened to her grandmother tell the story of Briar Rose. Rebecca's quest for the castle in the sleeping woods takes her from her home in New England to Poland, where she discovers that this story is, in truth, her grandmother's *own* story. Rebecca learns that the castle in the forest is the death camp known as Chelmno, created by the Nazis during World War II, where her grandmother was gassed and thrown into a pit with the other victims. Unlike them, she escapes the curse of the angel of death: she is pulled from the pit by members of a group of partisans; the man who breathes life into her mouth is known by his companions as Prince. The partisans take care of the girl and name her Princess Briar Rose. They take her away from the barbed wire and the sleepers who will never awake.

In an "Author's Note" at the end of the novel, Yolen reports that 320,000 people died at Chelmno between 1942 and 1945. However, she makes it clear to the reader that this novel is fiction. "All the characters are made up. Happy-ever-after is a fairy tale notion, not history. I know of no woman who escaped from Chelmno alive" (p. 186).

Unlike this realistic story of tragic events in recent history, Sherri Tipper's *Beauty* (1991) is science fiction. It is the story of Sleeping Beauty recorded in the journal of Beauty, daughter of the Duke of Westfaire. The first entry is made in April, 1347, not long before her sixteenth birthday. Other entries record her time travel forward into the twenty-first century, back into the 1990s, her return to her own time, the 14th and 15th centuries, as well as her travel into the world of Faery. Beauty's journey into the future reveals the dark side of the human psyche. She sees the terrible waste of natural resources, the manmade machines of destruction, the writers who create the terrors of bigotry, hatred, persecution, and violence. Her journey into a world without beauty and magic helps her understand the nature of her own gift to humanity.

Interwoven into this story of good and evil, love and loss, hope and despair, mortals and faery are characters and motifs from other traditional tales such as "The Frog Prince," "Snow White," and "Rapunzel."

Margaret Mahy's *The Changeover: A Supernatural Romance* (1984) also has its roots in "Sleeping Beauty," and motifs and themes from other ancient tales are woven into this modern story of a young woman's maturation and inner journey and of the power of love over evil. When Laura Chant's three-year-old brother, Jacko, becomes the victim of an evil stranger with magical powers, she knows that only by gaining supernatural powers herself will she be able to fight for her brother's life. Like the heroines in old fairy tales, she risks her life to save her beloved Jacko. She enters into a supernatural rite, the "changeover" — she must find her way through the forest and the briars, the terror and the pain, on her own. At the end of her journey, she looks into the mirror and "...she saw plainly that she was remade, had brought to life some sleeping part of herself, extending the forest in her head... through the power of charged imagination, her own and other people's, had made herself into a new kind of creature" (p. 152).

Watching the Roses by Adéle Geras (1992) is about Alice, an English girl whose life resembles a modern version of "Sleeping Beauty." She is raped on her eighteenth birthday and withdraws into a coma-like silence. As she lies in her childhood bedroom, the activity in the household also stops, and the roses grow wild like a thorny wall. But Alice initiates her own healing process as she writes in her diary about events before her birth, the curse of Aunt Violette at her christening, her family life, her boarding-school life — all the events leading up to the trauma.

This novel is a sequel to *The Tower Room* (1992), in which one of Alice's boarding-school roommates, Megan, is the central character in a contemporary tale drawn from "Rapunzel." Readers of this novel also meet the third room-mate, Belle, who, like Snow White, has a vain and jealous stepmother who gives Belle apples that almost cause her to choke to death. Belle is very independent and goes through the forest to a secret meeting with a group of seven jazz musicians to prepare to sing in a nightclub. Of course, this incident is of special interest to students who have already encountered a remarkably similar scene in *Snow White in New York* (French, 1986).

The Wedding Ghost is a sophisticated picture book created by Leon Garfield and Charles Keeping (1985). The story of Sleeping Beauty is woven into a contemporary narrative that begins with the hectic preparations for the wedding of Jack and Gillian (Jill). The only one who hadn't been invited to the wedding was Jack's old nurse. A mysterious, anonymous wedding gift — an old map — leads Jack on a journey into a supernatural world where he makes his way through a dense forest of brambles and thorns and skulls and skeletons until he sees a mansion, the palace of the Sleeping Beauty. When he sees her, he longs to awaken her with a kiss. "Yet he did delay… He was about to betray one love for another. What of Jill, whom he loved dearly?" (p. 46). His decision to kiss the beautiful princess means she will always be with him — "And it would be a strange life, with two wives" (p. 64).

This ancient tale has also been a source of inspiration for poets: Hayden Caruth's *The Sleeping Beauty* (1982) is a book-length poem; Anne Sexton's *Transformations* (1971) is a collection of poem-stories of Grimm fairy tales that includes "Briar Rose (Sleeping Beauty)" (pp. 107-112).

About the Sleeping Beauty (Travers, 1975) is recommended for teachers and students who develop a special interest in exploring some of the history of this tale. This volume includes five traditional variants which have come to us from different cultures: Germany, France, Italy, Ireland, and Bengal. Travers includes her own version of this tale as well as an essay about the meaning and mystery of "The Sleeping Beauty."

Jack-the-Giant-Killer by Charles de Lint (1987) is another fantasy novel that is included in the Fairy Tales series conceptualized by Terri Windling. In this re-creation of "Jack the Giantkiller" and "Jack and the Beanstalk," the central character is Jacky Rowan and the setting is modern-day Canada. Jacky is a young woman who lives a fairly ordinary and predictable life until the evening she encounters Urban Faerie and finds the red cap that enables her to see into the Faerie world. She is involved in a battle against the dark forces of evil that threaten both the human world and the brighter creatures of the Faerie world.

The writer weaves other traditional story characters and motifs into this high fantasy. For example, one of Jacky's companions on her heroic quest is her best friend Kate, known in the Faerie world as Kate Crackernuts (p. 68). Another companion is Eilian Dunlogan, a man who can wear the shape of a swan and uses a nettle tunic for his transformation (p. 100).

"Stalking Beans" by Nancy Kress is a short story based on the traditional tale of "Jack and the Beanstalk." This story of an older, more experienced "Jack" is part of a collection of adult fairy tales, *Snow White, Blood Red*, edited by Ellen Datlow and Terri Windling (1993).

Betsy Hearne's *Beauty and the Beast: Visions and Revisions of an Old Tale* (1989) is recommended as a rich resource for teachers and students interested in exploring the history of this story, its transformations as an art form, and its enduring core.

Other selections for those interested in this tale include: *Beauty* (McKinley, 1978), a fantasy novel narrated in the first-person by a young girl nicknamed "Beauty"; "A Beauty in the Beast," a contemporary version included in a collection of short stories, *Untold Tales* (Brooke, 1992); and *Beauty and the Beast*, retold by Nancy Willard and illustrated by Barry Moser (1992). The latter is a sophisticated picture book with black-and-white wood engravings that extend the text and convey a sense of American gothic gloom. The setting for this tale, New York City and the New York countryside early in the twentieth century, is portrayed in rich detail through the collaboration of author and artist. This retelling is significantly longer than the average picture book so that the central characters can be well-developed, three-dimensional people with the complexities of real human beings.

A comparative analysis of the diverse retellings and revisions of "The Beauty and the Beast" tale can include the recent animated film version produced by Walt Disney Pictures in November 1991, as well as the video-tape of this film which became available in October 1992, as a Bueno Vista Home Video, and the picture book edition, *Beauty and the Beast*, published by Disney Press in 1991.

"Rapunzel," like the stories reviewed above, can be studied by comparing the works of writers using diverse literary forms to revise or retell this traditional tale. Two of the tales included in the collection *Snow White, Blood Red* are based on the traditional Rapunzel tale: "The Root of the Matter" by Gregory Frost (pp. 162-195) and "The Princess in the Tower" by Elizabeth A. Lynn (pp. 197-213). "Rapunzel" is also one of the poems included in Anne Sexton's collection, *Transformations* (pp. 35-42), and it is the basis for the novel, *The Tower Room* (Geras, 1992).

Melisande was written by E. Nesbit over a hundred years ago and first published as a picture book in 1989, with illustrations by Patrick Lynch. It is a fairy tale that draws from "Rapunzel" and "Sleeping Beauty" as well as *Alice in Wonderland* and *Gulliver's Travels*.

Swan's Wing by Ursula Synge (1981) is the story of the fate of the eleventh prince from Hans Christian Andersen's "The Wild Swans," the prince whose transformation from a swan was incomplete because the nettle shirt woven for him by his sister lacked a sleeve. In Synge's tale, Lord Lothar is a winged man who travels the land, seeking a cure for his affliction, searching for someone who can make him whole again. References to other fairy tales are woven into this fantasy-sequel: Gerda the goose-girl is Lothar's companion on his quest, and they encounter Lady Almira, white as snow, who has much in common with the Snow Queen.

"The Springfield Swans" by Caroline Stemmer and Ryan Edmonds is one of the short stories included in *Snow White, Blood Red* (Datlow and Windling, 1993, pp. 272-280). This retelling of "The Wild Swans" is a humorous tale, set in a small Midwestern town, about baseball and a family named Swenson. When the nine Swenson boys are changed into swans by their stepmother, their sister silently sews nine baseball jerseys. Her task is almost completed on the day of the first game of the season. The nine brothers change into boys again, just in time to play against the Albert Lea team. The youngest brother's jersey wasn't quite finished: "His right sleeve fluttered in the breeze... about like a wing almost" (p. 279). But when he pitched, he was amazing, and he eventually played in the major league clubs.

Like Ursula Synge, David Henry Wilson creates a new story about a minor character in an old story, "Cinderella." *The Coachman Rat* (1989), is a first-person account of the rat who had been transformed into Robert the Coachman by Amadea's fairy godmother. When he is changed back into his animal form after one night of enchantment, Robert retains the power of human speech but can no longer utter or comprehend the language of rats. When he is cast out of the rat community, Robert sets out in search of the Woman of Light, who has the power to change him back to a man. When Robert becomes a man and enters into the human world, he encounters evil and ignorance and brutality as well as man's ability to triumph over evil. The second part of the novel is drawn from the old tale of the Pied Piper of Hamlin and, in the end, Robert is faced with a terrible dilemma: He is asked to lure the rats (his own people) into the river with his recorder in order to save humanity from the plague. This is a haunting fantasy about love and revenge and the nature of the human experience.

Two poems about the Cinderella story offer new ways of looking at this old tale: "Knives" by Jane Yolen is included in *Snow White, Blood Red* (pp. 357-358) and "Cinderella" by Anne Sexton is included in her collection, *Transformations* (pp. 53-57). "The Fitting of the Slipper" by William Brooke is a short story that is included in his collection *A Telling of the Tales* (1990, pp. 51-74). In this retelling, the prince discovers that it is better for him to make a shoe that fits the one he loves. "It's madness to try to make the foot fit the shoe" (p. 73).

In the novel *Sleeping in Flame* (Carroll, 1989), the tale of "Rumpelstiltskin" is woven into the lives of the two central characters, Walker and Maris. As the love between them deepens, Walker discovers that he has had many past lives, reaching back to the time that he was stolen by a little man from his mother, the queen, who had broken her promise to give him her baby. In each generation, this small, magical man has raised this child as his own son, but caused tragedy to strike whenever his "son" gave his love to a woman. Now, the lives of Maris and Walker and their baby are threatened unless Walker is able to discover the secret name of this evil man who is Walker's "Papa." Walker manages to resurrect the two sisters who originally told the Rumpelstiltskin tale to the Grimm brothers who, in turn, edited it before printing it in 1812. These two sisters from Kassel, Germany, reveal to Walker the real name of his "Papa," and they revise the ending of their original tale so that Walker and his loved ones are able to escape from the curse that threatened to destroy them. *Sleeping in Flame* is a fascinating fantasy that explores dreams, myths, and the supernatural, and celebrates the power of love in overcoming evil.

Anne Sexton's poem "Rumpelstiltskin," in her collection *Transformations* (pp. 17-23), suggests another way of thinking about this old tale. Students are encouraged to read the poem along with the novel, as well as a translation of the Grimm tale, and to look for connections and contrasts.

Reading-Dialogue-Writing Connections, Continued

As in the initial part of this Focus Unit experience, students are invited to share their personal experiences evoked by these novels, short stories, and poems in their journals and/or in group settings. Their next step is to engage in literary analysis: to identify literary techniques explored earlier and to find additional examples of authors' craft; to identify narrative elements and their interrelationships; to identify connections between modern selections and traditional literature; and to find connections between modern stories and poems, with special emphasis on theme, style, technique, and roots.

These reading experiences and the literary analysis of these complex works set the stage for writing. Some students may choose to write interpretive essays about the prose or poetry they've experienced; others may decide to write a comparative analysis of modern retellings and revisions of a single traditional tale; still others may be interested in creating their own prose or poetry, drawing from their knowledge of traditional literature and their experiences with some of the authors discussed above.

Students who are especially interested in illustration are encouraged to experiment with visual representation of characters and settings. Betsy Hearn's *Beauty and The Beast: Visions and Revisions of an Old Tale* includes examples of the work of diverse artists who have illustrated this tale over the years. The wide variety of artistic elements (color, line, shape, texture), styles, and media used by these artists to create many different interpretations of this single tale suggest rich possibilities for young artists. Cooper Edens' *The Three Princesses —* *Cinderella, Sleeping Beauty, and Snow White* (1991) is another rich resource for student artists. Edens has compiled the work of 25 master illustrators who have interpreted these three tales for the past 125 years. Some students may choose to collaborate as author and artist teams to create illustrated editions of new stories or poems that have roots in traditional literature.

Literary Learning

A central goal of this Focus Unit is to provide students with a context in which to learn about the connections between traditional and modern literature and the ways modern writers draw from our literary heritage to create new prose and poetry. In her eloquent essays about folklore and fantasy in *Touch Magic* (1981), Jane Yolen focusses on these connections:

> Folklore is, in part, the history of mankind... Folklore is, of course, imperfect history because it is history constantly transforming and being transformed... but... it is the perfect guidebook to the human psyche; it leads us to the understanding of the deepest longings and most daring visions of human-kind...
>
> So when the modern mythmaker, the writer of literary fairy tales, dares to touch the old magic and try to make it work in new ways, it must be done with the surest of touches. It is, perhaps, a kind of artistic thievery, this stealing of old characters, settings, the accoutrements of magic. But then, in a sense, there is an element of theft in all art; even the most imaginative artist borrows and reconstructs the archetypes when delving into the human heart (Yolen pp. 50-51).
>
> Stories lean on stories, art on art. This familiarity with the treasure-house of ancient story is necessary for any true appreciation of today's literature... the child who has never known dryads or fauns will not recognize them in Narnia,

or find their faces on museum walls or in the black silhouettes on Greek vases (Yolen, pp. 15-16).

This chapter, "Modern Fairy Tales and Traditional Literature: Revisions and Retellings," is presented as an invitation to teachers to explore this "treasure-house of ancient story" on their own and to introduce their students to their literary heritage, the roots of modern literature. In this Focus Unit, the study of modern fairy tales is an integral part of a larger context in which students explore the connections between traditional and modern literature in order to understand the meaning of "artistic thievery" and Yolen's claim that: "Stories lean on stories, art on art."

References

Barnes, Douglas. (1975). *From Communication to Curriculum.* New York: Viking Penguin.

Chukovsky, Kornei. (1963). *From Two to Five.* Translated and edited by Miriam Morton. Berkeley, CA: University of California Press.

Edens, Cooper, comp. (1991). *The Three Princesses: Cinderella, Sleeping Beauty, and Snow White.* New York: Bantam.

Favat, F. André. (1977). *Child and Tale: The Origins of Interest.* Urbana, IL: NCTE.

Hearne, Betsy. (1989). *Beauty and the Beast: Visions and Revisions of an Old Tale.* Chicago: University of Chicago Press.

Travers, P.L. (1975). *About the Sleeping Beauty.* New York: McGraw-Hill Book Co.

Yolen, Jane. (1981). *Touch Magic: Fantasy, Faerie, and Folklore in the Literature of Childhood.* New York: Philomel.

Zipes, Jack. (1986). *Don't Bet on the Prince. Contemporary Feminist Fairy Tales in North America and England.* New York: Methuen.

Bibliography: Modern Fairy Tales

Alcock, Vivien. (1993). *Singer to the Sea God.* New York: Delacorte.

Arnold, Tedd. (1988). *Ollie Forgot.* New York: Dial.

Baumann, Hans. (1976). *The Hare's Race.* New York: William Morrow.

Berenzy, Alix. (1989). *A Frog Prince.* New York: Henry Holt.

Berson, Harold. (1980). *Charles and Claudine.* New York: Macmillan.

Brooke, William. (1990). *A Telling of the Tales.* New York: Harper.

Calmenson, Stephanie. (1989). *The Principal's New Clothes.* New York: Scholastic.

Carroll, Jonathan. (1989). *Sleeping in Flame.* New York: Doubleday.

Carruth, Hayden. (1982). *The Sleeping Beauty.* New York: Harper and Row.

Castle, Caroline, reteller. (1985). *The Hare and the Tortoise.* New York: Dial.

Cole, Babette. (1987). *Prince Cinders.* New York: G. P. Putnam's Sons.

Cole, Brock. (1986). *The Giant's Toe.* New York: Farrar Straus & Giroux.

Coville, Bruce. (1992). *Jennifer Murdley's Toad.* San Diego, CA: Harcourt Brace Jovanovich.

Datlow, Ellen and Terri Windling, eds. (1993). *Snow White, Blood Red.* New York: Morrow.

deRegniers, Beatrice Schenk, reteller. (1987). *Jack The Giant Killer: Jack's First and Finest Adventure Retold in Verse as Well as other Useful Information About Giants.* New York: Atheneum.

Desy, Jeanne. (1982). "The Princess Who Stood on Her Own Two Feet." in *Stories for Free Children,* ed. by L. C. Pogrebin. New York: McGraw Hill.

Dinardo, Jeffrey. (1989). *The Wolf Who Cried Boy.* New York: Grosset.

Emberly, Michael. (1990). *Ruby.* Boston: Little, Brown.

French, Fiona. (1986). *Snow White in New York.* New York: Oxford University Press.

Gardner, John. (1971). *Grendel.* New York: Knopf.

Gardner, John. (1976). *Gudgekin the Thistle Girl and Other Tales.* New York: Alfred Knopf.

Gardner, John. (1975). *Dragon, Dragon and Other Tales.* New York: Alfred Knopf.

Gardner, John. (1977). *The King of the Hummingbirds and Other Tales.* New York: Alfred Knopf, Inc.

Garfield, Leon and Charles Keeping. (1985). *The Wedding Ghost.* New York: Oxford University Press.

Geras, Adéle. (1992). *The Tower Room.* San Diego, CA: Harcourt Brace Jovanovich.

Geras, Adéle. (1992). *Watching the Roses.* San Diego, CA: Harcourt Brace Jovanovich.

Graham, Kenneth. (1938). *The Reluctant Dragon.* New York: Holiday House.

Gray, Nigel. (1987). *The One and Only Robin Hood.* Boston: Little Brown.

Gwynne, Fred. (1990). *Pondlarker.* New York: Simon and Schuster.

Hayes, Sarah. (1987). *Bad Egg — The True Story of Humpty Dumpty.* Boston: Little, Brown.

Heide, Florence, and Sylvia Van Clief. (1978). *Fables You Shouldn't Pay Any Attention To.* Philadelphia, PA: J.B. Lippincott.

Herman, Harriet. (1974). *The Forest Princess.* New York: Over the Rainbow Press.

Hooks, William. (1989). *The Three Pigs and the Fox.* New York: Macmillan.

Isadora, Rachel. (1989). *The Princess and the Frog.* New York: Greenwillow.

Kellogg, Steven. (1985). *Chicken Little.* New York: Morrow.

Lee, Tanith. (1973). *Princess Hynchatti and Some Other Surprises.* New York: Farrar, Straus & Giroux. (See: "Princess Dahli," p. 95.)

Levine, Arthur. (1993). *The Boardwalk Princess.* New York: Tambourine.

Lurie, Alison, ed. (1993). *The Oxford Book of Modern Fairy Tales.* New York: Oxford University Press.

McKinley, Robin. (1981). *The Door in the Hedge.* New York: Morrow.

Mahy, Margaret. (1984). *The Changeover: A Supernatural Romance.* New York: Atheneum.

Marshall, James, reteller. (1988). *Goldilocks and the Three Bears.* New York: Dial.

Marshall, James, reteller. (1990). *Hansel and Gretel.* New York: Dial.

Marshall, James, reteller. (1987). *Red Riding Hood.* New York: Dial.

Marshall, James. (1989). *The Three Little Pigs.* New York: Dial.

Miles, Bette. (1974). "Atlanta," in *Free to Be... You and Me.* Edited by Carole Hart, Letty Pogrebin, Mary Rodgers, Marlo Thomas. New York: McGraw-Hill.

Myers, Bernice. (1985). *Sydney Rella and the Glass Sneaker.* New York: Macmillan.

Nesbit, E. (1980). *The Last of the Dragons.* New York: McGraw-Hill Books.

Paterson, Katherine. (1992). *The King's Equal.* New York: HarperCollins.

Perrault, Charles. (1983). *Cinderella*. (Illustrated by Roberto Innocenti.) College Station, TX: Creative Publications.

Pomerantz, Charlotte. (1982). "The Princess and the Admiral," in *Stories for Free Children*, edited by Letty Cottin Pogrebin. New York: McGraw-Hill.

Ross, Tony. (1982). *The Three Pigs*. New York: Pantheon.

Scieszka, Jon. (1991). *The Frog Prince Continued*. New York: Viking.

Scieszka, Jon. (1992). *The Stinky Cheese Man and Other Fairly Stupid Tales*. New York: Viking.

Scieszka, Jon. (1989). *The True Story of the Three Little Pigs by A. Wolf*. New York: Viking.

Sexton, Anne. (1971). *Transformations*. Boston: Houghton Mifflin.

Singer, A.L., adaptor. (1991). *Beauty and the Beast*. New York: Disney Press.

Stamm, Claus, trans. (1982). "Three Strong Women," in *Stories for Free Children*, ed. by L. C. Pogrebin. New York: McGraw-Hill.

Stevens, Janet, adaptor and illustrator. (1984). *The Tortoise and the Hare: An Aesop Fable*. New York: Holiday House.

Stevens, Janet, adaptor and illustrator. (1987). *The Town Mouse and the Country Mouse*. New York: Holiday House.

Storr, Catherine. (1955, 1979). *Clever Polly and the Stupid Wolf*. London: Faber and Faber, Ltd.

Synge, Ursula. (1981). *Swan's Wing*. London: The Bodley Head.

Turkle, Brinton. (1976). *Deep in the Forest*. New York: Dutton.

Vesey, A. (1985). *The Princess and the Frog*. New York: The Atlantic Monthly Press.

Williams, Jay. (1979). *The City Witch and the Country Witch*. New York: Macmillan.

Williams, Jay. (1978). *The Practical Princess and Other Liberating Fairy Tales*. New York: Parents' Magazine Press.

Williams, Jay. (1972). *Seven at One Blow*. New York: Parent's Magazine Press.

Wilson, David Henry. (1989). *The Coachman Rat*. New York: Carroll and Graf Pub.

Yolen, Jane. (1992). *Briar Rose*. New York: A Tom Doherty Associates Book.

Yolen, Jane. (1976). *Moon Ribbon and Other Tales*. "The Moon Ribbon," pp. 1-15. Cromwell.

Yolen, Jane. (1981). *Sleeping Ugly*. New York: Coward-McCann.

Yolen, Jane. (1980). "The White Seal Maid," in *The Hundredth Dove*. New York: Schocken.

Foot Notes:

1. Norton Juster. (1961). *The Phantom Tollbooth*. New York: Random House.
2. Lewis Carroll. (1963, 1865, 1872). *Alice's Adventures in Wonderland*. New York: Macmillan.
3. Iona and Peter Opie. (1974). *The Classic Fairy Tales*. New York: Oxford University Press.

DILEMMAS AND DECISIONS: INTERNAL CONFLICT IN REALISTIC FICTION

All the way home, Skip was aware of Jean's approving arm around her shoulder. Jean had just told her she was her best friend again. That was worth stealing for (Slepian, *Risk N' Roses*, 1990, p. 131).

In Jan Slepian's novel, *Risk N' Roses*, eleven-year-old Skip is driven by a desperate need to belong and to be liked. In order to become a member of a gang and gain the approval of the leader of the gang, Skip chooses to engage in activities that she knows are cruel and wrong. But she is torn by guilt and divided loyalties and struggles to gain the inner strength necessary to resist peer pressure and the powerful control of the gang leader.

Characters in realistic novels for the middle grades often struggle with internal conflicts and may be forced to make moral decisions in moments of crisis. Protagonists engaged in the process of making moral decisions may reflect on their personal values and rule systems: questions of rights and responsibilities, conflicting loyalties, and consequences for self and others. Middle-grade students are ready to explore the moral complexities presented in these realistic novels. They are ready to enter into serious dialogue about the decision-making process of story characters, to consider the options open to these characters and alternative responses which would have produced different outcomes and consequences. Most middle-grade students have begun to move beyond the notion of right and wrong as a rigid dichotomy to an awareness of the gray areas, alternate points of view, and legitimate differences of opinion. They have the intellectual maturity and experience to judge a character's behavior in terms of intention, motivation, and context.

Middle-grade readers are invited to step into the lives of these characters and to experience vicariously their inner struggles and emotional turmoil, their feelings of guilt and confusion, and to live through the experience of making moral choices and facing the consequences of these choices. Unlike story characters, readers are able to respond to the moral dilemma or moment of crisis in the novel without risk and from a safe distance.

Focus On Internal Conflict

Each of the Focus Units described in this book invites students to explore the content of literary texts, the craft of the authors, and the connections between diverse texts selected for the Focus Unit experience. These units are designed to help students understand the formal elements of literature and how authors use these literary elements to create stories so that, as readers, they can reach for deeper understanding of each story as a whole. Students are encouraged to analyze narrative fiction in terms of elements of setting, characterization, plot, theme, style, and viewpoint, as well as the interdependence of the elements within a given story. The Focus Unit described in this chapter is designed to help students learn about literary analysis by focusing on one of these elements, plot, and, in particular, on the nature of internal conflict.

Plot and conflict are intrinsically linked; conflict is usually the source of plot and creates the tension in the story. Rebecca J. Lukens[1] discusses four types of conflict found in literature:

1. *Person-against-person* conflict involves a struggle between a protagonist and an antagonist.

2. *Person-against-society* conflict is one in which society or a representative of society acts as an antagonist (p. 64).

3. *Person-against-nature* conflict involves a protagonist who is threatened by nature or "a component of nature, the antagonist" (p. 64).

4. *Person-against-self* conflict is "an internal conflict of feelings within the protagonist" (p. 62).

Internal conflict is usually intertwined with one or more of the external kinds of conflict to create a strong story. The decision to isolate internal conflict in realistic fiction and use it as a focus for this literature unit was based on instructional objectives: to reinforce and extend literary skills by calling attention to a specific literary element and providing opportunities to study the use of this element in diverse, age-appropriate novels. In this Focus Unit, the study of literary craft is integrated with personal responses to literary content. The focus on internal conflicts of central characters in selected novels allows middle-grade readers to gain insights about themselves as they experience the inner turmoil of a fictional character. Many readers recognize the fear, confusion, self-doubt, and guilt of a particular character in themselves and discover that they are not the only one facing difficulties.

The Focus Unit: Internal Conflict In Realistic Fiction

A collection of contemporary and historical realistic novels is displayed in the classroom. Students are asked to look through the collection, read summaries on book flaps or reviews on back covers, and choose one book to read independently. Several copies of popular titles are included in the collection. Students are given time each day to read silently and to respond in their literary journals. They are also encouraged to take books home for further independent reading.

After all the students have selected a novel for independent reading, the teacher introduces the Newbery Award Winner, *Shiloh* (Naylor, 1991), to the whole class in a series of shared reading sessions. Students are asked to share their personal responses to the story and to identify the setting, characters, plot, viewpoint, and themes. The teacher introduces questions to call attention to the internal conflict of the central character and the relationship between the setting — including time, place, and significant characters — and this conflict. This literary analysis, which highlights the internal conflict in the book selected for a shared reading experience, is intended to prepare students to respond in their literary journals to the novels they have selected for independent reading. They are asked to write about the central character in this self-selected book in terms of his/her internal conflict and to discuss the interrelationships between the internal and external conflicts, as well as the other literary elements. Students are also asked to look for connections between the internal conflict in *Shiloh* and the internal conflict confronting the protagonist in their self-selected novels. As students record their responses in their literary journals, they gain experience in analyzing single texts and comparing multiple texts. The journal serves as a context for developing literary skills and provides the teacher with information about the nature of the thinking and literary response of each student.

Students are asked to present to the class brief book-talks to introduce their self-selected novels in terms of setting, central characters, and conflict. Those reading the same title work together to plan a book talk which will be presented by one member of the group. These book talks are intended to provide brief outlines of diverse novels and expose students to additional titles which can expand their understanding of internal conflict in fictional characters and suggest new possibilities for independent reading. Students are also encouraged to recommend other relevant titles for the classroom collection.

The Shared Reading Experience: *Shiloh*

Shiloh is the story of eleven-year-old Marty Preston who lives with his parents and two younger sisters in the town of Friendly, West Virginia, which is set in the Bible Belt countryside. Hunting is an integral part of this world; it is a way of putting food on the table. But Marty loves animals and is very uncomfortable with the thought of shooting deer and rabbits. The story begins with Marty's encounter with a young beagle who has run away from his master, Judd Travers, who cruelly mistreats his hunting dogs. Marty gives the dog a name, Shiloh, and decides to rescue him from his brutal owner and to keep him hidden from his law-abiding parents. But his first lie leads to further deceptions that have an impact on his family and friends, and Marty must confront the complex moral dilemma generated by his actions.

As *Shiloh* is read aloud in a series of group sessions, students are invited to respond spontaneously to the unfolding story. At the completion of the narrative, students are asked to consider three questions:

1. **What did you learn about the central character, Marty Preston?**
2. **What was the nature of his internal conflict?**
3. **What was the relationship between the setting (time, place, and other significant characters) and Marty's internal conflict?**

In response to the first question, students identify clues that reveal the character of Marty Preston. For example, his deep feelings about animals is revealed in the opening scene of the book in which Marty struggles with thoughts of the rabbit that is the main dish at his family's Sunday dinner. The next clue is found in the scene on the second page: Marty is up in the hills with his .22 rifle, which he uses to shoot targets such as apples or cans, but never "...at anything moving..." (p. 12). The third clue is the delight he expresses during his first encounter with the little beagle and the pain he feels when he realizes the dog has been mistreated.

Another important dimension of the character of Marty Preston is his antipathy toward Judd Travers. In this first-person account, Marty lists the reasons he dislikes the man and describes Travers' cruel treatment of his hunting dogs. When Judd tells Marty that he had not fed Shiloh in order to teach him a lesson, Marty reveals his empathy, "My stomach hurts for Shiloh" (p. 35).

The second question focuses attention on the internal conflict. When Marty decides to rescue Shiloh from Judd, he must keep him hidden from his own family. To keep this secret he is forced to tell a series of lies to his family and to steal food to feed Shiloh. This is especially difficult for him because he is acutely aware of his family's financial problems.

In Chapter 6, Marty describes the shame he had experienced several years earlier when he had secretly taken his sister's Easter chocolate. He recalls his mother's words when she reminded him that he could not keep his secret from Jesus and warned him not to separate himself from God's love (p. 56). Now, when Marty tells Judd he hasn't seen his dog — knowing this is not the truth — he reaches out to Jesus in prayer. "Jesus," he asks, "which you want me to do? Be one hundred percent honest and carry that dog back to Judd so that one of your creatures can be kicked and starved all over again, or keep him here and fatten him up to glorify your creation?" (p. 57).

As he sees himself forced to tell one lie after another to protect his secret, Marty thinks, "Funny how one lie leads to another and before you know it, your whole life can be a lie" (p. 60).

Marty's inner turmoil and sense of personal guilt deepen when Shiloh is severely injured by a German shepherd and when he sees that his secret creates a wedge in his parents' relationship to each other and in their relationship with their neighbors.

Finally, Marty takes responsibility for his own actions, his commitment to Shiloh, and what is right by law. He works for Judd for two weeks to pay for Shiloh. The closing lines of the novel suggest Marty's growth as a result of his struggle with a complex ethical conflict: "...I'm thinking how nothing is as simple as you guess — not right or wrong, not Judd Travers, not even me or this dog I got here. But the good part is I saved Shiloh and opened my eyes some. Now that ain't bad for eleven" (p. 144).

The third question is intended to call attention to the role of setting in shaping character and plot development. The financial hardship faced by Marty's family in this poor community means that owning a pet is a luxury they cannot afford. Thus Marty is forced to steal food from the family table and to practice other forms of deception to feed Shiloh. Hunting is an economic necessity in this community and provides the context for this story about a boy, a hunting dog, and a hunter. This community is also set in the Bible Belt, where religious belief plays a major role in the daily lives of the people. Marty's religious training enters into his struggle to cope with his conflict in his own mind.

In this small rural community, people know each other and appear to live together in relative harmony. An unwritten code seems to govern the relationships between neighbors: neighborly acts of small kindnesses or cooperation are valued, but quarrels between neighbors are avoided. Marty's father reminds him on several occasions that they cannot interfere in a neighbor's business. Marty is acutely aware that his intrusion into Judd Travers' life makes his parents' life difficult. He knows that he does not act alone. He knows that his actions touch the lives of those around him. Marty lives among people who respect the law, the Bible, and each other. It is in this context that he strives to resolve his internal conflict and in which he grows as an individual.

After *Shiloh* is read aloud and discussed in the shared sessions, students are asked to write independently a portrait of Marty Preston. The three questions used to guide the group discussion are now used by students to help them plan what they will write about the central character and how they will organize and express their ideas.

Independent Reading

By this time, students will have had the time to read independently at least one novel from the collection of books selected for this Focus Unit and to record responses in their literary journals. When students are ready to present their book talks to the class, whole-group sessions are scheduled. After these books are introduced to the class, students are invited to find connections among these self-selected novels. As these connections are identified, the teacher records on a wall chart the titles of novels that are linked by a common theme, and students decide on appropriate headings for each group of related titles. Students sign their names next to the title of the novel they have read independently. Those students whose self-selected titles are listed under a particular heading form a dialogue group to engage in an in-depth comparative analysis of these novels. Some novels will be listed under more than one heading; students can choose to join the group which will focus on the theme of most interest to them. In the Focus Unit described in this chapter, four dialogue groups are formed to explore the titles under four headings: 1. "Tragedy and Responsibility"; 2. "Moral Dilemmas"; 3. "Peer Pressure"; and 4. "Choices and Consequence."

Students in each of these four groups are asked to use this comparative analysis of novels that are linked by a common theme to generate a series of questions. Each student is asked to select one of these questions as the focus for a written response to the novel he/she has read independently. Reviews of some of the novels discussed in each of the four dialogue groups, along with questions developed about these novels, are presented below.

Dialogue Groups: Comparative Analysis

1. Tragedy and Responsibility

The series of novels studied in the first dialogue group includes several stories with drowning incidents which suggest a basis for comparative analysis. For example, in *Good-bye, Chicken Little* (Byars, 1979), Jimmie is convinced that he didn't try hard enough to stop his Uncle Pete from walking across the river after his uncle had bragged to his friends from the bar that he could accomplish this stunt. But Uncle Pete falls through the thin ice in the middle of the river and drowns. When Jimmie's mother learns of the tragedy and, in her initial shock, accuses Jimmie of not stopping Pete, Jimmie's sense of guilt deepens. Later, his mother explains that she hadn't meant what she said, but the words are already deeply embedded in Jimmie's mind, and the guilt eats away at him.

In *Cousins* (Hamilton, 1990), Cammy grows up in a small, southern Ohio town in a loving family. But she does not love her too-perfect cousin Patty Ann, who is beautiful, bright, and talented. Patty Ann causes Cammy real distress, making her feel uncomfortable with herself. Cammy looks for her cousin's faults and tries to make her less than she is. But when another cousin, Elodie, falls into a dangerous flooded river, it is Patty Ann who sacrifices her life to save Elodie. Cammy, debilitated with guilt and grief, withdraws from life, haunted by nightmares in which Patty Ann returns.

Jesse Aarons reacts with a mixture of emotions when his best friend, Leslie Burke, drowns in the creek (Paterson, *Bridge to Terabithia*, 1977): denial, guilt, anger, betrayal, fear, grief. Deep down, Jesse knows that if he had asked Leslie to join him and Miss Edmunds for the day in Washington she would not have drowned in the creek. He knows that he had been unable to tell Leslie that he was afraid to cross the creek into Terabithia; she crossed it alone.

Marion Dane Bauer's *On My Honor* (1986) is another narrative about events leading up to and following a drowning tragedy. Joel had promised his father that he and his friend Tony will ride their bikes *only* to the park. He had promised with the words, "On my honor" (p. 8). But when Tony challenges him to swim in the treacherous Vermillion River, where swimming was not allowed, Joel reluctantly consents so that Tony will not think he's a coward. In the water, during a competitive interchange, Joel challenges Tony to swim out to the sandbar. Joel is a good swimmer and reaches the sandbar in good time. What he does not know is that the shallow river has holes of deep water and that Tony can not really swim. Only after Tony disappears does Joel discover the deep black hole and that Tony could not swim but had never revealed this secret about himself. "...the last thing in the world he was ever willing to do was admit that there was something he didn't know" (p. 27). Devastated and guilt-ridden,

Joel struggles to find the courage to face both sets of parents and to tell the truth about Tony's drowning.

In *Plague Year* by Stephanie Tolan (1990) the drowning scene occurs toward the end of a powerful drama of emotional and social upheaval and mob hysteria. When Bran Slocum first comes to the quiet town of Ridgewood and enters the high school, the students react negatively to his "weird" appearance, and he becomes a target for the verbal and physical assaults of bullies. When the town learns that Bran is the son of a suspected serial killer, almost everyone turns against him. Hysteria, hate, and fear spread like a contagious disease; individuals become a mob; voices of protest are silenced; terror and violence end in tragedy.

Only two students befriend Bran: Molly Pepper and Steve Watson reach out with humane concern and compassion to this gentle, thoughtful boy as the rest of the townspeople abandon their humanity in a mindless passion to rid their town of evil. But his two friends cannot protect Bran from those bent on destroying him. The story reaches its climax when the bullies from school corner Bran at the quarry one night and force him to fight for his life. Molly and Steve cannot save him; they cannot stop the events of the next moments as the boys, locked in struggle, slip into the water. Only one survives, the one who had finally taken Bran's life. Molly and Steve hear his voice in the water, saying "Help me" (p. 194), but... "Neither of us moved" (p. 194). Later, when they tell the police the story of the fight, they omit what happened after all three boys had fallen into the water. "...in all the news about it afterward, nobody ever said anything about a fight" (p. 195).

Later, after the "tragedy at the quarry" (p. 195), the townspeople do not speak of the mobs or the violence. "It was almost as if the month of October had never happened, except for that 'accident' at the end" (p. 196).

The story is narrated from the viewpoint of Steve. Toward the end of his narrative, he reflects on what had happened. "I thought about the plague a lot all winter, whatever it was had infected us all and turned ordinary people into people who could kill someone — or let someone die" (p. 197).

An excerpt from a comparative analysis of these novels in a dialogue group reveals students' exploration of issues such as responsibility and guilt:

- I don't think Cammy [*Cousins*] or Jimmie [*Good-bye, Chicken Little*] were *directly* responsible for what happened. But they had reasons to *feel* responsible.

- They both had problems with them [the victims] *before* the accident — so that has a lot to do with how they feel afterwards.

- If you wish for something bad to happen to someone you don't like — and it *does* — it's like you *caused* it, but not really.

- For Jimmie it was hard because of what his mom said. But she didn't realize how it hurt him. You can't erase words.

- Joel [*On My Honor*] pressured Tony to do something dangerous, so it was his fault.

- But he didn't know Tony couldn't swim, so I don't think he's responsible.

- But he knows if he *hadn't challenged* Tony, he'd be alive — so he's the cause even if he didn't mean it.

- Jesse and Joel were both kind of weak. Jesse was afraid to say he was afraid of the creek so she [Leslie] went alone. And Joel was afraid that Tony would think he's a coward if he didn't go in the river. I think *that's* why they feel guilty — they weren't strong — they're not *assertive* — they just let things happen.

- I think Molly and Steve [*Plague Year*] were *most* responsible, because they really could have saved that guy, but they didn't move—

- They didn't *want* to save him — but Joel really did... That's the difference.

- But that guy was a murderer!

- It's still wrong. That's what the courts are for!

- They have to always carry the secret.

- They tried so hard to save Bran. I think the people in that town are *really* responsible... I wonder if any of them *feel* guilty about what happened.

- I think that's why they tried to erase what happened... but you can't. You do stuff with a gang you *know* you'd never do alone — but then it's too late....

The comparative analysis of these and other novels studied by this dialogue group leads to the discovery of similarities and differences which provide the basis for developing a series of questions which will be used later by individual students for written analyses of their self-selected novels.

1. **What is the relationship between the central character(s) and the victim(s)?**

2. **What is the role of the central character(s) in the events leading up to the tragedy and the moment of crisis itself?**

3. **What is the degree of his/her responsibility for the tragedy?**

4. **What is the degree of guilt felt by this character? What is his/her response to the tragedy?**

5. **What is the response of others to the tragedy and to the central character?**

6. **Who is most supportive and helpful in his/her response to the central character?**

2. Moral Dilemmas

The second dialogue group engages in a comparative analysis of novels that feature complex moral dilemmas.

Shiloh portrays a character caught between his humane determination to save a beagle from the abuse of its cruel master, the moral teachings of his family, and the law.

Poor Badger (Peyton, 1990), set in England, is the story of nine-year-old Ros who loves horses and develops a special attachment to a handsome black-and-white pony she discovers one day in a field and names Badger. Ros is shocked to see that Badger is neglected and brutally mistreated by his owner. She cannot bear to see Badger's suffering. Ros, like Marty Preston, decides to rescue the animal from such cruel treatment. She steals him in the middle of the night and hides him in a place where he will be free and safe. Like Marty, Ros is caught between feelings of compassion for an abused animal and the law. Her rescue is a humane act, and she knows it is the right thing to do. She also knows it is against the law and that she is a thief.

Fox in a Trap (Thomas, 1987) is the story of Daniel, who longs to leave his family's Michigan farm and to live an exciting life like his Uncle Pete, an outdoorsman and writer. He is determined to prove to his parents and uncle that he is mature and brave enough to become a hunter. However, when Uncle Pete begins to teach him how to trap foxes, Daniel finds himself caught between his dream of hunting polar bears in the Arctic and his own deep feelings about living creatures. Daniel is shocked to discover that kittens are used for bait, but when he is confronted with the reality of a trapped fox, watches his uncle kill it, and holds the dead fox in his arms, his inner struggle reaches a climax. He knows he cannot bear to see an animal in pain or being killed. Daniel resolves his moral dilemma the next morning when he sets out to spring all of the traps and returns to his family with new insights about himself and a deeper understanding of the meaning of courage.

Shades of Gray (Reeder, 1989) is an historical novel whose action takes place at the end of the Civil War. Twelve-year-old Will Page has lost all of his immediate family and is sent from his city home to live in the Virginia countryside with his aunt and the uncle he considers a traitor because of his pacifist attitudes and his refusal to fight against the Yankees. Will is forced to accept his uncle's hospitality and to become part of a rural life he has never known. As Will works alongside his uncle in their fight for survival, he initially is consumed with anger, hostility, and contempt for this man who refused to fight for his country. But his anger eventually turns to respect and admiration for his uncle, who takes pride in hard work and "in doing things for himself" (p. 35). Will struggles to understand the meaning of honor and pride and to see beyond the simple dichotomy of right and wrong. He discovers that the enemy, the Yankee soldiers, are men with families, hopes, and dreams like his own. He realizes that good people can hold opposite views, and finally understands that it had taken courage for his uncle to refuse to fight in a war he thought was wrong (p. 145).

Stepping on the Cracks (Hahn, 1991) takes place during World War II. Eleven-year-old Margaret and her best friend next door both have brothers fighting overseas against Hitler. The girls' own private war is with Gordy, the sixth grade bully. When they discover Gordy's secret hideout and that he and his friends have been hiding Gordy's brother, an Army deserter who cannot kill a human being and who is convinced that killing is wrong, Margaret struggles to decide whether to turn him in or to help protect a deserter. Later, when Margaret's mother discovers that her daughter has protected a deserter, she says, "...desertion is wrong — you could get into trouble if anyone finds out what you did" (p. 205). But Margaret questions this attitude and begins to see the validity of other perspectives: "...but if you truly believe killing is wrong, what are you supposed to do?" (p. 205).

Waiting for Anya (Morpurgo, 1990) also takes place during World War II, but this historical novel is set in Vichy, France. Jo is a twelve-year-old boy who takes care of the sheep in the absence of his father, who was taken as a prisoner-of-war in Germany. Jo's small village is occupied by German soldiers who patrol the border to prevent any attempts to escape into Spain. The soldiers have orders to shoot anyone helping fugitives. Jo has discovered, on the farm of a reclusive widow, a secret hideout in which a band of Jewish children are waiting to escape into Spain. For months Jo helps the widow and her son-in-law Benjamin get food for these children while they wait for the right time to cross the border. When they realize they cannot wait any longer, Jo decides to assist the twelve children who are trying to escape from the Nazis. He makes this decision with the clear knowledge that he will be shot if he is caught.

Ask Me No Questions (Schlee, 1976) is another historical novel set in Victorian England and based on actual events that occurred in the late 1840s. However, Laura is a fictional character who is sent to London to stay with her aunt and uncle in the country in order to escape the cholera. Laura discovers that the children in the orphan asylum next door to her uncle's farm are sick and starving. She also discovers that none of the adults around her are willing to see or do anything about the neglect and abuse of these poor children. Laura is determined to help them, to steal food for them, although she has been forbidden to talk to the children of paupers. She struggles with the need to violate the rigid code of behavior taught to her by the adults around her, to lie and steal in order to feed these hungry children. She is weighed down with a heavy burden of guilt because of her disobedience and immoral behavior, and by her anxiety that she will not be able to provide enough to help the children survive.

The Cry of the Crow (George, 1980) is set in the Piney woods of the Florida Everglades. Although Mandy Tressel's family must kill crows to protect their strawberry crop, she secretly cares for and tames a young crow, orphaned when her younger brother used crows for target practice. Mandy is torn between her desire to keep her pet and the warnings of her mother to return the bird to the wild. For a while she keeps the bird, ignoring the warnings and her own inner voices. But when the crow identifies Mandy's younger brother as the one who had shot the crow family, she attacks his face. The nature of Mandy's conflict changes as she confronts the danger to her brother, knowing that crows are vindictive. She makes the difficult decision to kill her pet crow to protect her brother.

In *Plague Year*, Steve has to decide whether to go along with his peers and the rest of the townspeople who see Bran as the "bad seed," or to ignore his father's warnings of danger and his own anxiety to stay with Bran and be his friend.

In *A Map of Nowhere* (Cross, 1988) Nick discovers that his older brother's motorcycle gang robs and wrecks shops in remote villages. When he is drawn into their plan to rob the store owned by the family of his friend, Joseph, Nick must decide where his loyalties lie. He must decide whether the quest for adventure and loyalty to his brother are more important than the lives of other people or the rules of right and wrong. In making his decision, he must confront what kind of person he wants to be. At the end of the story, he must make a difficult choice. Should he tell the truth to allow the innocent to go free but in the process reveal, at risk to himself, his own guilt or should he save himself and let the others get convicted?

Questions generated by a comparative analysis of the series of novels listed under the second heading are included below:

1.　What is the nature of the moral dilemma?

2.　What are the personal risks the central character must consider as he/she tries to resolve the dilemma or make a choice?

3.　In what way does the central character's moral decision affect his/her family?

4.　What does the central character learn about the nature of right and wrong, good and evil, justice and mercy, and conventional codes of behavior?

5.　What do the central characters learn about other people as they struggle to resolve their moral dilemma? What do they learn about themselves?

3.　Peer Pressure

Risk N' Roses (Slepian, 1990) is set in the Bronx in 1948. Eleven-year-old Skip longs to join the street gang in her neighborhood led by tough, magnetic Jean Persico. Skip's desperate need to belong drives her to turn her back on family rules and her responsibility for caring for her gentle, mentally-handicapped sister, Angela. When she joins Jean's gang, Skip discovers there are no rules; nothing is too dangerous or forbidden. Lying, stealing, and cruelly harassing an old man are all part of belonging to Jean's inner circle. In order to be accepted as a member of Jean's gang, each girl must complete a "dare" set up by Jean, who appeals to the wildness and rebelliousness in each of them to lure them beyond mischief to cruel and immoral deeds. Skip is torn between loyalty to family and to peers, and she struggles with guilt about deserting her sister, violating her father's trust, and participating in deeds she knows are wrong and cruel. But her fear of losing Jean and being forced to leave the club overpower all other considerations.

The plot of *The Truth or Dare Trap* (Hopper, 1985) is similar to that in *Risk N' Roses,* although the characters in the latter are more richly developed, the inner struggle of the central character is described in greater depth, and the plot is more complex. Megan is a member of a gang of middle-grade girls. Their leader, Angie, uses a "truth or dare" game to hold the group together and to keep things interesting. Like Jean, Angie knows the weakness of each girl and sets up a dare that would be most difficult and painful for each one. And, like Jean, Angie sets up each dare as the price of her friendship. That the truth and dare game will become less innocent and more cruel and dangerous is foreshadowed on page 7: "And before the end of the summer — that innocent little game was going to lead us into more trouble than I'd ever dreamed possible."

In the novel *On My Honor*, peer pressure plays an important role. Joel does not have the inner strength to resist Tony's challenges to engage in activities Joel knows are dangerous and forbidden. In fact, Joel hoped that his father would help him by making the decision for him. But his father demonstrated his trust in his son and put him "on his honor" to do the right thing.

In *Salted Lemons* (Smith, 1980), ten-year-old Darby has moved with her family from Washington, D.C. to Atlanta during World War II. She has difficulty adjusting to a new way of life and is viewed with suspicion by the neighborhood children, who see her as an outsider, a foreigner, a Yankee. Darby discovers that these children follow a leader, Gordon, the "general of the neighborhood," who is much like Jean and Angie in *Risk N' Roses* and *The Truth and Dare Trap*. Led by "General Gordon," the children have targeted others as their enemies: the grocer who is a German; Yoko who is a Japanese-American; and the children who live on the other side of the city limits, the city kids. Hatred, fear, ignorance, and the need for power infect the social context in which Darby must learn to live. Darby is unwilling to submit to the authority of Gordon as the price for acceptance into the neighborhood group. She manages to challenge his authority, prove her courage, and earn the respect of her peers — including Gordon. Darby also refuses to participate in the group's attacks against anyone who is different or suspect. In contrast, she reaches out to build a friendship with Yoko in spite of being called a "yellow Jap lover." Later, when a new girl is treated cruelly because of her religious beliefs, Darby reaches out in empathy and friendship. She remembers when she, too, was the new girl, the enemy.

In the novel, *Out of Control* (Mazer, 1993), sixteen-year-old Rollo Wingate is a follower, a "go-along." He and his two best friends do everything together, and Rollo depends on them to lead the way. He doesn't think about what he does; he simply goes along with whatever they do as if nothing matters except their friendship. Rollo goes along when they attack a classmate, Valerie, in a deserted hallway at school. He goes along when his friends, the principal, and their parents decide to conceal the truth as if nothing happened. But it did happen. Valerie is suffering, and Rollo is haunted by what he has done, by his own role in an incident that got "out of control."

The story is told as a third-person narration which alternates between the viewpoints of Rollo and Valerie. Rollo tries to understand who he is, what he has done, how it happened. As he begins to confront the truth, he can't escape thoughts like these: "if only it hadn't happened... If only he had said something... If only... you could turn back the clock" (p. 137). Valerie tries to cope with the fear, the humiliation, the hatred, and, finally, the anger. It is only when Valerie becomes involved with a group of girls at school who know about sexual harassment from personal experiences that she is able to talk about what happened. For the first time she feels she is not alone. In the end, she decides to write to the editor of the newspaper "to simply make clear what happened to her that day..." (p. 212). She decides to bring out in the open an act of violence that has been concealed to protect the school, the faculty, the boys, and their parents.

When Rollo is forced to think about what he has done to Valerie and to step into her shoes as a victim, he knows he can no longer "go-along." He knows he must begin to take responsibility for his own actions. His first step in this direction occurs in the final scene: Rollo walks away from his two best friends.

This novel can provoke serious debate among older students about sexual harassment, moral responsibility, and individual accountability. Significant differences in the nature of reader response related to gender can play an important role in this dialogue.

Questions derived from a comparative analysis of this group of novels include:

1. Identify the opposing characters. What are the significant differences between them? How do these differences highlight and/or shape the central conflict in the story?

2. Identify the character whose magnetic and charismatic qualities enable him/her to lead and control others. What did you learn about the "leader" in this novel? What personal problems drive him/her to gain power over others?

3. Identify characters who appear to be "followers." What needs or weaknesses drive these followers to submit to the pressure and control of a leader? What kinds of conflicting loyalties and moral dilemmas are associated with this submission to peer pressure?

4. Identify characters who gain enough insight and strength to stand up to a leader or to resist peer pressure.

5. Identify characters who resist peer pressure and who refuse to follow the crowd instead of their own wisdom and moral code.

4. Choices and Consequences

The fourth dialogue group focusses on a series of novels which show how one wrong choice or decision can set into motion a chain of events which can end in tragedy.

For example, in *Such Nice Kids*, (Bunting, 1990), Jason submits to the pressure of a persuasive friend and, against his better judgment, agrees to let another friend use his mother's car without parental permission. When this boy damages the front end of the car in a hit-and-run accident, the three boys drive late at night to a mechanic who agrees to fix the car secretly for $900.00. This leads them to commit robbery, to escape from the scene of the crime, and eventually to the final tragedy in which one of the three friends is killed.

The chain of events that leads to tragedy in *On My Honor* is set into motion by Joel's decision to accept Tony's challenge and to ignore his better judgment and inner warnings.

One-Eyed Cat (Fox, 1984) is about Ned, an only child in a loving family, who has learned to move quietly through their big old house so as not to disturb his invalid mother. When Ned's uncle gives him an air-rifle for his eleventh birthday, his father forbids him to use it and puts it in the attic, trusting Ned to leave it alone. But, wanting desperately to hold the gun just once, Ned violates his father's trust, takes the gun from the attic in the middle of the night, and carries it outside. He shoots in the dark at a shadow and only later, after days and nights of worrying about what he had done, he discovers that his target had been a cat. When Ned encounters the wild one-eyed cat, he knows that he had shot this living creature the night he had disobeyed his father (p. 67). Ned is plagued by feelings of guilt and struggles to make up for what he had done by caring for the injured cat. It is only when he finally brings himself to reveal his terrible secret that he begins to feel free of the heavy burden of guilt.

Nothing But the Truth: A Documentary Novel (Avi, 1991) is the story of Philip Malloy, a ninth grader who is determined to get back at Miss Narwin, his English teacher, when he is prevented from joining the track team because of a poor English grade. During Miss Narwin's homeroom, Philip hums along with the morning tape of "The Star-Spangled Banner," defying the school rule requiring students to "rise and stand in respectful, silent attention." In spite of repeated warnings, Philip continues this behavior until he is eventually suspended. Philip tells his parents that he has been suspended for singing along with the tape of "The Star-Spangled Banner," but his story does not include other relevant information regarding school rules, repeated warnings, his English grade, and being barred from the track team. The story his parents hear is about a boy who has been "suspended for patriotism," which is the story reported in the paper and on the radio. A chain of events is set into motion when the story gets into the public arena, where it is distorted and taken out of context and becomes the focus of a nationwide debate. Miss Narwin is portrayed as the villain in the public story and she eventually loses her job and her reputation. The reader is given enough information about Miss Narwin to see her as a heroine and a tragic victim.

Initially Philip acts out of personal frustration and anger, which he directs at Miss Narwin. His actions set the stage for a larger drama about rumor and innuendo, injustice and distortion of the truth, and the manipulation by the media. Philip could have interceded to change the course of events, but he remains silent and allows the drama to play itself out. He could have saved Miss Narwin and himself, but he does not act, and both are deeply scarred by the experience.

Ash Road (Southall, 1965) begins with three boys who trick their respective parents into giving permission for a camping trip in the bush. The story is set in Australia in mid-January, the time each year when the bush is a "firetrap, a fuse waiting to be lit by a spark or flash of lightning" (p. 6). The boys camp out by a stream and use a tiny heater to cook their dinner. In the middle of the night two of the boys awaken and decide to boil some coffee. A flame from the heater escapes and before they know it the fire is out of control and they must run for their lives. Firefighters from all around come to fight the fire, but the flames, whipped by the wind, spread rapidly.

As the fire rages through the bush, across farms, and into towns, the three boys are determined never to reveal that they are responsible for the ghastly fire and the terrible destruction in its wake. But it is too much for them to hold in the fearful knowledge that their thoughtlessness and one careless move have produced this roaring inferno.

Questions derived from the comparative analysis of the novels discussed in the fourth dialogue group are listed below:

1. Identify the first "wrong move" or choice made by the central character(s) that resulted in painful or even tragic consequences. What were the circumstances in which the choice or move was made?

2. Identify points in the drama at which the course of events could have been altered. Which characters could have interceded? What prevented them from taking action or choosing to speak out?

3. What were the consequences of the initial choice or "wrong move"? How did the experience affect the central character? How did he/she change?

4. Identify character(s) who provided emotional support for the central character.

From Dialogue to Writing

The students in each dialogue group share and compare the novels they have read independently. The common theme which connects the novels studied in each group and is reflected in the heading chosen to represent this group of novels serves as a starting point for a comparative analysis in each group. For example, the group studying novels listed under the heading, "peer pressure," may decide to begin their dialogue by focussing on the different responses of characters in each novel to peer pressure, the reasons why one character is able to resist this social pressure while another cannot, and the connections between peer pressure and internal conflict. As students in this group hear about characters in the other novels, they discover similarities and differences between these characters and those portrayed in their own selections. Some students may begin to view the characters in their own selections from a new perspective. Some may discover new ways to look at authors' craft. As students engage in this in-depth study of single novels and comparative analysis of the group of novels, they generate insights and discoveries which are recorded by a group scribe and are later transformed into questions about this group of novels. After the dialogue group has formulated a series of relevant questions, each student chooses one question to use as the focus or starting point for a written analysis of the novel he/she has selected for independent reading. Students are expected to support opinions or arguments with evidence from the text or with logical reasoning. The group dialogue is intended to enrich students' experience with literary analysis and to expand their understanding of the content and craft of their own selections through exposure to the ideas and interpretations shared by peers. This writing assignment is designed to be a natural extension of the dialogue experience.

Synthesis Through Writing

Questions generated by the teacher and students are used throughout the Focus Unit to stimulate and guide literary response and analysis in large- and small-group discussions, in literary journals, and in more formal written assignments. The focus of the ongoing oral and written response is on the nature of the internal conflicts within protagonists and the internal motives and emotions which are behind the words and actions of supportive characters and antagonists. By the end of the Focus Unit, each student will have read at least one novel in addition to *Shiloh*. Most students will have selected additional titles for independent reading because of interest sparked during the group discussions and book talks. For the final project of the Focus Unit, students are asked to make connections between the fictional worlds portrayed in these novels and their own worlds. Sets of questions are introduced to guide personal reflection and written explorations of the connections between the lives and conflicts of fictional characters and their own.

These questions, formulated by the teacher, are derived from oral and written comments of students in the course of the Focus Unit experience. As the teacher listens to whole-group discussions, reads literary journals, and moves from one dialogue group to the next to participate in their discussions, she/he gathers information about student perspectives and concerns and the personal connections they feel toward specific fictional characters. Students are asked to review the following sets of questions and to select *one* that they would like to use as a framework or springboard for writing an essay about internal conflict in fiction and in their own lives.

1. Think about characters you encountered in the novels you read or the novels presented in the book talks or shared in your dialogue group. Which character, confronted with a moral dilemma or faced with a complex moral choice, triggered a special sympathy or understanding because of a similar experience in your own life? Describe the nature of the conflict, your response, reasons for your response, and the consequences of your response. If you were able to "turn back the clock," what would you have done differently?

2. Think about characters who experienced a deep sense of guilt about something they did or failed to do. Identify one character with whom you can most easily identify. Discuss an experience that enables you to empathize with this character. How did you cope with your own guilt in this situation? Who was able to help you at this time?

3. Think about characters who submitted to peer pressure against their better judgment. Identify a character whose experiences remind you of your own. Under what circumstances did you give in to peer pressure? What were the consequences? What did you learn? Under what circumstances did you decide *not* to give in to peer pressure? What were the consequences? Under what circum-

stances did you put pressure on a friend to do something against his/her better judgment? What were the consequences? What did you learn?

4. Think about characters whose "one wrong move" escalated into tragedy. Have you ever been involved in an experience of this kind in which you were the one who initiated the chain of events or in which you were a participant? Describe the experience. Were there any points at which you or someone else could have changed the course of events? What would you do differently if you could "turn back the clock" and consider the consequences?

5. Think about characters who gained some insight about other people and themselves as a result of their experiences. Identify a character who learned something about life and human relationships that you, too, have discovered in your own experience. Write about these insights and discoveries.

6. In some of the novels in this collection, characters struggled with questions of right and wrong, good and bad. Most of them learned that these clear-cut dichotomies are blurred in the real world. They discovered that life is a melding of opposites: joy and sorrow, strength and weakness, good and evil. Write an essay about this insight about life based on examples from relevant novels and your own experiences.

7. Think about characters who acted as leaders. Identify "leaders" among your own peers. What qualities, positive or negative, do they have in common? How are they different? What qualities do their followers have in common?

Concluding Comments

In this Focus Unit, craft and content are explored together. Students learn about the literary tools authors use to create stories and readers use to analyze these stories. Students are given opportunities to use their growing knowledge of literary elements to study the inner lives of fictional characters, the impact of outside forces such as family, friends, and social contexts on these characters, and the interactions between external and internal conflicts. As students develop an understanding of the role of each literary element in a given story, they are ready to discover the interdependence of these elements within the story.

A major goal of this Focus Unit is to enable students to view the world through the eyes of a protagonist and to understand how his/her viewpoint is shaped by a social, emotional, historical, and cultural context. Literature provides readers with opportunities to share the experience and perspective of others. This Focus Unit provides students with opportunities to share the lives of characters who are experiencing internal conflicts and confronting complex moral challenges. As students live through the protagonist's struggle to cope with a particular challenge or dilemma, they can begin to develop feelings of empathy and compassion. Unlike the protagonist, students have the opportunity to stand back and observe the people and events in his/her life from a comfortable distance. Readers can "slow down" events to examine the causes of conflict, the nature of the dilemma, the risk-benefit ratio, the "decision points," the consequences, and the personal needs and social dynamics which drive behavior. They can sort out the complex process of making moral choices and responding to moments of moral crisis. After an objective analysis of all elements of the story, readers, unlike fictional characters, have time to reflect and to make use of their reasoning abilities to consider alternatives.

At the conclusion of this cumulative study of internal conflict in realistic novels, students are invited to move from fiction to reality: To make connections between the lives of fictional characters and their own lives and, in the process, to develop a deeper understanding of the complexity of human experience.

Bibliography: Dilemmas and Decisions

Avi. (1991). *Nothing But the Truth — A Documentary Novel.* New York: Orchard Books.

Bauer, Marion Dane. (1986). *On My Honor.* New York: Clarion Books.

Bunting, Eve. (1990). *Such Nice Kids.* New York: Clarion Books.

Byars, Betsy. (1979). *Good-bye Chicken Little.* New York: Harper and Row.

Byars, Betsy. (1968). *The Midnight Fox.* New York: Viking.

Cleaver, Vera, and Bill Cleaver. (1967). *Ellen Grae.* Philadelphia: Lippincott.

Cross, Gillian. (1989). *A Map of Nowhere.* New York: Holiday House.

Fox, Paula. (1984). *One-Eyed Cat.* New York: Bradbury.

George, Jean. (1980). *The Cry of the Crow.* New York: Harper.

Hahn, Mary Downing. (1991). *Stepping on the Cracks.* New York: Clarion Books.

Hall, Lynn. (1992). *Windsong.* New York: Scribner's.

Hamilton, Virginia. (1990). *Cousins.* New York: Philomel.

Hopper, Nancy J. (1985). *The Truth or Dare Trap.* New York: E.P. Dutton.

Mazer, Norma Fox. (1993). *Out of Control.* New York: Morrow.

Morpurgo, Michael. (1990). *Waiting for Anya.* New York: Viking Penguin.

Naylor, Phyllis Reynolds. (1991). *Shiloh.* New York: Atheneum.

Peyton, K.M. (1990). *Poor Badger.* New York: Delacorte.

Reeder, Carolyn. (1989). *Shades of Gray.* New York: Macmillan.

Schlee, Ann. (1976). *Ask Me No Questions.* Orlando: Holt, Rinehart and Winston.

Slepian, Jan. (1990). *Risk N' Roses.* New York: Philomel.

Smith, Doris Buchanan. (1980). *Salted Lemons.* New York: Four Winds Press.

Southall, Ivan. (1965). *Ash Road.* New York: Greenwillow Books.

Thomas, Jane Resh. (1987). *Fox in a Trap.* New York: Clarion Books.

Tolan, Stephanie. (1990). *Plague Year.* New York: Morrow.

van Stockum, Hilda. (1975). *The Borrowed House.* New York: Farrar, Straus & Giroux.

Foot Note:
1.   Rebecca Lukens. (1990). *A Critical Handbook of Children's Literature.* Glenview, IL: Scott, Foresman & Co. 61-65.

FAMILY STORIES

Selecting the Focus: Historical Perspective

Surveys of realistic fiction written for children reveal that a popular theme since the mid-nineteenth century has been the relationships of children within the family. Although contemporary family stories differ significantly from earlier ones, this theme continues to have broad appeal among young readers and suggests an interesting focus for a literature unit.

In her text, *Through the Eyes of a Child: An Introduction to Children's Literature,* Donna Norton includes an interesting segment on "Children and the Family in Children's Literature" (Norton, 1991, pp. 66-78), which highlights some of the distinguishing features of family life as reflected in children's books since 1856. Families in realistic fiction written between 1856 and 1903 are generally portrayed as warm, happy, and stable. Religion plays an important role; male and female roles are carefully delineated; the household often includes members of the extended family such as a grandparent or maiden aunt; and children respect adult authority. Problems experienced by the central characters are often associated with attempting to live up to social and parental expectations, adhering to a moral code, or coping with financial difficulties.

The family stories written between 1938 and 1960 continued to portray children who grow up in happy, loving, and secure settings, who respect their elders, and who accept the social roles imposed upon them. They are generally well-adjusted children who have few significant emotional problems. The plots tend to focus on everyday events and interesting adventures; problems are resolved to allow for happy endings:

...not only did the protagonists survive but they did so unscathed and unaltered... Their parents or other solicitous adults were there to protect them against any drastic consequence (Egoff, 1981, p. 34).

Thus, prior to the 1960s, realistic family stories featured traditional family structures, gender roles, and patterns of parent-child relationships in close-knit, stable family units. "Nontraditional families and family disturbances were virtually unrepresented in this literature" (Norton, p. 410).

By the late 1960s realistic fiction reflected major social changes that shaped attitudes toward children and the family in subsequent decades. Traditional family patterns that characterized the earlier stories are no longer typical in the stories written after the mid-1960s: "...the happy, stable unit of the earlier literature is often replaced by a family in turmoil as it adjusts to a new culture, faces the prospects of surviving without one or both parents, handles the disruption resulting from divorce, or deals with extended family, exemplified by grandparents or a foster home" (Norton, p. 75).

Many middle-grade readers today enjoy reading about children living in the secure, stable families of the past, such as in *Little Women* (Alcott, 1868); *The Moffats* (Estes, 1941); *All-of-a-Kind Family* (Taylor, 1951); and *Meet the Austins* (l'Engle, 1960). However, realistic fiction which focusses on the problems middle graders experience or are exposed to in their own lives has a more immediate appeal. This "new realism" which emerged out of the turmoil of the 1960s and its aftermath, addresses the issues and questions that confront young people growing up in today's complex world. The selection of the focus for this literature unit was based on students' reading interests as well as their personal concerns about family issues.

The Family Stories Unit

The Focus Unit described in this chapter features family stories for middle-grade students. The study of this group of realistic novels begins with a consideration of the family as the setting for character development, conflict, and growth in fiction and in life. Teacher-initiated questions are designed to draw attention to the role of the family in the lives of fictional characters and in the students' own lives. In addition to exploring character development in family settings, students are invited to engage in other aspects of literary analysis and to compare the nature of family stories written prior to and after the mid-1960s.

The first whole-class meeting begins with an invitation to the students to talk about the focus of this unit: What does the word "family" mean to them? What kinds of novels would they expect to be included in this collection? What family stories have they read? What titles would they like to add to the collection set up in the classroom? What categories might be used to organize the wide variety of novels about families gathered for this collection?

The Focus Units described in this book are characterized by a dual focus on story content and authors' craft. In the unit described in this chapter, the study of literary elements provides a context for studying the families and central characters in these stories. A review of these elements may be necessary during this introductory meeting and at other points in this Focus Unit experience. An excellent resource for teachers to use in preparing for such a review is Rebecca Lukens' *A Critical Handbook of Children's Literature* (1990).

After this introductory session, the teacher reads aloud a novel to the class during a series of shared reading sessions. The selection of this novel is based on students' interests and experience as well as the teacher's goals and curricular considerations. Thus, the specific title used for these read-aloud sessions will vary from one classroom to another. This shared reading experience enables the teacher to introduce the literary concepts that provide the context for studying family stories, and it provides the students with opportunities to make connections between the experiences of fictional characters and their own experiences as members of a family. Students are encouraged to enter into the lives of these fictional characters and to use their own experiences and insights to understand the thoughts, feelings, and behavior of these characters. In turn, they may gain new insights about themselves and others from their encounters with these fictional characters. This shared reading experience is intended to stimulate reflection about family issues and conflicts and to set the stage for a cumulative dialogue about family patterns and relationships, and the role of family in the lives of individuals.

The Family as Setting

In this chapter, *Building Blocks* by Cynthia Voigt (1984) is the novel used to introduce the unit on family stories and the notion of the family as setting for character development, conflict, and growth. This novel is classified as a modern fantasy because time warp is used as the vehicle for revealing to the central character significant elements of his family history to help him gain insight into the behavior of his own father. It is a believable story about a contemporary boy coping with problems of contemporary society.

Building Blocks opens with the words: "They were fighting again." This sentence creates a setting for the story of Brann, a twelve-year-old boy who one morning escapes from the fighting between his parents by going down to the cellar and climbing inside the fortress his father had constructed out of the old, oak building blocks that had been handed down from father to son. Here he can escape from the unhappiness of his mother, who wants to go to law school, and the stubbornness of his father, who refuses to sell the farm he has recently inherited to cover the expenses so that her dream can become a reality. Brann falls asleep inside the block building and awakes in the past, the time of his own father's childhood, 37 years before. In his father's childhood home, he encounters his father as a child.

The building blocks are the link between Brann's childhood and his father's; they serve as the literary device for the time warp that carries Brann into his father's life as a child. The time warp enables him to discover what it was like for his father to live in his family, to be the eldest son who is expected to assume responsibility for his siblings and aging grandparents and whose dreams, ideas, and talents must be hidden from his family. Brann learns what it means to live with a tyrannical father who beats him cruelly, an overworked but domineering mother who vents her anger at him, and siblings who mock and tease him. This child, Kevin, who is to become Brann's father, lives in constant fear and hopelessness within the tight prison of his harsh, unfeeling family. Brann enters into this life with Kevin, and even feels the pain of the belt when Kevin's father whips *him,* along with Kevin and his sister. "He didn't know how Kevin could stand it, with this horrible sister and that father and his mother who didn't even act like a human being" (p. 96). Brann gains insight about his father, his remarkable courage, his integrity, his keen mind and artistic ability, his sensitivity and honesty. Brann begins to understand why his father seems to have no ambition and to fear taking risks even to realize his own dreams. When Brann returns to the present and his own home, he reflects on his experience: "You didn't really know somebody unless you knew him when he was a kid... He could begin to know his father now" (p. 112). Brann's time-travel adventures teach him about the family interactions that shaped his father's personality and help him discover that building relationships with others is not unlike building with blocks: "Like with people, too, relationships get made piece by piece, don't they, that's the way to make relationships" (p. 72).

During this shared reading experience, students are invited to respond with personal thoughts and feelings as they live through these events with Brann and travel with him into his family's past. In addition, the teacher introduces questions to call attention to the notion of *family as setting* for character development, conflict, and growth, as well as the author's use of time warp as a literary device to build characters and action and to provide the key to resolve the central conflict in the novel.

The question, **"What is the significance of the lead sentence?"** invites students to focus on the tension between Brann's parents; the conflict between his energetic, ambitious mother and passive father; and the feelings of anger and resentment Brann has toward his father. He is ashamed of his father and sees him as a coward, a loser. The tension in the family can be viewed as the central aspect of the setting for Brann's story; it is this aspect of the setting that affects the way Brann is developed as a character and the nature of his conflict with his father. It is this tension that drives the plot. The teacher invites students to think beyond the familiar notion of setting as time and place. They are introduced to the idea of a psychological setting and asked to consider its function in the story. Rebecca Lukens (1990) describes five functions of setting: setting that clarifies conflict; setting as antagonist; setting that illuminates character; setting that affects mood; and setting as symbol (pp. 108-115).

Questions about the author's use of the time warp are introduced to generate reflection about the way a literary device enables the central character (Brann) to gain firsthand knowledge about his extended family and his own father's childhood and, in the process, to discover that this family setting *illuminates the character* of his father. Brann uses his time-warp adventure to find a solution for the problem that threatens to destroy the well-being of his family. Students are invited to identify other novels in which this device is used and to speculate about the author's purpose in using time warp for his/her story.

A question about the significance of the title is intended to highlight its multiple meanings and its use as a clue about the central theme of the novel. The oak building blocks provide the link between the childhoods of father and son and the vehicle for the time travel. Building blocks can also be interpreted to represent the factors contributing to personality development within the family setting, as well as the development of human relationships within and outside the family unit. Students are encouraged to stretch their minds to generate possible meanings for this title.

The final questions use the notion of building blocks to focus on connections between the world of the novel and the world of the students in the classroom:

- **What are the building blocks that contributed to the development of Brann and his father and their relationships to each other?**
- **What contributed to the change in Brann and the change in their relationship?**
- **What building blocks have contributed to your own development and your relationships within and outside your family?**

Independent Reading

After this novel has been shared with the whole class, students are invited to browse through the "family stories unit collection," which has been divided into categories representing different types of family stories suggested during the initial discussion of family. (See the Bibliography of Family Stories at the end of this chapter.) The teacher and students have worked together to arrange the novels in boxes, with one box for each category. Some of the titles fit in more than one category. A list of these categories and the titles selected for inclusion in each one is posted next to the collection:

EXTENDED FAMILY

Arthur for the Very First Time (MacLachlan, 1980)
Baby (MacLachlan, 1993)
Building Blocks (Voigt, 1984)
Cousins (Hamilton, 1990)
Cry Uncle! (Auch, 1987)
Dicey's Song (Voigt, 1982)
A Dig in Time (Griffin, 1991)
Edith Herself (Howard, 1987)
Homecoming (Voigt, 1981)
House of Wings (Byars, 1972)
Humbug (Bawden, 1992)
In Search of the Sandhill Crane (Robertson, 1973)
Journey (MacLachlan, 1991)
Julie's Daughter (Rodowsky, 1985)
The Midnight Fox (Byars, 1968)
My Brother Stevie (Clymer, 1967)
The Stone-faced Boy (Fox, 1968)
The Two Thousand Pound Goldfish (Byars, 1982)
Up a Road Slowly (Hunt, 1966)
The Village by the Sea (Fox, 1988)

SINGLE PARENT - DIVORCE - REMARRIAGE

Amazing Gracie (Cannon, 1991)
Angel's Mother's Wedding (Delton, 1987)
The Animal, the Vegetable and John D. Jones (Byars, 1982)
Blowfish Live in the Sea (Fox, 1970)
Dear Mr. Henshaw (Cleary, 1983)
The Divorce Express (Danziger, 1982)
Face To Face (Bauer, 1991)
Family Reunion (Cooney, 1989)
Fish Friday (Pearson, 1986)
Goodbye and Keep Cold (Davis, 1987)
Half Nelson, Full Nelson (Stone, 1985)
Last was Lloyd (Smith, 1981)
Maggie, Too (Nixon, 1985)
The Mockingbird Song (Amoss, 1988)
Mom, the Wolf Man and Me (Klein, 1972)
The Moonlight Man (Fox, 1986)
Moving In (Slote, 1988)
My War With Goggle-eyes (Fine, 1989)
The Night Swimmers (Byars, 1980)
Park's Quest (Paterson, 1988)
Patchwork Summer (Holl, 1987)
Pillow of Clouds (Talbert, 1991)
Something to Count On (Moore, 1980)
Taking Sides (Klein, 1974)
Where the Lilies Bloom (Cleaver, 1969)
The Wicked Stepdog (Benjamin, 1982)

FOSTER CARE AND ADOPTION

The Cat Who Was Left Behind (Adler, 1981)
The Finding (Bawden, 1985)
Foster Child (Bauer, 1977)
The Great Gilly Hopkins (Paterson, 1978)
Last Chance Summer (Wieler, 1991)
Mail Order Kid (MacDonald, 1988)
The Pinballs (Byars, 1977)
Sunday's Child (Mebs, 1986)

DOMESTIC VIOLENCE — ILLNESS — DRUGS — ALCOHOLISM — DEATH

The Bears' House (Sachs, 1971)
Beat the Turtle Drum (Green, 1976)
Cracker Jackson (Byars, 1985)
The Crazy Horse Electric Game (Crutcher, 1987)
Grover (Cleaver, 1970)
A Hero Ain't Nothing But a Sandwich (Childress, 1973)
A Horse Named Sky (Corcoran, 1986)

I Am the Universe (Corcoran, 1986)
It Ain't All for Nothing (Myers, 1978)
The Latchkey Kids (Terris, 1986)
The Long Way Home (Cohen, 1990)
Mama's Going to Buy You a Mockingbird (Little, 1984)
Missing May (Rylant, 1992)
My Brother Stealing Second (Naughton, 1989)
RoboDad (Carter, 1990)
A Summer to Die (Lowry, 1977)
So Long, Grandpa (Donnelly, 1981)
Trouble Half-Way (Mark, 1986)
Up Country (Carter, 1989)
Words of Stone (Henkes, 1992)

SIBLING RELATIONSHIPS; PARENT-CHILD RELATIONSHIPS

The Animal, The Vegetable and John D. Jones (Byars, 1982)
The Book of the Banshee (Fine, 1992)
Chinese Handcuffs (Crutcher, 1989)
Family Project (Ellis, 1986)
Fanny's Sister (Lively, 1980)
Homecoming (Voigt, 1981)
Jacob Have I Loved (Paterson, 1980)
Mama, Let's Dance (Hermes, 1991)
Mariposa Blues (Koertge, 1991)
My Brother Stealing Second (Naughton, 1989)
The Nickle-Plated Beauty (Beatty, 1993, 1985)
No More Cornflakes (Horvath, 1990)
The Purple Heart (Talbert, 1992)
Ramona Forever; Beezus and Ramona (Cleary, 1984, 1955)
Shabanu (Staples, 1989)
Sister (Greenfield, 1974)
The Summer of the Swans (Byars, 1970)
The Two Thousand Pound Goldfish (Byars, 1982)

NON-TRADITIONAL LIFE STYLES

Come Sing, Jimmy Jo (Paterson, 1985)
The Glory Girl (Byars, 1983)
The Midnight Hour Encore (Brooks, 1986)
Return to Bitter Creek (Smith, 1986)
Star Shine (Greene, 1985)
The Street Dancers (Hill, 1991)

MULTICULTURAL

Blue-Eyed Daisy (Rylant, 1985)
Charlie Pippin (Boyd, 1987)
Child of the Owl (Yep, 1977)

Circle of Fire (Hooks, 1984)
Danza! (Hall, 1981)
Dragonwings (Yep, 1975)
Felita (Mohr, 1979)
For the Life of Laetita (Hodge, 1993)
Going Home (Mohr, 1986)
The Gold Cadillac (Taylor, 1987)
A Jar of Dreams (Uchida, 1981)
Journey of the Sparrows (Buss, 1991)
Journey to Jo'burg (Naidoo, 1986)
Let the Circle Be Unbroken (Taylor, 1981)
Onion Tears (Kidd, 1991)
Roll of Thunder, Hear My Cry (Taylor, 1976)
Shabanu (Staples, 1989)
Sounder (Armstrong, 1969)
Sweetgrass (Hudson, 1989)
Words by Heart (Sebestyen, 1979)

HISTORICAL FICTION

A Bellsong for Sarah Raines (Cannon, 1987)
The Borning Room (Fleischman, 1991)
Borrowed Children (Lyon, 1988)
Carlota (O'Dell, 1981)
The Endless Steppe (Hautzig, 1968)
Ike and Mama and the Seven Surprises (Snyder, 1985)
Little House books (Wilder, 1953)
The Man Who Sang in the Dark (Clifford, 1987)
A Matter of Pride (Crofford, 1981)
Maudie in the Middle (Naylor, 1988)
The Mockingbird Song (Amoss, 1988)
Morning Girl (Dorris, 1992)
Nelda (Edwards, 1987)
The Nickle-Plated Beauty (Beatty, 1993)
One-Way to Ansonia (Angell, 1985)
Place for Allie (Carey, 1985)
Prairie Songs (Conrad, 1985)
Sarah Plain and Tall (MacLachlan, 1985)
The Sky Is Falling (Corcoran, 1988)
Skylark (MacLachlan, 1994)
View from the Pighouse Roof (Olsen, 1987)
Year Walk (Clark, 1975)

When students have had time to look through the collection, read jacket flaps, back cover summaries, etc., the teacher presents a series of book talks to help them select books for independent reading. For example, the book-talk session might begin with an introduction to a group of realistic novels about the Tillerman family by Cynthia Voigt, author of *Building Blocks: Homecoming*

(1981); *Dicey's Song* (1982); *The Runner* (1985); *Sons from Afar* (1987). A book talk about Katherine Paterson's *Park's Quest* (1988) highlights the connection between this novel and Voigt's *Building Blocks* in terms of content and craft. *Park's Quest* is about a boy's search for answers to questions about his father who died in Vietnam eleven years before. A trip to his grandfather's farm in rural Virginia provides the opportunity for Park to learn the truth about his father's past. Like Brann in *Building Blocks*, Park's experience with extended family enables him to form a clearer picture of his father. Thus, both central characters learn about the past so that they might more fully understand the present. However, Voigt uses a fantasy device to achieve this end; Paterson creates a journey into the past that is grounded in reality.

Another novel featuring time-travel and extended family, *A Dig in Time* (Griffin, 1991), is about twelve-year-old Nan and her younger brother Tim, who discover how to travel into their family's past during a summer visit with their grandmother in San Antonio, Texas.

The book-talk session includes brief comments about one or two titles listed in each category and about differences between these novels that are related to authors' craft. For example, many of the novels in the family-story collection are serious in tone, whereas others are lighthearted and humorous. Light comedy novels such as *Family Reunion* (Cooney, 1989), *No More Cornflakes* (Horvath, 1990), and *The Book of the Banshee* (Fine, 1992) are contrasted with serious novels such as *The Bears' House* (Sachs, 1971), *Shabanu* (Staples, 1989), and *Jacob Have I Loved* (Paterson, 1980), as well as novels in which humor is woven into narratives featuring serious subjects, as in Betsy Byars' *Cracker Jackson* (1985), a story about an eleven-year-old boy who tries to save his ex-babysitter from wife-abuse.

During the book-talk session, students are again invited to share with the group any family stories they have enjoyed reading prior to this literature unit and to suggest additional titles for the classroom collection. They are also encouraged to add personal comments about books in the collection and to recommend favorite titles. This session is designed to prepare students for selecting books for independent reading and to encourage personal involvement in building up the collection of family stories.

When students select books for independent reading, they record their name and each title on a sign-up sheet attached to the appropriate category box. This record of their selections enables the formation of small dialogue groups in which participants discuss books within a particular category.

The Literary Journal

A notebook is given to each student so that he/she can record personal responses to novels read aloud in class or independently, as well as respond to specific assignments designed to reinforce the literary ideas explored in the shared reading experience. The first assignment is to write about Brann; how the family setting affects him; what he learns from his time-warp experience with his extended family; and how he changes as an individual. Subsequent assignments provide opportunities for students to write about the role of family settings in the development of central characters in self-selected novels; to engage in literary analysis of these texts; and to make connections between the lives of fictional characters and their own lives.

Suggestions for Literary Analysis

During the shared reading experience, students are introduced to the approach to literary analysis that emphasizes the notion of *family as setting* for character development. As the teacher and students discuss the shared text together, they generate and record suggestions for literary analysis of the self-selected novels. The book-talk sessions yield further ideas for literary analysis. A list of these suggestions derived from the combined input of teacher and students is posted on the wall near the family stories collection to guide literary analysis in the journals and in the dialogue groups. Students are invited to use the suggestions on the list that are relevant to the particular novels they have chosen to read independently. Not all students need to refer to this list, but many find that the suggestions are helpful as they read, discuss, and write about novels in which the family plays a significant role in the development of the central character. In the following discussion, seven Suggestions for Literary Analysis are presented. Summaries of relevant novels are included to provide teachers with suggestions for their own reading and study of literature.

1. **Discuss novel families that challenge central characters to change and grow.**

When the central character in *Edith Herself* (Howard, 1987) is orphaned by her mother's death, her older siblings send Edith, the youngest, to live with her oldest sister Alena and her family. Edith has difficulty adjusting to this stern Christian farming family, and the strain aggravates her epileptic seizures. Alena wants to teach Edith at home to protect her from the cruelty of children toward those who are different. Edith's brother-in-law insists that she attend school and helps her to find the courage to stand up for herself in the school setting. Edith comes to realize that in her own family she was the youngest child and was treated accordingly. In her sister's household she is the oldest child, and she learns to see herself as such and to behave accordingly.

The title and the nursery rhyme that precedes the first chapter in this historical novel can be used by students to generate analysis of Edith's growth toward independence and self-reliance.

The Moonlight Man (Fox, 1986) is about Catherine Ames, who has spent very little time with her father since her parents were divorced when she was three years old. Catherine spends a month with her father during her summer vacation and experiences intense fear and anger when she sees the way alcohol turns him from a charming individual into a sick and delirious old man. She learns that he has allowed drink to destroy his life, but this knowledge does not destroy her love for him. This experience with her father challenges her to come to terms with life's disparities. Instead of viewing people in terms of extreme polarities of good and evil, Catherine begins to accept the complex blend of opposites which is the reality of her father. She discovers she can love him without judging him.

In *Child of the Owl* (Yep, 1977), twelve-year-old Casey is sent to live with her maternal grandmother in San Francisco's Chinatown when her father is mugged and ends up in the hospital. Casey had been brought up by her father as an American child in an underworld of gambling. Living with her grandmother, Casey learns for the first time about her Chinese heritage and the Chinese language. This new family setting challenges her to struggle with cultural conflicts and eventually to grow toward a deeper understanding of her heritage and of herself as an integral part of a circle of family and friends, past and present.

The central character in *Mama's Going to Buy You a Mockingbird* (Little, 1984) is a sixth grade boy who must learn to cope with the death of his father. This tragic loss challenges Jeremy to reach outside of himself to offer the strength and support his younger sister and mother need. He learns to *give* comfort instead of expecting only to receive it. On the way to the funeral home, Jeremy takes his mother's hand and "...suddenly it came to him that he was old enough now to take her hand, not because he needed to cling to her but because he knew she needed him to be close" (Little, p. 118).

2. **Discuss novel families that provide the strength and support necessary to cope with external conflict.**

Rebecca Lukens (1990) defines conflict as the struggle between the protagonist and an opposing force or *antagonist* (p. 61). One type of conflict, identified as "person-against-society" (p. 63), involves a struggle between the protagonist and external forces such as racial hatred and discrimination. In plots driven by external conflict, the family often provides the love and support necessary for the central characters to deal with external threats to their dignity and self-respect and, in some cases, to their very survival.

A Jar of Dreams (Uchida, 1981) is a first-person account of a young Japanese girl growing up in California during the Depression. Rinko is part of a warm, loving, hard-working family. Her parents are determined to make it possible for their children to have a better life in spite of the fact that the Japanese are victims of hatred and discrimination in America. It is Aunt Waka, visiting from Japan, who helps Rinko and her family discover their own inner strengths and the confidence to realize their dreams. This is a proud family whose members stand up against those who try to humiliate and diminish them. In this family setting, Rinko learns that being different from other people "...doesn't mean you're not as good or that you have to dislike yourself" (Uchida, p. 125). She learns to accept her difference and to derive strength from her connections to her cultural heritage.

Mildred Taylor's *Roll of Thunder, Hear My Cry* (1976) and its sequel, *Let the Circle Be Unbroken* (1981) are novels about the Logans, a proud, close-knit African-American family living in rural Mississippi during the Depression. Strengthened by bonds of love, mutual respect, and personal courage, members of this family are able to stand up to racist cruelty and to maintain their self-respect and dignity in the face of prejudice and poverty. These stories of the Logan family portray the triumph of the human spirit over hatred, ignorance, and attempts to degrade and dehumanize them. It is the family unit that sustains each member through difficult times.

Words by Heart (Sebestyen, 1979) is another novel about an African-American family bound together by love, pride, and moral courage. Lena's father, Ben Sills, has brought his family out of an all-black community in the South to an all-white community in the West at the turn of the century because he wants his children to have the opportunities denied them in their former home. Although Ben is honest and works hard as a hired hand, the hatred and resentment of a neighboring tenant farmer toward him lead to violence and Ben's death. Lena carries with her the legacy of her father's inner strength and faith and forgiveness. This is a story of family love and solidarity, and it is in this setting that Lena builds the self-confidence and self-respect necessary to pursue her goals in the face of the hatred and violence directed against her family. It is another story of the power of the family unit to sustain its members in times of trouble and to provide the foundation for growth toward self-realization.

3. **Discuss novels in which the family seems to be antagonistic to the central character.**

Lukens includes "setting as antagonist" in her discussion of the functions of setting (p. 110-111). This Focus Unit features novels in which the family is the setting for character development; in some of these novels, the protagonist views his/her family as an opposing force or antagonist.

Katherine Paterson's novel of sibling rivalry, *Jacob Have I Loved* (1980), is narrated in the first person by Louise, who is driven by hatred and resentment of her beautiful twin sister, Caroline. Like Esau in the Biblical tale of sibling rivalry, Louise is convinced that Caroline has stolen her birthright: her parents' love and attention, her friends, and her chance for an education. Her grandmother reproaches Louise for her fierce resentment and teases her with quotes from the Bible: "Jacob have I loved but Esau have I hated." When Louise discovers that these are the words of God, she concludes, "It was God himself who hated me" (p. 181). She sees herself as the despised twin and feels that her family is against her. Her family, as antagonist, plays a powerful role in her development as an angry, bitter person. It is only when she eventually leaves her family as a young woman, has a family of her own, and becomes a midwife in a mountain community that she is able to move beyond this sibling rivalry to begin to realize her own potential as a capable individual.

In Paterson's Newbery acceptance speech for *Jacob Have I Loved*, which can be found in her book *Gates of Excellence* (1981), she observes: "...I do not think we can avoid the most obvious meaning of these stories [about sibling rivalry], which is that among children who grow up together in a family, there run depths of feeling that will permeate their souls for both good and ill as long as they live" (Paterson, 1981, p. 118).

It is interesting to contrast this tale of sibling rivalry with stories in which sibling relationships are not rooted in rivalry but in situations demanding protection and support. For example, *My Brother Stevie* (Clymer, 1967) is about Annie, a twelve-year-old girl who is given the responsibility of caring for her eight-year-old brother when their mother leaves them with their grandmother. In *Homecoming* (Voigt, 1983), the story of four children who have been abandoned by their mother, thirteen-year-old Dicey assumes the role of a parent and leads her younger siblings on a long journey in search of a home.

The Latchkey Kids (Terris, 1986) features an eleven-year-old girl, Callie, who is given after-school responsibility for her younger brother, Rex. Like Dicey and Annie, Callie assumes a parental role. The latchkey that unlocks the door to their empty apartment also locks them in. They are not allowed to leave the apartment, and they feel like prisoners in their own home. Callie's anger and resentment toward her parents and her confinement build as the burden of responsibility and the pressures of the family dynamics become too much for her to handle. For Callie, the family has become the antagonist.

The Bears' House (Sachs, 1971) is the story of nine-year-old Fran Ellen, one of five children crowded into a small apartment with an emotionally disturbed mother. Their father has deserted them, and the children live in fear that they will be placed in foster homes. Fran Ellen withdraws into a make-believe world as an escape from and defense against this family setting.

My Brother Stealing Second (Naughton, 1989) is the story of Bobby, a sixteen-year-old boy who suffers profound grief and shame after his older bother is killed in a car accident. According to the police report, his brother was driving with two other boys after a night of drinking and had hit another car, killing the couple in it. The victims were the parents of Bobby's classmate. Bobby's family moves to another part of town, where he and his parents withdraw into their separate inner worlds, unable to provide each other with the mutual support and understanding necessary for coping with the death of a family member. Bobby had always wanted to be like his brother, but now he is afraid he will follow in his footsteps; he fears that the alcoholism that runs in his family will take control of his life, too. When Bobby uncovers the terrible truth that his parents have accepted a bribe to protect the identity of the boy who was actually driving that night, he sees them as the enemy.

In *Chinese Handcuffs* (Crutcher, 1989), eighteen-year-old Dillon is haunted by the memory of his older brother's violent suicide. He, like Bobby, is determined not to follow in his brother's footsteps. As in *My Brother Stealing Second*, the relationship of the two brothers is revealed through flashbacks of significant scenes and incidents shared in the past. *Chinese Handcuffs* is told in part by Dillon in letters to his dead brother which are interwoven with a third-person narrative alternating between the viewpoints of Dillon, his friend Jen, and, occasionally, other key characters. As Dillon struggles to cope with the pain and guilt caused by his brother's tragic life and death, he becomes deeply involved in Jen's terrible secret: her stepfather, a prominent lawyer, sexually abuses her and threatens the life of her mother and sister if Jen reports him. When Jen attempts suicide, it is Dillon who saves her life, doing for her what he was unable to do for his brother.

Katherine Paterson's *Come Sing, Jimmy Jo* (1985) is the story of eleven-year-old Jamie's struggle to develop his own identity and self-confidence in the face of demands of a family who tend to be self-centered and preoccupied with their own lives as performers in the family's musical group in Appalachia.

In *The Street Dancers* (Hill, 1991), Fitzi, her parents, and grandfather are all performers. Fitzi feels trapped in this lifestyle and longs to live a normal life and to attend public school instead of doing street shows, commercials, and mime acts. She is ashamed of what her parents do for a living; she wants to separate herself from their life. When Fitzi finally explains to her parents that she wants to retire so she can go to school, they have difficulty understanding what she is saying. They seem to view their daughter only as part of their act; they do not see her as an individual with separate needs and dreams.

The Glory Girl (Byars, 1983) is the story of Anna Glory, who feels like an orphan and a misfit, because she is the only non-singing member of a gospel-singing family. She resents the fact that she is sent to the back of the auditorium to sell Glory records and cassette tapes whenever the Glory Gospel Singers perform. Anna feels a special kinship with her Uncle Newt. He helps Anna discover her own self-worth and to see herself as an individual who is defined, not by the standards her family has imposed on her, but by other standards that her parents and siblings would not comprehend.

The central character in *Ask Me Tomorrow* (Bates, 1987), fifteen-year-old Paige, feels trapped by his father's expectations that he will someday take over the family apple orchard business. In the beginning of the story, he sees the family as antagonist and is determined to escape to the city and a new life. However, when he meets Abby, who has come from Texas to spend the summer with her grandparents, Paige is given a new perspective of the Maine country-side that is his home. He gradually becomes aware of his own feelings about his surroundings and begins to rethink his decision to leave. His perception of his family changes as he gains a new sense of independence and control over his own future.

In *Mariposa Blues* (Koertge, 1991), thirteen-and-a-half-year-old Graham also feels trapped by his father's expectations and struggles to gain his independence and establish his own identity. When he returns with his parents to Mariposa Downs, where they train and race thoroughbreds during the summer, Graham resists his father's attempts to define and direct his life. He questions everything his father says and sees him as the antagonist who refuses to hear about his own son's feelings or to value his opinions.

Shabanu (Staples, 1989) is the story of the eleven-year-old daughter of a nomad in the Cholistan Desert in present-day Pakistan. Shabanu is an intelligent, spirited girl who loves the freedom of her childhood days. But now that she is becoming a woman, she must accept her father's decision to pledge her in marriage to an older man with several wives. Her duty as a daughter requires her to accept this arranged marriage which will bring prestige to the family but will commit her to a life of subjugation and emotional bondage. Shabanu knows that if she were to rebel against her father, she would bring shame and dishonor to her family and betray centuries of tradition. She knows that in order to fulfil her obligations to her family, she must give up thoughts of her own happiness.

4. **Discuss family settings that test the strength, courage, and values of the central character and illuminate his/her human qualities.**

I Am the Universe (Corcoran, 1986) is a first-person narration by Kit, a twelve-year-old girl who struggles to assume responsibility for her siblings and to cope with her own fears when her mother is hospitalized for brain surgery. But she finds the inner strength to weather this family crisis and comes through with a deeper understanding of herself as a person.

It Ain't All for Nothing (Myers, 1978) is about a twelve-year-old African-American boy who has been living a secure and quiet life in Harlem with his religious grandmother until she becomes ill and he is sent to live with his father in a world of crime, drugs, and violence. The boy, Tippy, struggles to maintain his self-respect and to adhere to the values taught by his Grandma Carrie, but at the same time he fears he will lose his father if he rejects his way of life. Living with his father proves to be a severe test of the strength of his values and his courage. Only after breaking his ties with his father can Tippy begin to take control of his own life.

Dicey, the thirteen-year-old girl in *Homecoming* (Voigt, 1981) who struggles to keep her two brothers and sister together and to find a home for the four of them, must find the strength and courage and inner resources to accomplish this mission.

In *Sweetgrass* (Hudson, 1989), a novel set in the western Canadian prairie in the nineteenth century, a fifteen-year-old Blackfoot Indian girl is called upon to demonstrate moral, emotional, and physical courage to provide the selfless care needed to save her family from a small pox epidemic.

Journey to Jo'Burg — A South African Story (Naidoo, 1986) is about thirteen-year-old Naledi, a black girl, whose emotional and physical courage is tested when she and her brother set out on foot to travel over 300 kilometers from their village to Johannesburg to seek help for their baby sister, who is dangerously ill. Their journey exposes them to the dangers of a country under apartheid and Naledi is challenged to think about the meaning of freedom and her own role in the movement to gain freedom.

5. **Discuss family novels in which interactions with extended family provide opportunities to discover significant information about family members, relationships, and history.**

In *Charlie Pippin* (Boyd, 1987), the central character learns from her grandfather about her father's experiences in Vietnam and as an African-American Vietnam veteran. She begins to understand why her father has become angry and demanding and why he keeps his bitter memories hidden. Charlie's search for understanding leads to a visit to the Vietnam Memorial Wall in Washington with her Uncle Ben. Her new knowledge and insight about her father allows Charlie to reach out to him and to begin to break down barriers which had been growing up between them.

Park's Quest (Paterson, 1988) is the story of Park's search for knowledge about his father, who was killed in Vietnam. His mother refuses to talk about his father, and it is only when he visits his grandfather's farm in Virginia that he gains new insights into the complex relationships in his family, as well as new understandings about himself. Like Charlie in *Charlie Pippin*, Park visits the Vietnam Memorial without parental approval. Like Charlie, who had traced the letters of the names of her father's friends, Park traces the letters of his father's name, feeling close to the man he had never known (pp. 31-32).

The Village by the Sea (Fox, 1988) is about Emma, whose father must have heart bypass surgery, and who is sent to spend two weeks with her aunt and uncle in their isolated seashore home. Here she learns about her family's history and the relationships that are the source of Aunt Bea's anger and resentment. These fierce emotions have eaten away at her and have driven her to strike out at those around her. Aunt Bea is known in the family as the "terror," but Emma's knowledge of the roots and the nature of this emotional illness melts the hatred she had felt toward her ever since she discovered it was Aunt Bea who had destroyed the tiny village by the sea she had created with her new friend.

Borrowed Children (Lyon, 1988) is the story of twelve-year-old Amanda, who lives with her family in the mountains of Kentucky during the Depression. When her mother almost dies giving birth to her sixth child, Amanda must care for the baby, her mother, her siblings, and the house. When her mother is well again, Amanda is invited to spend the Christmas holiday in Memphis, Tennessee, with her mother's parents and sister. During this experience with extended family, Amanda learns about the family relationships and history that shaped the lives of her mother and aunt. For the first time Amanda begins to appreciate her mother as an individual, and she begins to see how she, Amanda, fits into the family picture.

Return to Bitter Creek (Smith, 1986) is the story of twelve-year-old Lacey's return to the Southern Appalachian home and extended family she and her mother had left when Lacey was a baby. Here she learns about the differences and misunderstandings that have driven a wedge between family members.

Twelve-year-old Casey in *Child of the Owl* (Yep, 1977) learns from her maternal grandmother about the mother she never knew; about her father's ten-year search for a job and his turn to gambling in defeat; about her cultural heritage and even her real name. This knowledge of her family history and heritage changes her life and her sense of herself.

Like Cynthia Voigt's use of time-warp to enable the central character in *Building Blocks* (1984) to learn about his family's past, Jane Yolen uses the time-travel technique in *The Devil's Arithmetic* (1988) to enable a contemporary girl to learn about her family's experiences during the Holocaust. During a Passover seder with her relatives, Hannah opens the door for the prophet Elijah in the ancient tradition of the seder service and finds herself in a small Jewish village in Poland in the 1940s. She has become the girl, "Chaya", and enters into her world, the shtetl, and, as Chaya, is rounded up by the Nazi soldiers for transport with her family to a death camp. It is this terrifying experience that gives Hannah a glimpse of her family's history and why it is imperative for her to remember what happened to them and to the Jewish people.

Like Brann in *Building Blocks,* the central characters in each of the novels presented as examples for Suggestion 5 discover significant information about their family histories, which helps them understand current family problems and relationships.

6. **Discuss family stories in which a central character is forced to give up illusions about an absent parent and to confront the truth about him/her.**

Beverly Cleary uses letters and diary entries to reveal Leigh Botts' loneliness, his yearning for his father's return, and his feelings about his parents' divorce in *Dear Mr. Henshaw* (1983). In response to a classroom assignment, Leigh begins a correspondence with Mr. Henshaw, his favorite author. Later, the letters are largely replaced by diary entries that allow him to express his feelings and to see the changes in his own perceptions about and attitudes toward his father and the divorce.

Dear Mr. Henshaw reflects Beverly Cleary's response to the changing status of the family between the 1950s and the 1980s. Characters in her recent novels are faced with family problems which are part of the reality of today's complex world. Students are invited to compare some of Cleary's early family stories with her more recent writing and to look for evidence of changing views of childhood and the family over the years.

The Moonlight Man (Fox, 1986) portrays the relationship between Catherine and her divorced father. He is dishonest, unreliable, and drinks too much, but Catherine learns to accept him and to continue to love him after she has gotten over the initial shock of discovering the truth about him.

The Cat That Was Left Behind (Adler, 1981) is about thirteen-year-old Chad, who has been in many foster homes and is spending the summer on Cape Cod with yet another foster family, the Sorenics. He develops an attachment to a stray cat that was abandoned by summer people. As the cat learns to trust Chad, Chad learns to trust the Sorenic family, recognizing that they are *not* like the other foster families who had given up on him and sent him away. However, Chad continues to cling to the hope that he will be reunited with his real mother. It is not until he receives a letter from his mother that clearly spells out both her rejection of him and that she cannot be his mother that Chad is able to break free of this unrealistic dream. This cruel letter represents a turning point for Chad, enabling him to accept his growing attachment to this warm, caring family and to agree to join them as an adopted son.

When twelve-year-old Renny in *Foster Child* (Bauer, 1977), is sent to a foster home because the great-grandmother she lives with becomes ill, she clings to the hope that her beloved gran will get well and come for her. She also clings to dreams of the father she has never met, dreams in which he, too, comes for her. As in the story of Chad, it is only when Renny's illusions about an absent family are shattered that she is free to take the emotional steps necessary to become part of a new family.

Like Chad, Gilly, in Katherine Paterson's *The Great Gilly Hopkins* (1978), has been in a number of foster homes and carries with her the dream of living with her beautiful idealized mother. Gilly, too, must confront the truth about her mother and give up the dream she has created so that she, like Chad and Renny, can take the emotional steps necessary to begin to build a new life founded on a realistic base.

7. **Discuss family stories in which new family units are created and become new settings for growth and well-being.**

A Family Apart (Nixon, 1987) is the first of four historical novels, "The Orphan Train Quartet," based on the true stories of New York City slum children who were sent to new homes in the West on orphan trains during the years from 1854 to 1929. *A Family Apart* begins in 1860 in New York City. It is the story of the Kelly family, whose members live in extreme poverty. When their father dies, their mother realizes that she can no longer support her six children or protect them from the life of the streets. Because of her deep love for them and her desire to give them a good life, she makes the ultimate sacrifice: With the help of the Children's Aid Society of New York City, she sends them on the orphan train to live with farm families in Missouri. Each of the books in the

Quartet is one orphan's story. The first story is about thirteen-year-old Frances Mary, who is determined to keep her promise to her mother to take care of Petey, the youngest. Learning that many Western families prefer to adopt boys who can work on the farm, she decides to masquerade as a boy so that she and Petey will be adopted into the same family. Over time Frances and Petey become actively involved in their new life on the farm with Margaret and Jake Cummings, and a new family unit is created.

Sarah, Plain and Tall (MacLachlan, 1985), about a prairie frontier family, opens with the words: "'Did Mama sing every day?' asked Caleb" (p. 3). This line sets the stage for a story about a family that is incomplete after the mother dies. It is a quiet, somber atmosphere without Mama and her singing. When Papa's advertisement for a wife is answered by Sarah and she travels from her home in Maine to begin a trial visit with Papa, Caleb, and Anna, the mood changes. In poetic language, MacLachlan describes the initial tentative relationships formed as these four individuals become acquainted and begin to adjust to one another and eventually create a new family unit. In the sequel, *Skylark* (1994), a drought tests the strength of the relationships in this new family unit.

Summer, the twelve-year-old narrator of *Missing May* (Rylant, 1992), had been passed around among her Ohio relatives for years after her mother's death. When she was six-years-old, Uncle Ob and Aunt May took her home to their old trailer in Deep Water, West Virginia. They *wanted* her and gave her the love she needed. A new family unit emerged.

Now the family circle is broken. It has been nearly six months since May died. But by the end of the novel, Ob and Summer come together, forming a new family unit based on mutual love and support and shared memories of their beloved May.

The Man Who Sang in the Dark (Clifford, 1987) is an historical novel set in Philadelphia during the Depression. The family circle is broken when their father dies and ten-year-old Leah, four-year-old Daniel, and their mother must create a new life for themselves. They develop a close friendship with a blind man who lives in the boarding house which is their new home and with the Safers, a couple who owns the house. Over time these friendships deepen into closer bonds: the Safers become "adopted" grandparents to Leah and Daniel, and Gideon, the blind musician, and their mother decide to marry. Leah thinks about rebuilding a family in this way:

> It is as if, as separate people, some part of each of them was missing. Mama without a husband; Gideon alone and blind; Leah and Daniel needing a father; the Safers longing for grandchildren. They had all been like pieces of an unfinished puzzle; when fit together, the puzzle became a beautiful picture (p. 110).

Pillow of Clouds (Talbert, 1991) is the story of Chester, who must decide which of his divorced parents he will live with now that he is thirteen-years-old. He feels that his mother — unstable, depressed, and an alcoholic — needs him, and she pressures him to stay with her. But he really wants to live in Santa Fe with his father and his new wife. When he finally realizes that he cannot help his mother and that he is not to blame for her illness, he makes the decision to live with his father and his new wife. In the context of this new family unit, Chester can be himself, and he is given the love and support he needs to grow as an individual.

Dicey's Song (Voigt, 1982), a sequel to *Homecoming* (1981), focusses on Dicey's difficulty accepting a new life with Gram, the Tillerman's maternal grandmother. As Dicey matures and changes, so does her relationship with Gram. Over time, all four children adjust to their new home, and Gram adjusts her life to include them, until gradually a new family unit emerges.

From Journals to Dialogue

In their literary journals, students record their personal responses to the family stories they have selected to read independently. They are also expected to write an analysis of each novel, using the "family as setting" approach as a framework for their analysis. Students are encouraged to consult the list of suggestions for literary analysis to help them with this assignment. Students are encouraged to share their own unique interpretation and understandings as they develop their analyses and, at the same time, to use their new literary skills. The purpose of this assignment is to provide an opportunity for students to verbalize their understanding of their self-selected novels and to reinforce their grasp of the expanded concept of setting introduced in the shared reading experience and articulated in the "Seven Suggestions." In addition, the teacher can use these analyses as feedback to discover what students are learning, as well as what they need to learn.

Journal entries can be used as starting points for sharing and discussing novels within the small dialogue groups. A scribe in each dialogue group records significant discoveries, insights, and connections generated during the dialogue-group meetings. Teachers who wish to have a record of these dialogue sessions for evaluation purposes can request that one student in each group be responsible for taping the session.

After students have had ample time to read and write independently and to discuss their novels in a dialogue group, the whole class comes together in a series of sharing-comparing sessions. The scribes from the dialogue groups report on the work of each group. As the rest of the class listens to these reports, they are asked to look for connections between novels they have read and the novels read by classmates in other dialogue groups.

These whole-class sessions are extensions of the cumulative dialogue which began with the initial discussion of the meaning of family and continued through the shared reading experience and the small dialogue groups formed to study independent reading selections and to explore the notion of "family as setting" in these novels. After sharing and comparing the novels selected from the family stories collection, students are ready to move beyond a focus on single texts and the craft of specific authors to a focus on the stories as a whole. What does this group of authors say about family patterns and relationships and about the role of family in the lives of individuals? What do authors of historical fiction and of novels with copyright dates prior to 1970 say about family patterns and attitudes about the family as a unit? How do authors of more recent family novels address the issues and problems confronted by young people in contemporary society?

Narrative Writing

The concluding activity for this Focus Unit is a writing project, which is another extension of the cumulative dialogue. Discussing the family as a setting for the development of central characters in the family novels and exploring the wide range of family patterns and relationships serve as a preparation for this writing experience.

Students are given two options for the narrative writing assignment.

1. **Create a fictional family story in which the central character is significantly influenced by family dynamics, other family members, and/or a family event, problem, or conflict.**

2. **Write an autobiographical story in which you are the central character and your family is the setting. What relationships, events, challenges, changes, and conflicts have influenced you?**

Whichever option is chosen, the student is expected to use family as the setting for character development, conflict, and growth. These narratives can be lighthearted and humorous or serious in tone. Some students, inspired by the craft of Betsy Byars, may choose to weave humor into stories with serious themes.

Students are invited to share their completed narratives in the small dialogue groups or in whole-class sessions. These new family stories composed by student authors are discussed in terms of the suggestions used previously to explore the work of professional writers.

The writing assignment provides students with an opportunity to draw from their exploration of family stories in terms of content and craft to create their own family stories and to use the concept of "family as setting" as a way to think about the impact of family on the development of the central character in their story.

The Family Focus Unit:
Learning about Oneself and Others

At the end of this Focus Unit experience, students are encouraged to make connections between the lives of characters in the family stories (by student or professional authors) and their own lives. They are given opportunities to share these connections in contexts of their own choosing. Some students are willing to share personal experiences and perspectives in their dialogue groups; others prefer to put their thoughts on paper; others choose to talk privately with a teacher or peer. Students who feel uncomfortable about engaging in this personal reflection can choose not to participate in these sharing experiences.

This Focus Unit experience is designed to provide opportunities for students to discover themselves and their own families in literary texts as they enter into the lives of fictional characters struggling to cope with or to find solutions for problems confronting them. Students who do find personal relevance in a particular novel or a story written by a classmate may gain insights or a new perspective about conflicts and problems in their own lives. This Focus Unit is also designed to provide opportunities for students to learn about the diverse family patterns and problems which may be represented in their own classroom community and which reflect those found in the larger society. Realistic fiction about families can serve as a context for learning about oneself as well as others.

References

Egoff, Sheila. (1981). *Thursday's Child*. Chicago, IL: American Library Association.

Lukens, Rebecca. (1990). *A Critical Handbook of Children's Literature* (4th edition). Glenview, IL: Scott, Foresman.

Norton, Donna. (1991). *Through the Eyes of a Child: An Introduction to Children's Literature* (3rd edition). New York: MacMillan.

Paterson, Katherine. (1981). *Gates of Excellence*. New York: E.P. Dutton.

Bibliography: Family Stories

Adler, C.S. (1981). *The Cat That Was Left Behind*. New York: Clarion Books.

* Alcott, Louisa May. (1868). *Little Women*.

Amoss, Berthe. (1988). *The Mockingbird song*. New York: Harper and Row.

Angell, Judie. (1985). *One Way to Ansonia*. New York: Bradbury Press.

Armstrong, William. (1969). *Sounder*. New York: Harper.

Auch, Mary Jane. (1987). *Cry Uncle!*. New York: Holiday House.

Auch, Mary Jane. (1992). *Out of Step*. New York: Holiday House.

Bates, Betty. (1987). *Ask Me Tomorrow*. New York: Holiday House.

Bauer, Marion Dane. (1991). *Face To Face*. New York: Clarion.

Bauer, Marion Dane. (1977.) *Foster Child*. New York: Seabury.

Bawden, Nina. (1985). *The Finding*. New York: Lothrop Lee & Shepard.

Bawden, Nina. (1992). *Humbug*. New York: Clarion/Houghton.

Bawden, Nina. (1989). *The Outside Child*. New York: Lothrop Lee & Shepard.

Beatty, Patricia. (1993, 1985). *The Nickle-Plated Beauty*. New York: Morrow Jr. Books.

Benjamin, Carol Lea. (1982). *The Wicked Stepdog*. New York: Crowell.

Blume, Judy. (1981). *Tiger Eyes*. New York: Bradbury.

Boyd, Candy Dawson. (1987). *Charlie Pippin*. New York: Macmillan.

Brooks, Bruce. (1986). *Midnight Hour Encore*. New York: Harper.

Buss, Fran Leeper. (1991). *Journey of the Sparrows*. New York: Dutton.

Byars, Betsy. (1982). *The Animal, the Vegetable, and John D. Jones*. New York: Delacorte.

* published before 1960

Byars, Betsy. (1988). *Beans on the Roof.* New York: Delacorte.

Byars, Betsy. (1985). *Cracker Jackson.* New York: Viking.

Byars, Betsy. (1983). *The Glory Girl.* New York: Viking.

Byars, Betsy. (1972). *The House of Wings.* New York: Viking.

Byars, Betsy. (1968). *The Midnight Fox.* New York: Viking.

Byars, Betsy. (1980). *The Night Swimmers.* New York: Delacorte.

Byars, Betsy. (1977). *The Pinballs.* New York: Harper & Row.

Byars, Betsy. (1970). *The Summer of the Swans.* New York: Viking.

Byars, Betsy. (1982). *The Two Thousand Pound Goldfish.* New York: Harper & Row.

Cameron, Eleanor. (1971). *Room Made of Windows.* Boston: Little, Brown.

Cameron, Eleanor. (1982). *That Julia Redfern.* New York: Dutton.

Cannon, A. E. (1991). *Amazing Gracie.* New York: Delacorte.

Cannon, Bettie. (1987). *A Bellsong for Sarah Raines.* New York: Charles Scribner's Sons.

Carey, Mary. (1985). *A Place for Allie.* New York: Dodd and Mead.

Carter, Alden. (1990). *Robodad.* New York: G.P. Putnam's Sons.

Carter, Alden. (1989). *Up Country.* New York: G.P. Putnam's Sons.

Childress, Alice. (1973). *A Hero Ain't Nothing But a Sandwich.* New York: Coward, McCann.

Clark, Ann Nolan. (1975). *Year Walk.* New York: Viking.

* Cleary, Beverly. (1955). *Beezus and Ramona.* New York: Morrow.

Cleary, Beverly. (1983). *Dear Mr. Henshaw.* New York: Morrow.

Cleary, Beverly. (1977). *Ramona and Her Father.* New York: Morrow.

Cleary, Beverly. (1979). *Ramona and Her Mother.* New York: Morrow.

Cleary, Beverly. (1984). *Ramona Forever.* New York: Morrow.

Cleaver, Vera and Bill Cleaver. (1970). *Grover.* Philadelphia, PA: Lippincott.

Cleaver, Vera and Bill Cleaver. (1969). *Where the Lilies Bloom.* Philadelphia, PA: Lippincott.

Clifford, Eth. (1987). *The Man Who Sang in the Dark.* Boston: Houghton Mifflin.

Clymer, Eleanor. (1967). *My Brother Stevie.* New York: Holt.

Cohn, Barbara. (1990). *The Long Way Home.* New York: Lothrop, Lee & Shepard.

Conrad, Pam. (1985). *Prairie Songs.* New York: Harper and Row.

Cooney, Caroline. (1989). *Family Reunion.* New York: Bantam Books.

Corcoran, Barbara. (1986). *A Horse Named Sky.* New York: Atheneum.

Corcoran, Barbara. (1986). *I Am the Universe.* New York: Atheneum.

Corcoran, Barbara. (1988). *The Sky Is Falling.* New York: Atheneum.

Crew, Linda. (1991). *Nekomah Creek.* New York: Delacorte.

Crofford, Emily. (1981). *A Matter of Pride.* Minneapolis, MN: Carolrhoda Books.

Crutcher, Chris. (1989). *Chinese Handcuffs.* New York: Greenwillow.

Crutcher, Chris. (1987). *The Crazy Horse Electric Game.* New York: Greenwillow.

Danziger, Paula. (1982). *The Divorce Express.* New York: Delacorte.

Davis, Jenny. (1987). *Good-bye and Keep Cold.* New York: Orchard.

Delton, Judy. (1987). *Angel's Mother's Wedding.* Boston: Houghton Mifflin.

Donnelly, Elfie. (1981). *So Long, Grandpa.* New York: Crown Publishers.

Dorris, Michael. (1992). *Morning Girl.* New York: Hyperion.

Edwards, Pat. (1987). *Nelda*. Boston: Houghton Mifflin.

Ellis, Sarah. (1986). *A Family Project*. New York: Macmillan.

* Enright, Elizabeth. (1941). *The Saturdays*. New York: Holt.

* Estes, Eleanor. (1941). *The Moffats*. San Diego, CA: Harcourt Brace Jovanovich.

Fine, Anne. (1992). *Book of the Banshee*. Boston: Little, Brown.

Fine, Anne. (1989). *My War with Goggle Eyes*. Boston: Little, Brown.

Fleischman, Paul. (1991). *The Borning Room*. New York: Zolotow/Harper.

Fox, Paula. (1970). *Blowfish Live in the Sea*. New York: Bradbury.

Fox, Paula. (1987). *Lily and the Lost Boy*. New York: Orchard Books.

Fox, Paula. (1991). *Monkey Island*. New York: Orchard/Watts.

Fox, Paula. (1986). *The Moonlight Man*. New York: Bradbury.

Fox, Paula. (1980). *A Place Apart*. New York: Farrar, Straus, and Giroux.

Fox, Paula. (1968). *The Stone-Faced Boy*. New York: Bradbury.

Fox, Paula. (1988). *The Village by the Sea*. New York: Watts.

Green, Connie Jordan. (1992). *Emmy*. New York: McElderry.

Greene, Constance. (1976). *Beat the Turtle Drum*. New York: Viking.

Green, Constance. (1985). *Star Shine*. New York: Viking Kestrel.

Greenfield, Eloise. (1974). *Sister*. New York: Crowell.

Griffin, Peni R. (1991). *A Dig In Time*. New York: McElderry.

Guy, Rosa. (1989). *The Ups and Downs of Carl Davis III*. New York: Delacorte.

Hahn, Mary Downing. (1985). *The Jelly Fish Season*. New York: Clarion Books.

Hamilton, Virginia. (1990). *Cousins*. New York: Philomel.

Hall, Lynn. (1981). *Danza!* New York: Charles Scribner's Sons.

Haseley, Dennis. (1991). *Shadows*. New York: Farrar, Straus, and Giroux.

Hautzig, Esther. (1968). *The Endless Steppe*. New York: Harper.

Henkes, Kevin. (1992). *Words of Stone*. New York: Greenwillow.

Hermes, Patricia. (1991). *Mama, Let's Dance*. Boston: Little Brown.

Hill, Elizabeth Starr. (1991). *The Street Dancers*. New York: Viking.

Hill, Kirkpatrick. (1990). *Toughboy and Sister*. New York: Macmillan.

Hodge, Merle. (1993). *For the Life of Laetitia*. New York: Farrar.

Holl, Kristi. (1987). *Patchwork Summer*. New York: Atheneum.

Holman, Felice. (1990). *Secret City, U.S.A*. New York: Scribner.

Hooks, William. (1984). *Circle of Fire*. New York: Atheneum.

Horvath, Polly. (1990). *No More Cornflakes*. New York: Farrar Straus Giroux.

Howard, Ellen. (1987). *Edith Herself*. New York: Atheneum.

Hudson, Jan. (1989). *Sweetgrass*. New York: Philomel.

Hunt, Irene. (1966). *Up a Road Slowly*. Englewood Cliffs, NJ: Follett.

Hurmence, Belinda. (1980). *Tough Tiffany*. New York: Doubleday.

Hurwitz, Johanna. (1978). *The Law of Gravity*. New York: William Morrow.

Kidd, Diana. (1989, 1991). *Onion Tears*. New York: Orchard Books.

Klein, Norma. (1972). *Mom, the Wolf Man and Me*. New York: Pantheon.

Klein, Norma. (1974). *Taking Sides*. New York: Pantheon.

Koertge, Ron. (1991). *Mariposa Blues*. Boston: Little, Brown.

Lasky, Kathryn. (1981). *The Night Journey*. New York: Warne.

* L'Engle, Madeleine. (1960). *Meet the Austins*. New York: Vanguard.

Levin, Betty. (1992). *Mercy's Mill*. New York: Greenwillow.

Little, Jean. (1984). *Mama's Going to Buy You a Mockingbird*. Kestral Books.

Lively, Penelope. (1980). *Fanny's Sister*. New York: Dutton.

Lorentzen, Karin. (1983). *Lanky Longlegs.* New York: Atheneum.

Lowry, Lois. (1977). *A Summer to Die.* Boston: Houghton Mifflin.

Lowry, Lois. (1987). *Rabble Starkey.* Boston: Houghton Mifflin.

Lyon, George Ella. (1988). *Borrowed Children.* New York: Orchard Books.

MacLachlan, Patricia. (1980). *Arthur for the Very First Time.* New York: Harper.

MacLachlan, Patricia. (1993). *Baby.* New York: Delacorte.

MacLachlan, Patricia. (1991). *Journey.* New York: Delacorte.

MacLachlan, Patricia. (1985). *Sarah, Plain and Tall.* New York: Harper and Row.

MacLachlan, Patricia. (1994). *Skylark.* New York: HarperCollins.

Mann, Peggy. (1973). *My Dad Lives in a Downtown Hotel.* New York: Doubleday.

Mann, Peggy. (1977). *There are Two Kinds of Terrible.* New York: Doubleday.

Mark, Jan. (1986). *Trouble Half-Way.* New York: Atheneum.

McDonald, Joyce. (1988). *Mail-Order Kid.* New York: G.P. Putnam.

Mebs, Gudrun. (1986). *Sunday's Child.* New York: Dial.

Mohr, Nicholasa. (1979). *Felita.* New York: Dial.

Mohr, Nicholasa. (1986). *Going Home.* New York: Dial.

Moore, Emily. (1980). *Something to Count On.* New York: E.P. Dutton.

Myers, Anna. (1992). *Red-Dirt Jessie.* New York: Walker.

Myers, Walter Dean. (1978). *It Ain't All for Nothing.* New York: Viking.

Myers, Walter Dean. (1982). *Won't Know Till I Get There.* New York: Viking.

Naidoo, Beverley. (1986). *Journey to Jo'burg — A South African Story.* New York: Harper and Row.

Naughton, Jim. (1989). *My Brother Stealing Second.* New York: Harper and Row.

Naylor, Phyllis. (1988). *Maudie in the Middle.* New York: Atheneum.

Nelson, Theresa. (1986). *The 25¢ Miracle.* New York: Bradbury Press.

Nixon, Joan Lowery. (1987). *A Family Apart.* New York: Bantam.

Nixon, Joan Lowery. (1985). *Maggie, Too.* San Diego, CA: Harcourt Brace Jovanovich.

O'Dell, Scott. (1981). *Carlota.* Boston: Houghton Mifflin.

Olsen, Violet. (1987). *View from the Pighouse Roof.* New York: Atheneum.

Park, Barbara. (1981). *Don't Make Me Smile.* New York: Knopf.

Paterson, Katherine. (1985). *Come Sing, Jimmy Jo.* New York: Dutton.

Paterson, Katherine. (1978). *The Great Gilly Hopkins.* New York: Crowell.

Paterson, Katherine. (1980). *Jacob Have I Loved.* New York: Crowell.

Paterson, Katherine. (1988). *Park's Quest.* New York: Lodestar Books.

Pearson, Gayle. (1986). *Fish Friday.* New York: Macmillan.

Peck, Richard. (1991). *Unfinished Portrait of Jessica.* New York: Delacorte.

Roberts, Willo Davis. (1990). *To Grandmother's House We Go.* New York: Atheneum.

Robertson, Keith. (1973). *In Search of a Sandhill Crane.* New York: Viking.

Rodowsky, Colby. (1985). *Julie's Daughter.* New York: Farrar, Straus & Giroux.

Rylant, Cynthia. (1985). *A Blue-Eyed Daisy.* New York: Bradbury.

Rylant, Cynthia. (1988). *A Kindness.* New York: Orchard.

Rylant, Cynthia. (1992). *Missing May.* New York: Orchard.

Sachs, Marilyn. (1971). *The Bears' House.* New York: Doubleday.

Sachs, Marilyn. (1973). *The Truth About Mary Rose.* New York: Doubleday.

Sachs, Marilyn. (1987). *Fran Ellen's House.* New York: E.P. Dutton.

Sebestyen, Ouida. (1979). *Words By Heart.* Boston: Little, Brown.

Shreve, Susan. (1979). *Family Secrets: Five Very Important Stories.* New York: Knopf.

* Sidney, Margaret. (1980). *Five Little Peppers and How They Grew.*

Singer, Marilyn. (1988). *Several Kinds of Silence.* New York: Harper and Row.

Slote, Alfred. (1988). *Moving In.* Philadelphia, PA: Lippincott.

Slote, Alfred. (1990). *The Trading Game.* New York: HarperCollins/Lippincott.

Smith, Doris. (1983). *The First Hard Times.* New York: Viking.

Smith, Doris. (1981). *Last Was Lloyd.* New York: Viking.

Smith, Doris. (1986). *Return to Bitter Creek.* New York: Viking Kestrel.

Smith, Robert Kimmel. (1989). *Bobby Baseball.* New York: Delacorte.

Snyder, Carol. (1985). *Ike and Mama and the Seven Surprises.* New York: Lothrop, Lee & Shepard.

Staples, Suzanne Fisher. (1989). *Shabanu: Daughter of the Wind.* New York: Alfred Knopf.

Stone, Bruce. (1985). *Half Nelson, Full Nelson.* New York: Harper and Row.

Talbert, Marc. (1991). *Pillow of Clouds.* New York: Dial.

Talbert, Marc. (1992). *The Purple Heart.* New York: HarperCollins.

Taylor, Mildred. (1987). *The Gold Cadillac.* New York: Dial.

Taylor, Mildred. (1981). *Let the Circle Be Unbroken.* New York: Dial.

Taylor, Mildred. (1976). *Roll of Thunder, Hear My Cry.* New York: Dial.

* Taylor, Sidney. (1951). *All of a Kind Family.* Englewood Cliffs, NJ: Follett.

Terris, Susan. (1986). *The Latchkey Kids.* New York: Farrar Straus & Giroux.

Tolan, Stephanie. (1980). *The Liberation of Tansy Warner.* New York: Scribner's.

Uchida, Yoshiko. (1981). *A Jar of Dreams.* New York: Atheneum.

Voigt, Cynthia. (1984). *Building Blocks.* New York: Random House.

Voigt, Cynthia. (1982). *Dicey's Song.* New York: Atheneum.

Voigt, Cynthia. (1981). *Homecoming.* New York: Atheneum.

Voigt, Cynthia. (1985). *The Runner.* New York: Random House.

Voigt, Cynthia. (1984). *A Solitary Blue.* New York: Atheneum.

Voigt, Cynthia. (1987). *Sons from Afar.* New York: Atheneum.

Wieler, Diana. (1991). *Last Chance Summer.* New York: Delacorte.

* Wiggin, Kate Douglas. (1903). *Rebecca of Sunnybrook Farm.*

* Wilder, Laura Ingalls. (1953). *Little House in the Big Woods.* New York: Harper and Row. (Series)

Yep, Laurence. (1977). *Child of the Owl.* New York: Harper and Row.

Yep, Laurence. (1975). *Dragonwings.* New York: Harper and Row.

Yep, Laurence. (1991). *The Star Fisher.* New York: Morrow.

Yolen, Jane. (1988). *The Devil's Arithmetic.* New York: Viking Penguin.

ART AND ARTISTS:
FICTION AND NON-FICTION

In most middle-grade classrooms there are students who feel a special identification with Jesse Aarons, the central character in *Bridge to Terabithia* (Paterson, 1977) who loved to draw. There are other students who feel a personal connection with eleven-year-old Minna Pratt, a young cellist in search of her vibrato, in *The Facts and Fiction of Minna Pratt* (MacLachlen, 1988) or with twelve-year-old Littlejim, whose love of language and writing is viewed with contempt by his stern father who believes that reading and writing are not manly interests (*Littlejim*, Houston, 1990).

There are a few students who can empathize with Peter, whose secret love of ballet is in conflict with his public image as a basketball player and "one of the boys" (*A Special Gift*, Simon, 1978) or with Willie, who thinks of nothing but dancing and must defy his father to pursue his dream (*Nobody's Family is Going to Change*, Fitzhugh, 1974).

Fictional accounts of young people who experience personal anxiety and frustration and encounter social disapproval and rejection as they struggle to pursue their dreams provide mirrors for readers who recognize themselves in these characters.[1] Often these readers find support and encouragement as they enter into the lives of fictional characters whose dreams and dilemmas seem to reflect their own.

For students who are not involved or interested in the world of art, fiction and non-fiction about artists, their lives, and their work serve as windows into another way of life, another world. Portraits of artists in fiction and non-fiction reveal what it is like to be deeply immersed in the creative process of dance, sculpture, drama, music, painting, drawing, and writing. Readers are introduced to individuals with an intense inner drive to express their feelings, ideas, and experiences through a particular art form.

For all students, literature about the lives of artists presents models of motivated, self-directed, independent people with rich inner lives and the capacity for the self-discipline and self-control required for the growth and refinement of talents and skills. For some students, a particular fictional or biographical account of an artist may serve as an inspiration to stretch and reach beyond what they are and toward what they can become.

The focus for the unit described in this chapter was selected in response to students with special interests in particular art forms or artistic endeavors. In addition, this Focus Unit was developed to provide opportunities for all students to expand their own worlds and to learn about and from those whose lives are different from their own.

Planning A Focus Unit About Art and Artists

A Focus Unit featuring art and artists can be developed for the class as a whole or as an independent study for individual students or small groups. A loose-leaf notebook provides the structure for this unit. The notebook contains *booklists* of relevant fiction and non-fiction available in a classroom collection or school and public libraries; a series of *questions* about selected texts; and a variety of *suggestions* for special projects.

The Notebook is intended to be an open-ended resource which evolves out of a collaboration between teacher and students as they engage in the process of reading widely and deeply and constructing meanings throughout this cumulative learning experience. It is used as a framework for planning, implementing, revising, and expanding the Focus Unit experience. In the initial stages, the teacher (1) selects the *focus* for the unit; (2) compiles a preliminary list of titles of relevant books and other reading and audio-visual materials; and (3) generates questions about the literature for this unit and suggestions for special projects designed to enrich experience with texts. The focus of this literature unit, "Art and Artists," and the Notebook are introduced to the class in an initial whole-group session. Students are invited to share their personal experiences with particular art forms and to express feelings and attitudes (positive or negative) about art and artists. At the conclusion of this first session, students generate a list of the different artistic endeavors in which they are involved as active participants and/or interested spectators.

In the second whole-class session, the three components of the Notebook are reviewed: the preliminary lists of titles, questions, and suggestions. Students are asked to offer ideas for organizing, revising, and expanding the contents of the Notebook so that it can become a practical, easy-to-use tool or resource. One of these ideas — to organize the notebook in terms of the art forms that are of interest to students in the class and are featured in fiction and non-fiction texts included in the initial list of titles — is used to organize the Notebook described in this chapter. Students are invited to help the teacher divide up the initial list of books into separate lists for each of the different types of artistic endeavors and create separate sections in the Notebook; each section would include relevant titles, questions, and project suggestions for a particular type of artistic endeavor. Students are requested to add their own ideas for titles, questions, and special projects to each section of the Notebook during the course of the

Focus Unit experience. They are encouraged to do their own library research to locate appropriate titles.

After the Notebook has been introduced and organized, the teacher and students plan the next steps in the process of developing this unit. If the whole class is to be involved in this unit, the teacher plans a series of shared reading experiences to read aloud and discuss one or more of the novels selected for this unit. The teacher presents brief summaries of a number of novels that might have broad appeal to help students choose a title (or titles) for this shared experience. Like the other Focus Units, this shared experience sets the stage for small *dialogue groups* to explore self-selected novels in terms of personal response and literary craft and content. Participants in each dialogue group will be responsible for analyzing self-selected books and contributing relevant questions and project suggestions to the Notebook. Students also record their responses to and analysis of self-selected texts in their *literary journal*. Journal entries may be generated by questions in the Notebook or they may include questions to add to the Notebook. Journal entries can also be used as starters for discussions in the small dialogue groups.

The Notebook can also be used by individuals or small groups as a guide for *independent study*. Many of the Focus Units described in this book can be adapted for use as frameworks for independent study. The Notebook provides a useful structure for students who engage in independent study within a given discipline or in interdisciplinary study. Students may choose to work alone or in a small group to pursue a special interest in a particular art form; they will use the appropriate section in the Notebook to help them plan and implement their independent study. For example, students with special interests in visual arts would begin with the preliminary content in this section of the Notebook and then add to or revise it as they become involved in reading, writing, and dialogue with group members and/or the teacher. In some school settings, arrangements can be made for these students to work on their study of fiction and non-fiction featuring the visual arts in collaboration with their art teacher and their English or Language Arts teacher. The study of literature across the curriculum is made possible in school settings in which interdisciplinary thematic teaching in encouraged and supported.

In the remainder of this chapter, contents of the Notebook used to develop this Focus Unit are presented in more detail. This Notebook is organized in terms of four types of artistic endeavors: Writing, Music, Dance, and Visual Arts. Each of the four sections begins with a particular novel selected for use as a *springboard* for discussion and writing and for exploring other novels and non-fiction about the art form featured in that section or the literature in other sections. At least one of the four Springboard Books is read aloud and discussed in the shared reading experience or read independently by small groups or individuals working on their own.

When a whole class is involved in the Focus Unit, students select at least one fiction and one non-fiction text from one of the sections of the Notebook to read independently. Small dialogue groups are formed to enable students to share and compare their self-selected books with classmates who have selected books from the same section. After the students in each dialogue group have an opportunity to discuss their books and to formulate questions and suggestions for the Notebook, the whole class comes together to engage in a comparative analysis of fiction and non-fiction listed in all four sections. Questions introduced by the teacher and the student scribes from each dialogue group are used to initiate the search for connections between these books.

Each of the sections in the Notebook can be used as a separate unit for independent study or as an integral part of a Focus Unit featuring different types of artistic endeavors and designed to meet the diverse needs and interests and to broaden the horizons of all the students in a particular class.

An overview of this Focus Unit is presented below. It is organized into two parts: (1) bold print is used to indicate the contents of each section of the Notebook, and (2) standard print is used to indicate analysis of selected titles in terms of craft and content and connections with other books in any of the four sections. This second part of the overview offers examples of the Focus Unit experience in which the entire class is involved in experiencing, exploring, and comparing texts representing all four types of artistic endeavors.

THE NOTEBOOK

SECTION I: WRITING

The Springboard Book

Littlejim by Gloria Houston (1990) is used to introduce fiction and non-fiction selections featuring writers (see Bibliography at the end of this section, page 114). Littlejim is a twelve-year-old boy who lives with his family on a farm in a rural North Carolina community in the early years of the twentieth century. His mother, his sister Nell, and his teacher recognize his special gift as a writer, and they support him in his pursuit of this interest. However, his father expresses only contempt for his son. To his father, reading and writing are not manly activities. He feels that Littlejim should be cutting timber, hunting, and working on the farm. Littlejim is deeply hurt by his father's contempt and struggles to earn his approval and respect. When an essay contest is announced at his school and Littlejim learns that the winning essay will be printed in the newspaper, his first thought is of his father. "In his mind he was already seeing a rare smile lighting his father's face as he read the essay his only son had written right there in print in the *Kansas City Star*" (p. 20). Even after his father forbids him to waste his time on this contest, Littlejim is determined to enter the competition and to work on his essay in secret. His decision to defy his father in order to prove his own worth and to earn his father's respect sets the stage for this story of a boy coming into manhood.

Connections: Conflict

After students have an opportunity to share their personal responses to this historical novel, they are invited to identify and discuss the central conflict that drives the plot and to find connections between the father-son conflict found in this story and similar conflicts found in stories in this and other sections selected for independent reading. The Notebook includes questions initiated by the teacher to generate this dialogue:

1. What is the conflict between the central character and his/her father?

2. In what way does this conflict shape or influence the experiences, feelings, goals, and behavior of the central character?

3. In what way is the conflict resolved for the central character? For the father?

A Special Gift (Simon, 1978)[2] is about Peter who keeps his love of dance a secret until he decides to audition for a part in the annual Nutcracker ballet. When his secret becomes public knowledge, he must face his father's anger and disapproval, as well as the cruelty and ridicule of his peers. His father and his father's close friend pressure Peter to pursue his athletic interests; they suggest that this interest in ballet is not natural for a boy. At the same time, Peter is struggling with his own inner doubts about his identity as a male.

In *Thursday's Children* (Godden, 1984),[3] Doone Penny, the youngest son of a London greengrocer, is also determined to become a ballet dancer in spite of the disapproval of his father and the ridicule of his siblings and peers. He, too, keeps his study of dance a secret from his father until he appears in a public performance. Like Littlejim and Peter, Doone is a gifted and dedicated artist who pursues his interests against all odds.

Jesse, in *Bridge to Terabithia* (Paterson, 1977),[4] is another young boy whose artistic interests are kept secret from his father to avoid his anger and disapproval.

A central character in *Nobody's Family Is Going To Change* (Fitzhugh, 1974)[5] is Willie Sheridan, an African-American boy whose father is intensely opposed to his son's dream of becoming a dancer. Willie's dancing triggers a deep emotional response from his father: "You've got to think of all the people who have bled and died so other people don't look at you and see nothing but a minstrel show. You want to take all that and throw it in their faces..." (p. 48).

In *Summer Light* by Zibby O'Neil (1985)[6] is about the relationship between seventeen-year-old Kate and her father, a famous painter. Kate has been deeply involved in painting since childhood, but when she wins first prize for a painting at her school, her father refuses to respond to it seriously. Kate has tried all her life to get her father to take her seriously as an individual, and her own response to this incident is to stop painting and to change her major. Only when Kate begins to realize that her father feels threatened by her and begins to see herself as an individual identity, separate from her father, does she return to her painting.

Connections: Writers in Fiction and Non-fiction

Students select fiction and non-fiction about writers for independent reading. These books are shared in a small dialogue group and, along with the springboard novel, *Littlejim*, become the basis for a comparative study of writers in novels and in real life. The following questions are derived from this comparative analysis and can be used to initiate further dialogue and/or to suggest topics for written response.

1. In which novels is the central character's interest in writing a source of conflict or significant problem for that character? Which biography or autobiography portrays an author with similar conflicts or problems?

2. In the fictional and non-fictional accounts of writers, identify individuals who were supportive and helpful. Identify those who worked against these writers or made it more difficult for them to pursue their interest in writing. What patterns do you find?

3. Identify the childhood settings of writers in fiction and non-fiction. What influence did this setting have on their writing and their life experiences?

4. Which writers (in fiction and non-fiction) use writing as a way of coping with personal problems and engaging in self-reflection? Give evidence of this from the texts.

5. What obstacles were encountered by the writers in these novels and biographical accounts? How did each writer deal with these obstacles?

6. Which accounts provided insight or information about the writing process? Find examples in the texts.

7. After reading and thinking about the writers portrayed in novels and in biographical accounts, what connections do you find between the fictional writers and those in real life?

8. What connection do you find between these writers and yourself?

This list of questions, representing the combined input of teacher and students, is derived from connections discovered in the process of comparative analysis.

For example, in *A Sound of Chariots* (Hunter, 1972), Bridie McShane describes the pain she feels when her teacher changes and marks out words in her essay with red pencil (p. 53). "It had been a wonderful feeling when it was finished. But now she was staring at the ruin of her lovely pattern of words..." (p. 55).

In *A Girl from Yamhill: A Memoir* (1988, p. 169), Beverly Cleary describes an eighth grade experience in which a teacher hands back a paragraph of description "inflamed with red pencil corrections," which made her stop writing descriptions for years. [See questions 5 and 7.]

In *Libby on Wednesday* (Snyder, 1990), Libby is a young writer who records her observations and impressions of people, her accounts of books she's read, her inner thoughts and feelings, and her experiences at home and at school in a set of journals that she keeps in the tree house where she does her writing.

The Newbery award winner, Betsy Byars, writes in a personal memoir, *The Moon and I* (1991): "Plenty of good scraps are as important in making a book as in the making of a quilt. I often think of my books as scrapbooks of my life, because I put in them all the neat things that I see and read and hear. I sometimes wonder what people who don't write do with all their good stuff" (p. 39). [See questions 6 and 7.]

These questions are included in the Notebook to suggest ideas for writing. Students select one or more of these questions to use as a starting point for writing about the writers they have encountered in fiction and non-fiction; what they have learned about the writing process and becoming a writer; what they've learned about themselves. For example, a young writer who read *Libby on Wednesday* and *The Moon and I* recognized her own habit of recording thoughts and feelings; observations and impressions; personal experiences and dreams; and questions, clues, and discoveries about human nature in small spiral notebooks. [See question 8.] A student who was especially impressed with the tree house in *Libby on Wednesday* and had expressed her longing for a private space for her own writing, found that other artists she encountered in fiction and non-fiction had created their own "special places to work alone and be themselves." When she conducted an informal survey of students and teachers about this issue of personal space, one teacher told her about Virginia Woolf and her book *A Room of One's Own*.[7]

Suggestions for Special Projects

1. Interview local authors or poets or those who visit your school or community. Construct questions for this interview by drawing from your study of the books in this section.

2. Write a profile of one of the central characters in the novels you read.

3. Read one or more of the books written by an author whose biography or autobiography you have read. What connections did you find between the author's life and work?

4. Read about a writer. Construct questions to use for a hypothetical interview. Record your questions and the responses you think he/she would offer, based on information you have collected from biographical accounts.

5. Write an original story or poem. As you write, think about what personal experiences, knowledge, feelings, and beliefs you bring to this creative process.

6. Write about your own experiences as a writer in or outside of school. If you are especially interested in writing, write about someone who has significantly influenced, encouraged, or inspired you. What obstacles, frustrations, and problems have you encountered as a writer?

7. Try some of the techniques used by writers in novels and biographical accounts. For example, try some of the journal ideas found in *Libby on Wednesday* or form a writers' club like the one featured in this novel.

BIBLIOGRAPHY: WRITING

Fiction

Alcott, Louisa May.(1869). *Little Women.*

Bedard, Michael. (1992). *Emily.* New York: Doubleday (picture book).

Cameron, Eleanor. (1971). *A Room Made of Windows.* Boston: Little, Brown.

Fitzhugh, Louise. (1964). *Harriet the Spy.* New York: Harper and Row.

Houston, Gloria. (1990). *Littlejim.* New York: Philomel.

Hunter, Mollie. (1972). *A Sound of Chariots.* New York: Harper and Row.

Mills, Claudia. (1986). *The One and Only Cynthia Jane Thornton.* New York: Macmillan.

Montgomery, Lucy Maud. (1908). *Anne of Green Gables.*

Schami, Rafik. (1990). *A Hand Full of Stars.* New York: Dutton.

Snyder, Zilpha Keatley. (1990). *Libby on Wednesday.* New York: Delacorte.

Wiggin, Kate Douglas. (1903). *Rebecca of Sunnybrook Farm.*

Non-fiction

Barth, Edna. (1979). *I'm Nobody! Who Are You? The Story of Emily Dickinson.* New York: Clarion.

Bauer, Marion Dane. (1992). *What's Your Story? A Young Person's Guide to Writing Fiction.* New York: Clarion.

Benét, Laura. (1950). *Famous American Poets.* Dodd.

Blair, Gwenda. (1981). *Laura Ingalls Wilder.* New York: Putnam.

Block, Irving. (1973). *The Lives of Pearl Buck: A Tale of China and America.* Thomas Crowell.

Bober, Natalie. (1991). *A Restless Spirit: The Story of Robert Frost.* New York: Holt.

Byars, Betsy. (1991). *The Moon and I.* New York: Julian Messner.

Cleary, Beverly. (1988). *A Girl from Yamhill: A Memoir.* New York: William Morrow.

Dahl, Roald. (1984). *Boy: Tales of Childhood.* New York: Farrar, Strauss.

Duncan, Lois. (1982). *Chapters, My Growth as a Writer.* Boston: Little, Brown.

Fakuda, Hanako. (1970). *"Wind in My Hand": The Story of Issa, Japanese Poet.*

Franchere, Ruth. (1958). *Willa.* (Willa Cather's childhood.) Thomas Crowell.

Fritz, Jean. (1985). *China Homecoming.* New York: Putnam.

Fritz, Jean. (1982). *Homesick: My Own Story.* New York: Putnam.

Gherman, Beverly. (1992). *E.B. White — Some Writer!* New York: Atheneum.

Hurwitz, Johanna. (1989). *Astrid Lindgren: Storyteller to the World.* New York: Viking.

Johnston, Norma. (1991). *Louisa May: The World and Works of Louisa May Alcott.* New York: Four Winds.

Kamen, Gloria. (1985). *Kipling: Storyteller of East and West.* New York: Atheneum.

Kyle, Elisabeth. (1968). *Great Ambitions: A Story of the Early Years of Charles Dickens.* New York: Holt.

Little, Jean. (1987). *Little by Little.* New York: Viking.

Little, Jean. (1991). *Stars Come Out Within.* New York: Viking.

Longsworth, Polly. (1965). *Emily Dickinson: Her Letter to the World.* Thomas Crowell.

Lyttle, Richard. (1992). *Ernest Hemingway: The Life and the Legend.* New York: Atheneum.

May, Jill. (1991). *Lloyd Alexander.* New York: Twayne.

Meltzer, Milton. (1988). *Starting From Home: A Writer's Beginnings.* New York: Viking Kestrel.

Naylor, Phyllis Reynolds. (1978). *How I Came To Be A Writer.* New York: Atheneum.

Olsen, Victoria. (1990). *Emily Dickinson: Poet.* New York: Chelsea House.

Rylant, Cynthia. (1992). *Best Wishes.* Katonah, NY: Richard C. Owen. (Meet the Author series)

Singer, Isaac Bashevis. (1969). *A Day of Pleasure: Stories of a Boy Growing Up in Warsaw.* New York: Farrar.

Vipont, El Frida. (1966). *Weaver of Dreams: The Girlhood of Charlotte Brontë.* Walck.

Walker, Alice. (1974). *Langston Hughes, American Poet.* Thomas Crowell.

Wilder, Laura Ingalls. (1974). *West from Home: Letters of Laura Ingalls Wilder, San Francisco, 1915.* New York: Harper.

Yates, Elizabeth. (1983). *My Widening World.* Westminster.

Yolen, Jane. (1992). *A Letter From Phoenix Farm.* Katonah, NY: Richard C. Owen. (Meet the Author series).

Zindel, Paul. (1992). *The Pigman and Me.* New York: Harper Collins.

Zinsser, William, editor. (1990). *Worlds of Childhood: The Art and Craft of Writing for Children.* Boston: Houghton Mifflin.

SECTION II: MUSIC

The Springboard Book

The Pennywhistle Tree by Doris Buchanan Smith (1991) is about eleven-year-old Jonathan and his three best friends. Jonathan is a musician. Music is a significant part of his identity. He is a serious student of the flute and the piano, and he relaxes in his special tree by playing his pennywhistle.

Unlike Littlejim, Jesse, Doone, and Peter, Jonathan's parents and peers accept and appreciate his musical interest and talents. The source of conflict in this novel is not the artistic interests of the central character but the appearance of a new boy who moves with his parents and six younger siblings into a house on Jonathan's street. The newcomer is Saunders George, a belligerent, aggressive boy who pushes himself into Jonathan's life, invades his privacy, annoys him at school, and causes a breach between Jonathan and his friends.

A question introduced in the Notebook to call attention to the role of music in the development of plot in this novel is, **"How did music help to bridge the gap between Jonathan and Saunders?"**

Saunders' aggressive and irritating behavior sets him apart as the "enemy" as far as Jonathan's group of friends is concerned, but Jonathan looks beneath the surface of this overt behavior. He discovers Saunders' gift for music and becomes aware of Saunders' courageous struggle to maintain his dignity and to earn the acceptance of his peers.

When Jonathan reaches out to Saunders and gives him his own pennywhistle, an act of kindness and compassion, his friends turn against him. They see Jonathan as a traitor who is helping the enemy. But Jonathan no longer sees Saunders as the enemy. He is a human being who has never had what Jonathan has always taken for granted: loving parents, music, old friendships, books and musical instruments, space and privacy.

Connections: Characters who are defined by their artistic interests and talents.

The central character in *The Pennywhistle Tree* is defined as a musician. Jonathan sees himself as a musician, and his family and friends acknowledge and appreciate his musical talent. Music is part of him; it is part of his world. Most of the novels selected for this Focus Unit portray characters who are also defined by their special interests and talents. Students are invited to engage in a comparative study of central characters in diverse novels, using *The Pennywhistle Tree* as the starting point.

The following questions initiated by the teacher and recorded in the Notebook, guide this comparative study and call attention to craft, content, and connections:

1. **How does the author develop the character who is defined by his/her involvement in a particular art form? Find passages in the text that reveal the authors' craft or techniques used to portray the character.** For example, in *The Pennywhistle Tree*, Jonathan's family and peers recognize his musical talent and accept his intense involvement with music. The reader is drawn into Jonathan's inner world as he practices the piano and "struggles with the complicated phrases of the Bach fugue... The room wrapped him, muffling the world until he was inside the music and the music was inside him and there was only him and the music and nothing else in the world" (p. 28).

    Another example is *The Cartoonist* (Byars, 1978).[8] Alfie's inner world is filled with new ideas and images for the cartoons he creates in the privacy of his attic room. People and events in his life provide an ongoing source of material for his cartoons.

    Libby On Wednesday (Snyder, 1990)[9] offers a portrait of a writer. Eleven-year-old Libby has been writing for years in her notebooks, in the privacy of her tree house. She writes about herself and others; she writes short stories and novels; she writes about her day, her experiences, her problems with family and classmates. She absorbs impressions, analyzes motives, and records them in her notebooks. It is a way of life for her.

    The One and Only Cynthia Jane Thornton (Mills, 1986)[10] is about a fifth grader who sees herself as a writer. On a class trip, Cynthia is struck by the beauty of the shafts of sunlight streaming through thick clouds (p. 52); she can't wait to capture this image with words in her notebook. On rainy Saturdays she wakes up early and recites poems in her head (pp. 57-58).

2. **What role does the character's identity as a dancer, writer, musician, or artist play in the development of the plot?** Unlike Jonathan (*The Pennywhistle Tree*), who is confident about himself as a musician, Cynthia (in *The One and Only Cynthia Jane Thornton*) has doubts about her identity until she finally understands that it isn't being a writer that makes her unique and special; it is her drive to write and the content and quality of her work that is important. The plot revolves around her search for identity.

   In *Bridge to Terabithia* (Paterson, 1977)[11] drawing is a significant part of Jesse's life, but the novel focusses more attention on friendship, growth, family relationships, and death.

   The plot in *A Special Gift* (Simon, 1978)[12] is driven by Peter's struggle to reconcile his identity as a male with his identity as a dancer. Once he solves this dilemma for himself, he need not live a double life and can deal with the reactions of family and peers.

   In *A Sound of Chariots* (Hunter, 1972)[13] Bridie loves language, and she stores up "a whole rich gallery of impressions" (p. 215) to translate into poetry. The plot is driven by her struggle to cope with the death of her beloved father and the effect of this tragedy on her growth as an individual. Bridie is a writer, and her writing is woven into the central plot.

   Ten-year-old Jon, in *Carver* (Radin, 1990)[14] wants to be a wood carver like his own father had been before he was killed in an accident. But Jon's quest is complicated by his blindness; he must prove that he can do what others assume he cannot do because of his visual handicap.

3. **Identify characters in these novels who provide significant help and encouragement as the central character pursues his/her artistic interests.**

   In *Bridge to Terabithia* Jesse's friend Leslie and one of his teachers recognize and appreciate his talent and help him to build on his inner strengths. Jon (in *Carver*) manages to get the best local carver, an angry recluse, to become his teacher.

   In *Thursday's Children* (Godden, 1984)[15] Doone Penny has a number of significant people in his life who help him realize his dream of becoming a dancer. There is Beppo, a former clown, who takes care of Doone as a child and teaches him about love and acrobatics and discipline. There is Mr. Felix, the piano teacher who works secretly with Doone. There are other teachers and artists who appreciate his gifts and the intensity of his dedication to dance.

4. **Identify novels in which the central character is the only member of a family who is unable to participate in the artistic endeavors that identify the family as a unit.**

The Glory Girl (Byars, 1993) is about Anna Glory, the only non-singing member of a gospel-singing family who treat her as a misfit. She struggles to establish her own identity and to discover her own self-worth.

In *Yang the Youngest and His Terrible Ear* (Namioka, 1992), Yingtao, the youngest Yang, is expected to play the violin with his family of talented musicians. But Yingtao does not have an ear for music; he is the only musically untalented member of the family.

After a comparative study of central characters in diverse novels, students are invited to discuss or write about personal connections to these fictional characters. The following questions are included in the Notebook to generate personal responses:

1. **What connections do you see between a particular story character and yourself?**

2. **What connections do you see between a particular character and someone you know?**

3. **What can you learn about yourself and/or other people by reading about fictional characters and entering into their personal lives?**

Connections: Musicians in Fiction and Non-Fiction

As in the first section which focusses on writers, students who select titles from the bibliography of fiction and non-fiction about musicians look for connections between these and the springboard book. Questions are derived from this comparative analysis and recorded in the Notebook. Later, these questions will be used as a source of suggestions for writing about musicians in fiction and non-fiction.

1. **Identify fiction and non-fiction about individuals whose interest in music is a source of conflict.**

2. **In fiction and non-fiction stories of musicians, identify individuals who helped or inspired them to pursue their interests. What other factors in their lives helped these musicians reach their goals?**

3. **In fiction and non-fictional about musicians, who attempted to impede their progress toward their goals? What other obstacles did these musicians encounter? How did they cope with these problems?**

4. **What sacrifices were required for individual musicians in fiction and non-fiction to pursue their dreams?**

5. **Which fictional or non-fictional books provided insights and information about the world of music, the lives of musicians, and the art of the musician?**

6. What connections do you find between musicians in fiction and musicians portrayed in biographies and memoirs?

7. What connections do you find between these musicians and yourself?

8. What did you learn about the process of becoming a performer in the world of music?

9. What did you learn about different kinds of music?

Suggestions for Special Projects

1. Interview professional musicians in your school or community or classmates who are musicians. Use what you've learned about musicians from reading fiction and non-fiction to construct a list of questions to use as you conduct the interview and to help you organize your notes as you write a profile of this person.

2. Select one of the biographies of a well-known musician. Construct a set of interview questions as suggested above to create a hypothetical interview with this individual. Record your questions and the responses you assume he/she would give *if* it were possible to meet with him/her in person.

3. If you are a musician, write about your own history and experiences with music.

4. If you play a musical instrument, identify classmates who also play an instrument and form a musical group as in *The Facts and Fictions of Minna Pratt* (MacLachlan, 1988).

5. If you are interested in writing music, compose an original piece with a friend as Sibilance and her father did in *Midnight Hour Encores* (Brooks, 1986).

BIBLIOGRAPHY: MUSIC

Fiction

Bell, Mary S. (1992). *Sonata for Mind and Heart*. New York: Atheneum.

Brooks, Bruce. (1986). *Midnight Hour Encores*. New York: Harper and Row.

Byars, Betsy. (1983). *The Glory Girl*. New York: Viking.

Clifford, Eth. (1987). *The Man Who Sang in the Dark*. Boston: Houghton Mifflin.

Duder, Tessa. (1986). *Jellybean*. New York: Viking.

Guy, Rosa. (1992). *The Music of Summer*. New York: Delacorte.

Higginsen, Vy with Tonya Bolden. (1992). *Mama, I Want to Sing*. New York: Scholastic.

LeGuin, Ursula. (1976). *Very Far Away From Anywhere Else*. New York: Atheneum.

MacLachlan, Pat. (1988). *The Facts and Fictions of Minna Pratt*. New York: Harper and Row, 1988.

Namioka, Lensey. (1992). *Yang the Youngest and His Terrible Ear.* Boston: Little Brown.

Paterson, Katherine. (1985). *Come Sing Jimmy Jo.* New York: Dutton.

Raymond, Patrick. (1990). *Daniel and Esther.* New York: Margaret Elderry Books.

Smith, Doris Buchanan. (1991). *The Pennywhistle Tree.* New York: Putnam.

Non-fiction

Beirne, Barbara. (1990). *A Pianist's Debut: Preparing for the Concert Stage.* Minneapolis: MN: Carolrhoda.

Gutman, Bill. (1977). *Duke: The Musical Life of Duke Ellington.* New York: Random House.

Haskins, James. (1980). *I'm Gonna Make You Love Me: The Story of Diana Ross.* New York: Dial.

Haskins, James. (1983). *Lena Horne.* Coward.

Jones, Hettie. (1974). *Big Star Fallin' Mama: Five Women in Black Music.* New York: Viking.

Krementz, Jill. (1991). *A Very Young Musician.* New York: Simon and Schuster.

Krull, Kathleen. (1993). *Lives of the Musicians: Good Times, Bad Times.* San Diego, CA: Harcourt.

Lasker, David. (1979). *The Boy Who Loved Music.* New York: Viking.

Mathis, Sharon Bell. (1973). *Ray Charles.* Crowell.

Monjo, Ferdinand. (1975). *Letters to Horseface: Being the Story of Wolfgang Amadeus Mozart's Journey to Italy 1769-1770 When He Was a Boy of Fourteen.* New York: Viking.

Nichols, Janet. (1992). *Women Music Makers: An Introduction to Women Composers.* New York: Walker Books.

Paolucci, Bridget. (1990). *Beverly Sills.* New York: Chelsea House.

Salerno-Sonnenberg, Nadja. (1989). *Nadja on My Way.* New York: Crown.

Tames, Richard. (1991). *Giuseppe Verdi.* New York: Watts.

Tames, Richard. (1991). *Wolfgang Amadeus Mozart.* New York: Watts.

Thompson, Wendy. (1991). *Ludwig van Beethoven.* New York: New York: Viking.

Tobias, Tobi. (1972). *Marion Anderson.* Crowell.

Ventura, Piero. (1989). *Great Composers.* New York: Putnam.

Wolff, Virginia E. (1991). *The Mozart Season.* New York: Henry Holt.

SECTION III: DANCE

The Springboard Book

In *Thursday's Children* (Godden, 1984), Doone Penny, the unwanted sixth child of a London greengrocer, is determined to become a ballet dancer. Readers are given a glimpse into the world of ballet training and performance as Doone moves from a local class to a Ballet School to a role in "Leda and the Swan" at the Royal Theater in London. Readers discover the rigors and pain of training, as well as the joy of creating art and beauty through control of one's body. This is a quest tale about a boy who sets his goal, overcomes obstacles, and through hard work, endurance, and self-discipline, reaches this goal.

Connections: Dreams and Discipline

Many of the novels in this Focus Unit offer portraits of serious artists whose dreams can only be realized through hard work, discipline, and sacrifice. A comparative study of these novels is initiated by questions recorded in the Notebook:

1. Which novels feature central characters who are serious artists?

2. What do you discover about the training and commitment required to develop and refine skills for a particular art form?

3. What qualities do these central characters share?

Like *Thursday's Children,* the novel *A Special Gift* (Simon, 1978) provides a picture of the rigorous training required for those who want to dance and what life is like for those who perform on stage. *As the Waltz Was Ending* (Butterworth, 1982) is an autobiographical account of the author's experience as a ballet student at the Vienna State Opera House prior to and during World War II. Before the bombings, blackouts, hunger, and terror, Emma lives in a world of music and dancing. She is immersed in her study of ballet; hers is a life of hard work and dedication.

Daniel and Esther (Raymond, 1990) takes place in the pre-war years. Daniel is a difficult, defiant teenager living in a progressive private boarding school in England. When a music professor discovers Daniel's musical gifts, Daniel puts his energy into the serious study of composing.

Midnight Hour Encores (Brooks, 1986) portrays a sixteen-year-old musical prodigy who is ranked among the world's greatest cellists. In her first-person narrative, Sibilance describes what it's like to be a teen prodigy, to travel around the world on concert tours or for international competitions, and to be immersed in a world of music. Her position as a world-class cellist and the depth and breadth of her knowledge of music reflect many years of hard work, self-discipline, and intense involvement as a student. Her narrative makes it clear that her dedication to music has required her to sacrifice the social life most teenagers enjoy.

A Sound of Chariots (Hunter, 1972) and *Libby on Wednesday* (Snyder, 1990) provide portraits of serious young writers who are driven to record their experiences, feelings, and impressions by writing about them and to struggle to express themselves and capture images and ideas in words.

In *The Monument* (Paulson, 1991)[16] thirteen-year-old Rocky learns to see through the eyes of an artist who comes to her small Kansas town to create a war memorial. The artist shares his own insights about the creative process with Rocky and helps her develop techniques of line, color, and shading. He urges her to keep drawing and to keep working: "You must do this and do this — for years. Draw and draw until you think your hands will fall off. Just to know the line — the way the line works" (p. 90). Following his advice, Rocky draws everything she sees and then begins "to see things for the first time that I had been looking at forever" (p. 100).

Connections: Fiction and Non-fiction

Students who select fiction and non-fiction about dancers to read independently look for connections between these self-selected books and the springboard novel. Questions derived from this comparative analysis are recorded in the Notebook to suggest ideas for writing about dancers in fiction and non-fiction.

1. Compare fiction and non-fictional accounts of dancers in which the pursuit of their dream is a source of conflict.

2. Compare fiction and non-fictional accounts of dancers in which sex-role stereotyping plays an important role in the life of the artist.

3. Identify individuals who help or inspire dancers in fiction and non-fiction. Explain their role in the lives of these dancers.

4. Identify individuals in fiction and non-fiction who try to discourage dancers from pursuing their artistic interests or to prevent them from reaching their goals.

5. Compare fiction and non-fictional stories of dancers in which the social context functions as antagonist in their lives.

6. Compare fiction and non-fictional stories of dancers in terms of the role of their artistic endeavors in their growth as individuals.

7. Compare fiction and non-fictional stories of dancers in terms of the hardships they endure and overcome and the sacrifices they are required to make for their art.

8. What did you learn about the training and discipline of dancers in the fiction and non-fictional accounts?

9. What did you learn about the preparation required for public performances?

10. What did you learn about different types of dance?

11. What insights and information do fiction and non-fictional accounts of dance offer about the world of dance and the world of theater?

12. What connections did you find between the dancers portrayed in fiction and non-fiction and yourself?

Suggestions for Special Projects

1. Interview a professional dancer who comes to your school or community. Write a profile of this person.

2. Select one of the biographies of a well-known dancer and construct a hypothetical interview with this individual. Record your questions and the responses you would expect on the basis of what you have read about him or her.

3. If you are a dancer, write about your own training and experiences.

4. Read some of the stories of the well-known ballets such as "Swan Lake," "The Firebird," "The Nutcracker," and "Sleeping Beauty." If possible, plan to attend a live performance of one of these ballets scheduled at your local theater. Another possibility is to borrow video tapes of selected ballets from your local library. How does the knowledge of the story help you to appreciate and enjoy the performance of the ballet?

5. Read "Leda and the Swan" before reading *Thursday's Children*. Read "The Nutcracker" before reading *A Special Gift*. How does your knowledge of the ballet story enrich your reading of the novel in which it appears?

6. Select a favorite ballet and illustrate scenes from the story or create a diorama to represent the stage setting. Examine single illustrated editions of well-known ballets to discover how diverse artists have used the picture-book format to recreate these stories.

7. Create an illustrated dictionary of special terms used by professional dancers.

8. Read about other forms of dance such as modern dance, tap dance, soft shoe, and folk dances of particular countries. If possible, plan to attend live performances or view some of these dance forms on video tape.

BIBLIOGRAPHY: DANCE

Fiction

Ackerman, Karen. (1988). *Song and Dance Man*. New York: Knopf (picture book).

Asher, Sandy. (1982). *Just Like Jenny*. New York: Delacorte.

Betancourt, Jeanne. (1992). *Kate's Turn*. New York: Scholastic.

Butterworth, Emma. (1982). *As the Waltz Was Ending*. New York: Macmillan.

Fitzhugh, Louise. (1974). *Nobody's Family is Going to Change*. New York: Farrar, Straus & Giroux.

Godden, Rumer. (1984). *Thursday's Children*. New York: Viking.

Hill, Elizabeth Star. (1991). *The Street Dancers*. New York: Viking.

Isadora, Rachel. (1993). *Lili at Ballet*. New York: Putnam (picture book).

Lee, Jeanne. (1991). *Silent Lotus*. New York: Farrar (picture book).

Pendergraft, Patricia. (1988). *Hear the Wind Blow*. New York: Philomel.

Simon, Marcia. (1978). *A Special Gift*. San Diego, CA: Harcourt Brace Jovanovich.

Smith, Doris Buchanan. (1987). *Karate Dancer*. New York: Putnam.

Voigt, Cynthia. (1986). *Come A Stranger*. New York: Atheneum.

Non-fiction

Barboza, Stephen.(1992). *I Feel Like Dancing: A Year With Jacques D'Amboise and the National Dance Institute*. New York: Crown.

Brighton, Catherine. (1992). *Nijinsky: Scenes from the Childhood of the Great Dancer*. New York: Doubleday.

Chevance, Audrey. (1992). *Tutu*. New York: Dutton.

Fonteyn, Margot. (1989). *Swan Lake*. San Diego, CA: Harcourt Brace Jovanovich.

Ford, Thomas. (1992). *Paula Abdul*. New York: Dillon Press.

Krementz, Jill. (1976). *A Very Young Dancer*. New York: Knopf.

Morris, Ann. (1991). *On Their Toes: A Russian Ballet School*. New York: Atheneum.

Terry, Walter. (1975). *Frontiers of Dance: The Life of Martha Graham*. Thomas Crowell.

Tobias, Tobi. (1975). *Arthur Mitchell* (founder of the Dance Theater of Harlem). Thomas Crowell.

Tobias, Tobi. (1970). *Maria Tallchief*. Thomas Crowell.

Verdy, Violette. (1991). *Of Swans, Sugarplums and Satin Slippers: Ballet Stories for Children*. New York: Scholastic.

Werner, Vivian. (1992). *Petrouchka: The Story of the Ballet*. New York: Preiss/ Viking.

SECTION IV: THE VISUAL ARTS (Painting, Drawing, Carving)

The Springboard Book

Randall's Wall (Fenner, 1991) is the story of eleven-year-old Randall, who loves to draw and is a gifted artist. Randall's father is rarely home, and his mother is not well enough to care for him and his siblings. The family lives in poverty. The dirty, frightened boy is shunned by his classmates and barely tolerated by his teachers. He builds an inner wall of dreams to keep out the harsh world around him. And he draws his dreams. Drawing helps him survive as he lives his life alone inside his protective wall.

When one of his classmates reaches out to Randall and establishes a relationship with him, Randall's wall weakens. When his teacher discovers his drawings hidden in his desk and shares his remarkable work with others, the wall collapses and Randall is pulled into the outside world. The novel ends on a note of hope for Randall and his family. In the end, it is his artistic gift that calls attention to him and the plight of his family.

Connection: Art and the Inner Life

Randall found solace in his drawing and used it to cope with the deprivation, neglect, and cruelty in his life. He was able to draw his dreams to replace a painful reality. This connection between one's art and one's inner life and, in particular, the use of art as a coping mechanism is found in other novels. For example, in *Libby on Wednesday* (Snyder, 1990), Libby finds that writing helps her deal with anger and frustration: "Writing a tantrum had taken the place of having one, and writing a confusion had sometimes cleared it up" (p. 49). For Libby, writing is a vehicle for exploring feelings, clarifying experiences, and coping with personal problems. When she joins a small writers' club at school, she discovers that by sharing their writing in the group, they share themselves. Libby realizes that through their writing, these students reveal a great deal about their personal lives and enable the others to see beneath the surface to gain significant insights about them as individuals and to feel compassion.

The central character in *The Cartoonist* (Byars, 1978), Alfie, longs for his mother's attention and love but is acutely aware that his older brother is the one his mother has always idolized. Alfie feels disconnected from his peers and his family, and he retreats into the world of cartoons. His cartoons keep him going. He can ease the pain of his real world by the humor of his cartoon world.

The Dollmaker (Arnow, 1954), set during World War II, is about Gertie, a strong young woman who loves to whittle, drawing from her own inner life to bring life out of wood. As she struggles to deal with personal tragedy, poverty, and the confinement and stress of life in a Detroit housing project, Gertie turns to her carving to express herself and to find release from the daily fight for survival. For Gertie, art is a luxury, and at the end of this novel, she is forced to sacrifice her carving to feed her children.

Connections: Fiction and Non-Fiction

Questions derived from a comparative analysis of fiction and non-fiction featuring visual artists are recorded in the Notebook and used to stimulate ideas for writing about visual artists.

1   Compare fiction and non-fiction about visual artists whose artistic dreams and endeavors are a source of conflict.

2. Identify fiction and non-fiction about visual artists in which gender issues play a role in the conflicts that confront these artists.

3. Discuss hardships and obstacles encountered by visual artists in fiction and non-fiction. What character traits enable them to cope with the hardships and overcome the obstacles?

4. Identify individuals in fiction and non-fiction about visual artists who help or inspire them in the pursuit of their artistic goals. What character traits distinguish these supportive individuals?

5. Identify individuals in fiction and non-fiction about visual artists who attempt to block their efforts to succeed in the world of art. What character traits distinguish these antagonists?

6. Identify visual artists in fiction and non-fiction whose art reflects their inner lives. Find examples in the texts.

7. Identify visual artists in fiction and non-fiction whose art helps them cope with external conflict and internal turmoil. Find examples in the texts.

8. Compare fiction and non-fiction about visual artists in which personal sacrifice is required in the pursuit of artistic endeavor.

9. What insights and information about visual arts and artists did you gain from the fiction and non-fiction in this section?

10. What connections did you find between the visual artists portrayed in fiction and non-fiction and yourself?

11. Identify stories of fictional or living artists who were a source of inspiration for you. Explain.

12. What character traits did you especially admire in a visual artist you encountered in fiction or non-fiction?

13. Identify fiction or non-fictional selections that helped you understand and appreciate particular works of art. Explain.

Suggestions for Special Projects

1. Interview artists in your school or community. Use information you have acquired about art and artists to formulate your questions for the interview. Use your notes from the interview to write a profile of that person.

2. Write a profile of a fictional artist in one of the novels selected for this section.

3. Visit a local art gallery. Prepare for your visit by reading about famous artists whose work is exhibited in the gallery and about different types of art included in the collection. Invite someone from the gallery to visit the classroom in order to assist in this preparation.

4. Using Rocky (*The Monument*) as a model, carry a sketchbook with you for a week. Draw whatever you see. At the end of the week, write about this experience and what you notice about the contents of your sketchbook.

5. Read biographies of artists whose illustrated picture books you enjoyed when you were younger. Locate in the library picture books they have illustrated. Give a class presentation about one or more of these illustrators and show their work as you talk. Invite your classmates to identify favorite illustrators they recall from their early years. Share personal responses to these illustrations.

6. Examine a variety of Caldecott Award books in terms of the artists' styles and the media and techniques they used to illustrate these picture books. What are the connections between the illus-

trations and the subject or theme of each book? What artistic criteria do you think were used in the selection of each of these award winners? What social or political issues might have informed this decision-making process? Create a display of these books in chronological order. Invite your classmates to compare the earlier publications with the more recent ones and record their observations and discoveries. [*Picture Books for Looking and Learning* (Marantz, 1992) would be a useful resource for this project.]

7. Select a well-known painter or sculptor. Read about this individual and find reproductions of his/her work in art books. Write a profile which includes connections you find between his/her history and his/her art.

8. Write about your own experiences as an artist. Who has helped or encouraged you? What kinds of media and artistic techniques do you enjoy using?

9. Select an artist whose work is familiar to you. Look at examples of his/her work in a gallery or in art books with reproductions. Identify the kinds of media this artist uses (watercolor, oil, woodcut, collage, etc.) and his/her style (representational, abstract, impressionistic, expressionistic, folk art, etc.). Determine the nature of this work: themes, mood, subjects, etc. Write an analysis of the work of this artist.

10. Select a popular fairy tale that has been illustrated by diverse artists. Examine these illustrated editions of the same tale and identify significant similarities and differences. In what ways do particular illustrations change, diminish, enrich, or expand the story itself?[17]

BIBLIOGRAPHY: THE VISUAL ARTS

Fiction
Arnow, Harriette. (1954). *The Dollmaker*. New York: Macmillan.
Byars, Betsy. (1978). *The Cartoonist*. New York: Viking.
Cole, Brock. (1989). *Celine*. New York: Farrar, Straus & Giroux.
Fenner, Carol. (1991). *Randall's Wall*. New York: Macmillan.
O'Neal, Zibby. (1985). *In Summer Light*. New York: Viking.
Paterson, Katherine. (1977). *Bridge to Terabithia*. New York: Harper and Row.
Paulson, Gary. (1991). *The Monument*. New York: Delacorte.
Radin, Ruth. (1990). *Carver*. New York: Macmillan.

Non-fiction
Aldis, Dorothy. (1969). *Nothing is Impossible: The Story of Beatrix Potter*. New York: Atheneum.

Ayer, Eleanor. (1992). *Margaret Bourke-White: Photographing the World*. New York: Dillon.

Bang, Molly. (1991). *Picture This: Perception and Composition*. Boston: Little Brown.

Barnes, Rachel. (1990). *Artists By Themselves: Degas; Van Gogh; Renoir; Monet*. New York: Knopf.

Beardsley, John. (1991). *Pablo Picasso*. New York: Abrams.

Bernard, Bruce. (1993). *Van Gogh*. New York: Dorling Kindersley (Eyewitness Art Series).

Blegvad, Erik. (1979). *Self-Portrait; Erik Blegvad*. Boston: Addison-Wesley.

Blizzard, Gladys. (1992). *Come Look With Me: Animals in Art*. Charlottesville, VA: Thomasson-Grant.

Blizzard, Gladys. (1990). *Come Look With Me: Enjoying Art with Children*. Charlottesville, VA: Thomasson-Grant.

Blizzard, Gladys.(1992). *Come Look With Me: Exploring Landscape Art With Children*. Charlottesville, VA: Thomasson-Grant.

Bober, Natalie. (1991). *Marc Chagall: Painter of Dreams*. Philadelphia, PA: Jewish Publication Society.

Bolton, Linda. (1993). *Hidden Pictures*. New York: Dial.

Cole, Alison. (1993). *Perspective*. New York: Dorling Kindersley (Eyewitness Art Series).

Cummings, Pat. (1992). *Talking With Artists*. New York: Bradbury, 1992.

deMejo, Oscar. (1992). *Oscar deMejo's ABC*. New York: HarperCollins, 1992.

Dobrin, Arnold. (1975). *I am a Stranger on the Earth: The Story of Vincent Van Gogh*. New York: Warne.

Drucker, Malka. (1991). *Frida Kahlo: Torment and Triumphs in Her Life and Art*. New York: Bantam.

Edens, Cooper, ed. (1991). *The Three Princesses*. New York: Bantam.

Everett, Gwen. (1992). *Li'l Sis and Uncle Willie: A Story Based on the Life and Paintings of William H. Johnson*. National Museum of American Art, Smithsonian, New York: Rizzoli.

Feelings, Tom. (1972). *Black Pilgrimage*. New York: Lothrop, Lee & Shepard.

Fisher, Maxine. (1988). *Walt Disney*. New York: Watts.

Gardner, Jane Mylum. (1993). *Henry Moore*. New York: Four Winds Press.

Gherman, Beverly. (1986). *Georgia O'Keeffe: "The Wideness and Wonder" of Her World*. New York: Atheneum.

Greenberg, Jan. (1991). *The Painter's Eye: Learning to Look at Contemporary American Art*. New York: Delacorte.

Greenfield, Howard. (1967). *Marc Chagall*. Englewood Cliffs, NJ: Follett.

Greenfield, Howard. (1971). *Pablo Picasso: An Introduction*. Englewood Cliffs, NJ: Follett.

Heslewood, Juliet. (1993). *Introducing Picasso*. Boston: Little, Brown.

Howard, Michael. (1993). *Gauguin*. New York: Dorling Kindersley (Eyewitness Art Series).

Hyman, Trina Schart. (1981). *Self-Portrait: Trina Schart Hyman*. Boston: Addison-Wesley.

Janson, H.W. and Anthony Janson. (1992). *History of Art for Young People*, 4th edition. New York: Abrams.

Lipman, Jean and Margaret Aspinwall. (1981). *Alexander Calder and His Magical Mobiles*. New York: Hudson Hills.

Livingston, Myra Cohn. (1992). *Light and Shadow*. New York: Holiday House.

Lyttle, Richard. (1989). *Pablo Picasso: The Man and the Image*. New York: Atheneum.

Marantz, Sylvia and Kenneth. (1992). *Artists of the Page: Interviews with Children's Book Illustrators*. Jefferson, NC: McFarland.

Marantz, Sylvia.(1992). *Picture Books for Looking and Learning*. Phoenix, AZ: Oryx.

Mayers, Florence. (1992). *A Russian ABC*. New York: Abrams.

Meryman, Richard. (1991). *Andrew Wyeth*. New York: Abrams.

Peet, Bill. (1989). *Bill Pete: An Autobiography*. Boston: Houghton Mifflin.

Pekarik, Andrew. (1992). *Painting*. New York: Hyperion (Behind the Scenes Series).

Pekarik, Andrew. (1992). *Sculpture*. New York: Hyperion (Behind the Scenes Series).

Raboff, Ernest. (1968). *Pablo Picasso*. New York: Doubleday.

Raboff, Ernest. (1968). *Paul Klee*. New York: Doubleday.

Raboff, Ernest. (1968). *Marc Chagall*. New York: Doubleday.

Richardson, Wendy and Jack. (1991). *Families: Through the Eyes of Artists*. Chicago: IL: Children's Press.

Richardson, Wendy and Jack. (1991). *Cities: Through the Eyes of Artists*. Chicago, IL: Children's Press.

Richardson, Wendy and Jack. (1991). *Entertainers: Through the Eyes of Artists*. Children's Press.

Richardson, Wendy and Jack. (1991). *Water: Through the Eyes of Artists*. Chicago, IL: Children's Press.

Roalf, Peggy. (1992). *Looking At Paintings*. (series) New York: Hyperion Books. (*Cats; Dancers; Families; Seascapes*)

Rodari, Florian. (1991). *A Weekend With Picasso*. New York: Rizzoli.

Rodari, Florian. (1993). *A Weekend With Velazquez*. New York: Rizzoli.

Schwartz, Gary. (1992). *Rembrandt*. New York: Abrams.

Sills, Leslie. (1989). *Inspirations: Stories About Women Artists*. Morton Grove, IL: Whitman.

Sills, Leslie. (1993). *Visions: Stories About Women Artists*. Morton Grove, IL: Whitman.

Skira-Ventura, Rosabianca. (1991). *A Weekend With Renoir*. New York: Rizzoli.

Sky-Peck, Kathryn, ed. (1991). *Who Has Seen The Wind?: An Illustrated Collection of Poetry for Young People*. New York: Rizzoli.

Sufrin, Mark. (1991). *George Catlin: Painter of the Indian West*. New York: Atheneum.

Tobias, Tobi. (1974). *Isamu Noguchi: The Life of a Sculptor*. Thomas Crowell.

Turner, Robyn Montana. (1991). *Georgia O'Keeffe*. Boston: Little, Brown (Series: Portraits of Women Artists for Children).

Turner, Robyn. (1992). *Mary Cassatt*. Boston: Little, Brown.

Turner, Robyn. (1991). *Rosa Bonheur*. Boston: Little, Brown.

Ventura, Piero. (1989). *Michelangelo's World*. New York: Putnam.

Waldron, Ann. (1991). *Claude Monet*. New York: Abrams.

Welton, Jude. (1993). *Monet.* New York: Dorling Kindersley (Eyewitness Art Series).

Williams, Helen. (1992). *Stories in Art.* Brookfield, CT: Millbrook.

Wilson, Ellen. (1971). *American Painter in Paris: A Life of Mary Cassatt.* New York: Farrar.

Wilson, Sarah. (1992). *Matisse.* New York: Rizzoli.

Winter, Jeanette and Jonah. (1991). *Diego.* New York: Knopf.

Woolf, Felicity. (1993). *Picture this Century: An Introduction to Twentieth-Century Art.* New York: Doubleday.

Zemach, Margot. (1978). *Self-Portrait; Margot Zemach.* Boston: Addison-Wesley.

Zhensun, Zheng, and Alice Low. (1991). *A Young Painter.* New York: Scholastic.

Concluding Comments

The Focus Unit outlined in this chapter is designed as a framework for a whole-class shared experience or for independent study by individuals or small groups. The Notebook serves as a central resource which evolves out of the collaborative involvement of teacher and students in the course of this cumulative literary experience. The dynamic nature of the Notebook is reflected in its "loose-leaves," allowing for an ongoing process of revision and expansion to incorporate discoveries of new titles; new insights and understandings about craft, content, and connections; questions derived from comparative analysis; and suggestions for special projects. Students are invited to create and recreate the Notebook with their teacher and to *use* the Notebook as a source of ideas for dialogue, writing, and projects to extend and enrich their experiences with fiction and non-fiction about art and artists. Students engaged in independent study can choose to use only one section of the Notebook as a framework for building an individualized Focus Unit experience around a personal interest in a particular art form or artistic endeavor.

For some students, the study of fiction and non-fiction about art and artists featured in this unit serves as a reaffirmation of and support for their personal interest in a particular art form. Other students may discover new interests to pursue on their own or gain a new perspective about the art world or revise old attitudes. All students who become involved in this unit are given opportunities to become acquainted with individuals who have set a goal for themselves and have worked long and hard to realize their goal. Students are exposed to individuals who are highly motivated to engage in a creative process requiring endurance, persistence, patience, dedication, and self-discipline. Thus, students are introduced to models of goal-oriented individuals who exemplify qualities that are critical for all human endeavors.

Foot Notes:

1. Rudine Sims Bishop, (Summer 1990), "Mirrors, Windows, and Sliding Glass Doors," in *Perspectives: Choosing and Using Books for the Classroom*, Vol. 6, No. 3, Norwood: MA: Christopher-Gordon Publishers.
2. Marcia Simon, (1978), *A Special Gift*, San Diego, CA: Harcourt Brace Jovanovich.
3. Rumer Godden, (1984), *Thursday's Children*, New York: Viking.
4. Katherine Paterson, (1977), *Bridge to Terabithia*, New York: Harper and Row.
5. Louise Fitzhugh, (1974), *Nobody's Family Is Going to Change*, New York: Farrar, Straus and Giroux.
6. Zibby O'Neal, (1985), *In Summer Light*, New York: Viking.
7. Virginia Woolf, (1929), *A Room of One's Own*, San Diego, CA: Harcourt Brace Jovanovich.
8. Betsy Byars, (1978), *The Cartoonist*, New York: Viking.
9. Zilpha Snyder, (1990), *Libby on Wednesday*, New York: Delacorte.
10. Claudia Mills, (1986), *The One and Only Cynthia Jane Thornton*, New York: Macmillan.
11. Katherine Paterson, (1977), *Bridge to Terabithia*, New York: Harper and Row.
12. Marcia Simon, (1978), *A Special Gift*, San Diego, CA: Harcourt Brace Jovanovich.
13. Mollie Hunter, (1972), *A Sound of Chariots*, New York: Harper and Row.
14. Ruth Radin, (1990), *Carver*, New York: Macmillan.
15. Rumer Godden, (1984), *Thursday's Children*, New York: Viking Press.
16. Gary Paulson, (1991), *The Monument*, New York: Delacorte.
17. Cooper Edens' The *Three Princesses: Cinderella, Sleeping Beauty, and Snow White* (Bantam, 1991) includes examples of the work of 25 master illustrators who have interpreted these tales for the past 125 years. This is an excellent resource for students who plan to write about the art of the fairy tale.

WAR AND PEACE:
HISTORICAL FICTION
AND NON-FICTION

Historical fiction can turn sterile facts and figures about the past into living human experience. Writers of historical fiction portray the human dimension of an historical period and invite their readers to respond to the people and events of the past intellectually as well as emotionally. The reader who is drawn into the historical reality created by the writer can begin to feel the pain, suffering, and despair as well as the joys, triumphs, and hopes of the people in this reality.

Both fiction and non-fiction are used to study history in the Focus Unit described in this chapter. In their Introduction to *The Story of Ourselves: Teaching History Through Children's Literature* (1993), Michael Tunnell and Richard Ammon emphasize the value of integrating the study of literature and history: "Ultimately, our task in teaching history is not so much to teach facts as to help students grapple with concepts. Part of this process dictates breathing life into the dusty past and presenting history from varying viewpoints. Trade books provide one of the best mechanisms for helping teachers achieve a livelier and more meaningful history curriculum" (pp. viii-ix).

Like other Focus Units outlined in this book, this literary-historical unit is characterized by a dual focus on craft and content. That is, students are given opportunities to engage in literary analysis and a careful study of authors' craft and, at the same time, to study human experience as portrayed in literature. The literary part of this integrated unit introduces the students to historical fiction as a literary genre and to the human dimension of the historical period selected for study.

In this Focus Unit, the study of the craft and content of historical fiction is integrated with a third focus: non-fiction sources about the historical period selected for study in this unit, the Second World War. Students are expected to read fiction and non-fiction as complementary sources for studying this historical period.

Phase One: Historical Research

Prior to the introduction to historical novels, students are given opportunities to learn about the World War II period, including the pre- and post-war years. Classroom textbooks and trade books selected for this unit are used as a starting point for gathering data about this historical period. After a survey of these non-fictional materials, students generate a list of significant topics for further study. Small research committees are formed as students select subjects of special interest to explore through collaborative inquiry. The diverse non-fiction titles placed in the classroom are used as resource material for these in-depth explorations. The school librarian is available to assist in the location and use of other reference material in the library. Public libraries can also be used in the search for relevant material. The findings of each committee are shared with the whole class so that all the students are provided with information about the causes of the war; key political and military figures; Hitler's rise to power; significant battles and weapons; the Nuremberg Laws, the persecution, internment, and extermination of the Jews; the underground resistance; the Nuremberg trials of the Nazis; the imprisonment of Japanese-Americans after Pearl Harbor; and the bombing of Hiroshima. The students construct a chronology of key events on a wall chart that has adequate space for additions and revisions as new information is accumulated.

Phase Two: Historical Novels

Background information acquired from textbooks and other resources provides the context necessary to generate meaning from the historical novels that are read aloud to the class and selected for independent reading during the second phase of this integrated unit. (A bibliography of relevant historical novels and non-fiction can be found at the end of this chapter.) The novels enable the students to enter into the lives of people who were profoundly affected by these historical events. As they live through these experiences, students are given opportunities to gain a deeper understanding of the realities and human costs of war and to respond with empathy and feeling as they study this period of history.

Friedrich (Richter, 1970) is read aloud and discussed in a series of shared reading sessions to introduce the historical novel as a literary genre and to set the stage for independent study of novels selected from the collection of diverse novels gathered for classroom use. *Friedrich* is a novel about the persecution of the Jews in Nazi Germany before and during World War II. The story is told from the viewpoint of a non-Jewish boy whose best friend, Friedrich Schneider, lives right above him in the same apartment house. It is the story of two boys and their families, one Jewish, the other non-Jewish. The narrator witnesses the persecution and destruction of a single Jewish family, his neighbors.

As this novel is read aloud, students are encouraged to live through the experience of two young boys growing up in Germany before and during Hitler's rise to power. They are invited to respond emotionally to the characters and events and to share their feelings of anger, frustration, shock, and sympathy as the story unfolds. The initial discussions provide time for personal reactions to the story and questions about the historical events that intervene in the lives of the characters. Students are asked to draw from their store of knowledge about this period and use the "Chronology" included at the end of the novel to make sense of the sequence of events in the narrative. Some of their questions generate further research. Thus, the historical novel becomes a springboard for purposeful study as students discover gaps in their knowledge and understanding, which they will want to fill. This inquiry is initiated during Phase III of this Focus Unit.

These learning strategies — using prior knowledge to make sense of an historical novel and using the novel as a springboard for further inquiry — are introduced during the initial sessions, in which *Friedrich* is read aloud and discussed. Students are encouraged to use these strategies to facilitate their own learning as they read other novels independently.

Following spontaneous, student-initiated discussions of the story, the teacher introduces or reviews literary elements and genres which will be used as the basis for developing questions to generate a detailed analysis of this novel and to offer a framework for independent interactions with other texts: viewpoint, setting, characters, plot structure, conflict, genre, and themes.[1] After a discussion of these literary elements and of historical fiction as a literary genre, the teacher offers suggestions for formulating questions and asks the students to work together with one or two classmates to develop a series of questions for an analysis of *Friedrich*. Each team selects one of these elements or the genre — historical fiction — to use as a basis for developing questions for this analysis. In classrooms in which multiple copies of this novel are available, students are encouraged to formulate questions related to specific scenes or details in the text. As students work with their partners, the teacher moves from team to team to help them clarify their ideas and find the language to turn these ideas into questions.

When the class reconvenes for a whole-group literary analysis of this novel, each team takes a turn leading the discussion by posing their questions. Students read aloud excerpts from the text which they have used in formulating specific questions. The following examples of questions derived from a consideration of each literary element represent the combined input of students and teacher.

I.   Viewpoint: Who tells the story? Why does the author use a first-person point of view? Why do you think the narrator's name is withheld? Why do you think the author selected Friedrich's friend to tell the story?

II.   Setting: What is the role of setting in this narrative? What important information is revealed in the first chapter, "Setting the Scene (1925)"? Why does the author follow each chapter heading with the date? In what way is 1933 a turning point in the story? In what ways do historical events change the lives of the central characters? What could be the significance of the fact that the author was born the same year as the narrator? What knowledge do you have about the setting — Germany between 1925 and 1942 — that helps you to understand each episode and its larger implications?

III.   <u>Characters</u>: How does the author reveal each character? Find scenes that help to clarify specific characters. For example, how does the episode, "Snow" (pp. 7-12) reveal the characters of Friedrich and his mother and their relationship? How does the conclusion of this scene reveal the character of Herr Resch, the landlord, and foreshadow subsequent events? How is the narrator's grandfather portrayed in the episode, "Grandfather" (pp. 12-16)? What is the significance of this episode? Why did the author include the Sabbath observance (pp.16-19) and the Bar Mitzvah (pp. 78-84)? How did the episode at the amusement park (pp. 19-25) reveal the characters of Friedrich's father and the narrator's father and the differences between the two families? What does the narrator discover about himself when he participates in the Pogrom (pp. 88-95)?

IV.   <u>Plot Structure</u>: What is the nature of the plot structure? How does the author select and arrange specific episodes so that the plot builds steadily toward the destruction of the Jewish family and the final tragedy at the conclusion of the story? What is the connection between the plot structure and the Chronology included at the end of the book? What are important turning points in the narrative? For example, what is the significance of "The Jungvolk" episode (pp. 32-38) and "The Hearing" (pp. 48-54) for Friedrich's growing understanding of the realities of the adult world? What is the significance of the scene (pp. 70-74) in which the narrator's father reveals to Herr Schneider that he has joined the Party and urges the Schneiders to leave Germany? Reread the opening lines on the first page and the final episode (pp. 137-138). Why does the author feature Polycarp, Herr Resch's garden dwarf, in these opening and closing scenes? What is the significance of Polycarp in the story?

V.   <u>Conflict</u>: What is the **external conflict** in this story? Why does the author choose two young boys who are the same age and best friends to be, respectively, a witness and a victim of war? What **internal conflict** is experienced by the narrator? Find scenes in the text which show his struggle to understand what he observes and what he does. How does his growing awareness of the realities of the adult world deepen his internal conflict? Discuss the conflict between what he is being taught about the Jews by his grandfather, the Jungvolk, etc., and what he knows about his best friend Friedrich and his family.

     What **internal conflict** is experienced by the narrator's parents? Find moments in the narrative in which they show their courage and friendship by reaching out to their Jewish neighbors. How does the **external conflict** which drives the story force them to be passive and therefore unable to resolve their **internal conflict**?

VI.   <u>Genre</u>: What kind of historical fiction is this? What is the relationship of the author to the events? What clues about the author suggest that he has drawn from personal experience to create this story?

VII.   <u>Themes</u>: What moral issues are explored in this story? What does the author say about the nature and consequences of prejudice, hatred, and persecution? What does he say about loss of innocence and confrontation with evil? What is said about family ties, friendship, and loyalty? How does the author juxtapose man's inhumanity to man and the dark side of human nature with humane behavior, compassion, and responsibility and the triumph of the human spirit? How does this novel illustrate the concept that historical events shape the lives of individuals?

Independent Reading and Writing

Selection of novels for independent reading begins after the shared reading session in which *Friedrich* is introduced. Each student is expected to choose at least one of the novels about World War II that have been placed in the classroom collection. Ample time for this independent reading is built into the schedule, although many students choose to read additional books from the collection during free periods or at home. Independent reading occurs concomitantly with the class discussions of *Friedrich* to allow students to make connections between this shared reading experience and their individual reading experiences.

Independent reading is complemented by independent writing in the literary journal. This journal is used to record spontaneous personal responses to the unfolding text as well as comments prompted by the questions about literary elements generated by the teams and used in the group discussion of *Friedrich*. Students may choose one or more of these elements for the focus of their journal entries. They are also encouraged to incorporate in their response any connections they have discovered between the book(s) they are reading and *Friedrich*.

Journal entries are used as a starting point for reading conferences with the teacher. In this one-to-one interchange the student discusses what he/she is reading and selects a favorite passage to read aloud. The teacher may use another literary element to generate further discussion of the story or focus on specific difficulties the student may have with the meaning-making aspects of the reading process. Journal entries provide a running record of student's responses to and understanding of self-selected texts and enable teachers to monitor each students' progress in terms of strengths and weaknesses, insights and confusion, and the quality of involvement in the Focus Unit experience.

Journal entries can also be used by students during the whole-class discussions. Some students prefer to share what they have written than to share spontaneously in a group setting. Often, this gives them an opportunity to gain the confidence to contribute their thoughts informally in later group discussions.

Book Talks: Preparing for Choice

In order to assist students in choosing a novel from the classroom collection for independent reading, the teacher presents a series of brief book talks about some of the titles in the collection. Students who are already familiar with one or more of the novels in the collection or have new titles to add to it are invited to join the teacher in this overview of historical novels about World War II. This book-talk presentation includes representative examples of the different types of stories in the collection (see categories below). The discussion of each example concludes with a reference to other novels with a common focus. These group-ings can be used as a framework for organizing the titles on a wall chart above or next to the shelf in which the classroom collection is arranged alphabetically by author. The purpose of the wall chart is to provide additional assistance as students select books for independent reading.

The wall chart includes a series of headings such as "Friendship" or "Hiding," with a list of related titles under each heading. For example, *Friedrich* is listed under the heading "Friendship" and *Anne Frank: Diary of a Young Girl* (Frank, 1967) is placed under the heading "Hiding." Of course, there is consid-erable overlap between these groupings since most novels have multiple themes and distinguishing features. Thus, *Anne Frank* could be placed under the heading "Hiding" as well as the heading "Autobiographical Accounts." After the initial book-talk session and introduction to the wall chart, students are invited to add new headings and relevant titles and to record titles already on the chart under other headings. They are encouraged to think of the chart as a "working list" which changes as new ideas emerge during their study of the novels in the collection.

The groupings used in the Focus Unit described in this chapter are listed below, along with examples of titles which fit under each heading. A survey of these titles suggests the variety of books available for independent reading.

Wall Chart Headings and Titles:

I.   EVACUATION OF ENGLISH CHILDREN

All The Children Were Sent Away (Garrigue, 1976)
Carrie's War (Bawden, 1973)
The Eternal Spring of Mr. Ito (Garrigue, 1985)
The Sky Is Falling (Pearson, 1990)
When the Sirens Wailed (Streatfield, 1976)

II.   HIDING

Anna is Still Here (Vos, 1993)
Anne Frank: Diary of a Young Girl (Frank, 1967)
The Upstairs Room (Reiss, 1972)
The Borrowed House (van Stockum, 1975)
Behind the Secret Window: A Memoir of a Hidden Childhood (Toll, 1993)
Children of Bach (Dillon, 1992)
Hide and Seek (Vos, 1991)

The Hideout (Heuck, 1988)
Jacob's Rescue (Drucker and Haperin, 1993)
Twenty and Ten (Bishop, 1964)
The Lily Cupboard (Oppenheim, 1992)
Star Without a Sky (Ossowski, 1985)
Waiting for Anya (Morpurgo, 1990)

III. FRIENDSHIP

Autumn Street (Lowry, 1980)
The Devil in Vienna (Orgel, 1978)
Friedrich (Richter, 1972)
The Moon Bridge (Savin, 1992)
Number the Stars (Lowry, 1989)

IV. SURVIVAL

Along the Tracks (Bergman, 1991)
Daniel's Story (Matas, 1993)
Fireweed (Walsh, 1969)
Gideon (Aaron, 1982)
The Island on Bird Street (Orlev, 1984)
The Kingdom by the Sea (Westall, 1991)
The Little Fishes (Haugaard, 1967)
North to Freedom (Holm, 1965)
Shadow of the Wall (Laird, 1989)
The Survivor (Forman, 1976)
Tug of War (Lindgren, 1990)

V. AUTOBIOGRAPHICAL ACCOUNTS

Alicia: My Story (Appleman-Jurman, 1988)
As the Waltz Was Ending (Butterworth, 1982)
Bad Times, Good Friends: A Personal Memoir (Vogel, 1992)
The Big Lie: A True Story (Leitner, 1992)
The Boys Who Saved the Children (Baldwin, 1981)
Don't Say a Word (Gehrts, 1975, 1986)
The Endless Steppe (Hautzig, 1968)
Fly Away Home (Nostlinger, 1975)
I Am Fifteen and I Don't Want to Die (Arnothy, 1986)
Mischling, Second Degree. My Childhood in Nazi Germany (Koehn, 1977)
To Life (Sender, 1988)
Touch Wood — A Girlhood in Occupied France (Roth-Hano, 1989)
Upon the Head of a Goat, A Childhood in Hungary, 1939-1944 (Siegel, 1981)
We Survived the Holocaust (Landau, 1991)

VI. RESISTANCE

Ceremony of Innocence (Forman, 1970)
Code Name Kris (Matas, 1989)

Gideon (Aaron, 1982)
In Kindling Flame: The Story of Hannah Senesh (Atkinson, 1985)
Lisa's War (Matas, 1989)
The Man From the Other Side (Orlev, 1991)
Number the Stars (Lowry, 1989)
Shadow of the Wall (Laird, 1989)
Snow Treasure (McSwigan, 1942)
Uncle Misha's Partisans (Suhl, 1973)

VII.   JAPANESE-AMERICAN EXPERIENCE

Baseball Saved Us (Mochizuki, 1993)
The Bracelet (Uchida, 1993)
Farewell to Manzanar (Houston, 1973)
The Invisible Thread (Uchida, 1992)
Journey Home (Uchida, 1978)
Journey to Topaz: A Story of the Japanese-American Evacuation
    (Uchida, 1971 [1984])
Kim/Kimi (Irwin, 1987)
Naomi's Road (Kogawa, 1988)

VIII.   CHANGING ATTITUDES

The Borrowed House (van Stockum, 1975)
The Devil's Arithmetic (Yolen, 1988)
I Was There (Richter, 1962)
The Last Mission (Mazer, 1979)
Petros' War (Zei, 1972)

IX.   POST WAR

Alan and Naomi (Levoy, 1977)
Annie's Promise (Levitin, 1993)
Briar Rose (Yolen, 1992)
Crutches (Hartling, 1986)
Grace in the Wilderness (Siegal, 1985)
To Life (Sender, 1988)
Rain of Fire (Bauer, 1983)
Sadako and the Thousand Paper Cranes (Coerr, 1977)

Dialogue Groups

A sign-up sheet divided into nine columns — one for each heading on the chart — is posted next to the chart to allow students to record under the appropriate heading the title they have chosen to read independently. Students whose names are in the same column form a small dialogue group to discuss these novels. Some members in each group select the same titles and may need to work out a plan to share a single copy from the classroom collection or to locate the title in a public library. Some students will find the title they have chosen to read listed under several headings on the wall chart. They can choose the focus which is of most interest to them and sign their name in the appropriate column. Students who select titles which are not on the chart record their names and title under the relevant headings or, if necessary, create new categories.

After students are given ample time to read their selections independently, they meet in the small dialogue groups to share and compare books with a common focus. Journal entries about personal responses to these novels can be shared with members of the group to initiate the dialogue. The questions formulated about the literary elements introduced in the beginning of this unit can be used to generate analysis of individual titles.

A scribe is selected in each group to record key insights, literary connections, and questions about these novels, as well as personal responses to the individuals living in the historical reality portrayed in each story. Later, the scribe represents his/her dialogue group when the whole class meets to share what they have discovered.

Comparative Analysis of Historical Novels

Students are also asked to engage in a comparative analysis of the novels that are shared and analyzed in their dialogue groups. Results of the comparative analyses can be shared as informal oral presentations in the whole-group sessions by the scribes of each dialogue group. In upper-level classrooms, students can work together to produce more formal written reports of the results of a more extensive comparative analysis.

The literary elements introduced in the beginning of this chapter are used as a framework for a comparative analysis of the historical novels. Some of the connections and contrasts which can be discovered through such an analysis are presented below to suggest ways authors' craft is used to study these novels

I. Viewpoint

Stories written as first-person accounts by victims of hatred and persecution can have a powerful emotional impact on the reader. The reader is invited to stand in the shoes of the narrator and to feel his/her pain, humiliation, terror, anger, and helplessness. *Touch Wood* (Roth-Hano, 1988) is an autobiographical novel set in Nazi-occupied France. The narrator is a young Jewish girl who flees with her family from Alsace and lives in Paris until the restrictions against the Jews become unbearable and one Jewish family after another is picked up by the police. The narrator and her sisters escape to Normandy where they are sheltered and "hidden" in a Catholic residence. In Paris, Jews must wear a Star of David on their jackets or coats at all times. Renée, the narrator, describes what it is like when she goes to school with the large yellow star on her jacket: "I feel a weight on my chest, and it grows heavier as we near school" (p. 99). As the anti-Jewish decrees accumulate and neighbors turn their backs on her, she feels humiliated and ashamed: "I hate the metro now that we've been ordered to ride in the last car — humiliated once more... I am ashamed. I no longer walk: I skim the walls. The few inches I've gained in height I am losing by shrinking. I am ashamed" (p. 106).

Stories written from the viewpoint of witnesses provide a different perspective. The narrator in *Friedrich* observes the destruction of a Jewish family from a safe distance. He observes the cruelty and greed of those who hate the Jews. He watches Herr Schneider and the Rabbi dragged away by the police. "[Herr Resch] was smiling and, rubbing his hands gleefully..." (p. 125). He sees Herr Resch the next morning as he searches for valuables in the Schneiders' empty apartment; he sees the shopping bag already filled with Herr Schneider's books and the silver Sabbath candleholder (p. 127). He watches as Herr Resch sends Friedrich out of the shelter to his death.

In *I Was There* (Richter, 1972) the same narrator, as a member of the Hitler Youth Movement, describes events from 1933 to 1943. In an introductory note that precedes the story, the author writes:

> I am reporting how I lived through that time and what I saw — no more. I was there. I was not merely an eyewitness. I believed — and I will never believe again.

On the last page of the book, under the heading, "About the Author", Dr. Richter confirms that both *Friedrich* and *I Was There* are autobiographical books. As he did in *Friedrich*, the author includes a chronology of political and military events which are the context for the narrative. This chronology begins on January 30, 1933, when Adolf Hitler becomes Chancellor of the German Reich, and ends in 1943 when "the last remnants of the Sixth Army surrender to the Russians at Stalingrad..." (pp. 193-204). The author also provides the reader with detailed "Notes about" specific terms and phrases used in the narrative (pp. 181-192). This segment includes a chart to explain the Hitler Youth Organization. These two segments, the "Notes" and "Chronology," provide students with relevant historical background for understanding the events witnessed and recorded by the author.

The Borrowed House (van Stockum, 1975) is also told from the viewpoint of an active member of the Hitler Youth, a twelve-year-old German girl, Janna, who has been indoctrinated in this organization for two years before she goes to Amsterdam to live with her actor parents in a magnificent house taken over from a Dutch family by the Germans. Her journey to Amsterdam is a journey of discovery. Janna becomes a witness to the cruel and ruthless occupation of the Netherlands by the Germans. She discovers that her new knowledge of the Dutch people contradicts all that had been instilled in her by the Hitler Youth Organization. She grows to love a young resistance fighter she has discovered hiding in the basement of the house. When she learns that he is a Jew, all her training about Jews as dangerous, evil, inferior beings is challenged. In her journey of discovery she struggles to sort out what she had been taught about the Aryans as the master race and about the Jewish people so that she can distinguish between the truth and lies and propaganda. Like the narrator of *I Was There*, Janna started out as a "believer," but her initial allegiance to Hitler is extinguished as she becomes aware of the shocking truth about the Nazis and Hitler.

In *Farewell to Manzanar* (Houston, 1973) the narrator tells her own story of her life behind barbed wire at Manzanar internment camp, where she and her family have been sent — along with 10,000 other Japanese-Americans during World War II. Again, this is a first-person account by a victim of racial injustice and isolation, and the reader is invited to live through the disgrace and humiliation as well as the physical deprivation experienced by this family.

Rose Blanche (Innocenti, 1985) begins as a first-person account: Rose Blanche, a young girl who lives in a small German town, describes what she observes when her town comes under Nazi rule. The story begins with Rose Blanche as a witness; the viewpoint changes to third person in the middle of the story as she becomes personally involved in helping the Jews behind barbed wire. The story ends tragically when Rose Blanche, too, becomes a victim.

The child who works in opposition to the Nazis in this story is given the name "Rose Blanche," which was the name of a group of young German university students who protested Hitler's policies and practices. All of these young people were killed. Herman Vinke tells the story of this underground movement in Hitler's Germany called "The White Rose" in his book, *The Short Life of Sophie Scholl* (1984). James Forman's *Ceremony of Innocence* (1970) is a novel about Hans Scholl and his sister, Sophie, who, as students at Munich University in 1942, produced and distributed "White Rose" pamphlets denouncing Nazism.

Code Name Kris (Matas, 1990) is a first-person fictional account of the Danish Resistance told by a non-Jewish member of this underground movement. These resistance fighters challenged the German occupation through an underground newspaper and sabotage, and they managed to smuggle 7,000 Jews out of the country. The narrator shares with the reader his excitement, fear, pain, and his deep pride in the Danish people who demonstrate their courage in rebelling against the Nazis.

Shadow of the Wall (Laird, 1989) is a third-person account of life in the Warsaw ghetto as the Nazis tighten their control and intensify their persecution and brutality against the Jews in 1942. The story is told primarily from the viewpoint of a fictional character, a young boy who struggles to keep his family alive by smuggling in food from the "outside." However, a central figure in the novel actually did live at this time. He was a Jewish pediatrician who set up an orphanage in the ghetto and devoted himself to improving the quality of life for children who confronted disease, starvation, death, and Nazi brutality on a daily basis. In 1942 he walked with the children of the orphanage to the freight car which would take them to Treblinka. He taught these children to live with dignity, courage, and compassion in a world of evil and death. This is a true story embedded within a fictional narrative.

II. Setting

In historical fiction, setting plays a significant role in the development of plot, character, and theme. Rebecca Lukens, in *A Critical Handbook of Children's Literature*, distinguishes between "two types of setting: (1) the *backdrop* or relatively unimportant setting and (2) the *integral* or essential setting" (p. 104).

In the historical novels studied in this integrated unit, the actual political, social, and military events associated with a given historical period provide the context in which the stories unfold. Prior knowledge of these events enables readers to generate meaning as they enter into the lives of the characters in the story. Thus, the introductory study of the causes and consequences of the political and social climate of this period, as well as the chronology of military events, provides students with at least some of the background necessary to understand the characters, conflicts, and themes in these novels.

Students can study the settings of the novels they read and discuss in the small dialogue groups by focussing on the *functions* the settings might serve (see Lukens, pages 108-115):

A. Setting can serve as *antagonist* in plots driven by conflicts caused by political and social attitudes and events. Nancy Bond, a writer of novels for young readers, identifies this type of external conflict as *global*. It involves a great many people at the same time. World War II affected millions of people in different parts of the world. "But out of that mass a writer takes on one person or family; he or she tells a single story about a human being..." (p. 299).

Background information about such complex subjects as fascism and anti-Semitism is critical for readers to understand historical novels in which these antagonists bring degradation and death to innocent victims. For example, in *Touch Wood* (Roth-Hano, 1988), the narrator shares with us her pain as she is deprived of her dignity and self-respect and suffers the loss of family and friends who are taken away by Nazi soldiers. In *Friedrich* we see the destruction of a single family — warm, generous, peace-loving individuals — caught in a web of hatred and fear. In *The Little Fishes* (Haugaard, 1967), war is Guido's enemy. In war-torn Naples he struggles to survive physically and emotionally as a homeless beggar confronting the hunger, loneliness, degradation, and death caused by the war. In *Crutches* (Hartling, 1986) a thirteen-year-old boy searches for his mother amidst the ruins of post-war Vienna. The war has deprived him of his home, his family, his childhood. When twelve-year-old David escapes from a prison camp in Eastern Europe in the novel *North to Freedom*, (Holm, 1965), he begins a search for freedom as well as for his own identity. Having lived most of his life in the camp, he has no memory of his parents, has never known a normal childhood, and has never had the opportunity to develop the basic trust necessary for normal social and emotional development.

Non-fiction, including biographical texts, introduces students to significant historical events; political and military figures; the roots of anti-Semitism; the development of ghettos and concentration camps; and Hitler's rise to power and the brutal and evil nature of his dictatorship. These resources provide a basis for understanding the global conflict in these novels as well as for evaluating the authenticity of the settings which have such a powerful impact on central characters.

B.   Authors use settings to *create mood*. The setting in the opening scene in *North to Freedom* is a gray, bare room in a concentration camp. When David is given the chance to escape, he carries with him the fear of capture and death which is a basic fact of life for prisoners. Readers can feel the terror and foreboding that permeate his escape-journey. Only at the end of the novel is the tension relieved; readers sense a mood of hope as David reaches Denmark, freedom, and his mother.

In contrast, the early episodes in *Friedrich* draw the reader into peaceful domestic scenes of children playing; making potato pancakes; building a snowman; celebrating the Sabbath. The shadow of anti-Semitism and Nazi persecution is kept in the background in these early scenes, but it gradually intrudes into the lives of the central characters. For example, the joyful mood of mother and child playing in the snow is suddenly shattered when Herr Resch yells at the child "...you dirty Jewboy you!" (p. 12). By the end of the book the shadow has spread and deepened; the mood is dark, somber, and hopeless.

As the Waltz Was Ending, (Butterworth, 1982), an autobiographical novel, begins with the narrator's childhood in pre-war Vienna. She is a student in the Ballet School at the Opera House, where she is immersed in the intense training required of the ballet student and in the beautiful fantasy world of the theater. The scene and mood change abruptly in the second half of the book when Hitler takes over Austria. Her sheltered life of music and dance is past and now her life is marked by fear and hunger in a world of bombings and blackouts, food lines and rationing, disease and death, and the dark shadow of the Gestapo.

C. Setting can also be used to *reveal characters.* Extreme conditions and crises test the strength and courage and human qualities of an individual. Characters are pitted against a reality that requires a great deal more of them than in normal times. The nature of the individual's response illuminates his/ her character: for some the dark side emerges; for others the nobler, humane side dominates.

In *The Endless Steppe* (Hautzig, 1968) and *The Little Fishes* the struggle to survive in the harsh setting of Siberia and the ruins of war-torn Italy is marked by the triumph of the human spirit. In *Lisa's War* (Matas, 1989), *Code Name Kris,* and *Number the Stars* (Lowry, 1989), we see the courageous response of the Danish people against the Nazis. Whether searching for food among the ruins of a bombed city or hiding from the Nazis in cramped spaces, central characters in these novels demonstrate an ability to adapt to the extreme conditions into which they are cast and to maintain humane qualities of compassion, loyalty, and personal integrity and dignity. In *Escape from Warsaw* (Serraillier, 1972), Ruth Balicki and her brother and sister are alone and homeless. Nazi Storm Troopers have arrested their mother and blown up their house; their father is in prison. But Ruth sets up a school in the cellar of a bombed house and works with other innocent young victims, stretching their minds and imaginations.

In *Alicia: My Story* (Appleman-Jurman, 1988), a personal narrative by a Holocaust survivor, Alicia was only thirteen when she began saving the lives of others. She risked her life to rescue Jews from the Gestapo and to save a group of Russian partisans who were fighting the Germans. At the end of the war, at age 15, she established an orphanage for Jewish children who had survived the camps, and she led groups of Jews in an underground route from Poland to Palestine. This is a story of survival, heroic action, and humane behavior in the context of evil.

In every novel in which some of the characters demonstrate their adaptability and their capacity for courage and compassion, there are others who are unable to adjust to a changed world or to accept its reality and who give in to despair. And there are characters, such as Herr Resch in *Friedrich,* who are filled with hostility and hatred and respond with cruelty and destructive actions. Novels about World War II and the Holocaust reveal the dark side of human nature, the human capacity for evil. Individuals like Herr Resch actively help to spread the evil; others passively allow it to spread.

D. Some authors develop settings that function as symbols. A *symbolic setting* is one which has a literal meaning in the story as well as a figurative or suggestive meaning. The reader looks for clues that suggest that symbolism is being used to develop a plot or character.

In the opening pages of *As the Waltz Was Ending,* the reader is introduced to the Cathedral where Emma was confirmed and the Opera House where she studied ballet. One building symbolizes a world of spiritual harmony and order; the other symbolizes a world of music and dance and cultural harmony. Both were bombed in 1945, symbolizing the destruction of a way of life.

For Helene Richter, *The House on Prague Street* (Dementz, 1970; 1980), the house where she spent her summers with her Jewish grandparents, was an idyllic, tranquil place. Her grandfather was rich and influential, a pillar of the community. The house symbolizes her life before the war, before the Germans take the house, before her grandparents and relatives are sent to death camps. The narrator begins her story with "I still have dreams about the old house" (p. 1). It is her link to the past, symbolic of all that she has lost — family and friends, a way of life, and the cherished remnants of a great family, including the rickety handcart that her great-great grandfather had brought out of the ghetto in Prague.

The Endless Steppe also begins with a description of the house and garden where the narrator had lived with her extended family before "...the end of my lovely world" (p. 1). She describes the garden as "...the center of my world, the place above all others where I wished to remain forever" (p. 1). Again, a house and garden symbolize the lovely world which is lost.

E. Integral settings play an important role in *theme development.* Recurring themes are found in historical novels about war: the consequences of hatred, persecution, and tyranny; questions about morality and the nature of evil; the realities of war and its impact on soldiers and civilians, young and old; patterns of loss, abandonment, and powerlessness; the struggle for freedom; patterns of response to extreme conditions; the triumph of the human spirit.

Sheila Egoff, in her book *Thursday's Child: Trends and Patterns in Contemporary Children's Literature* (1981), notes the difference between English-language novels (those set in Britain and the United States) and European novels in regard to war themes: "British and American writers ...probe deeply into the personal lives of their children, but one senses that the war itself does not matter that much; any traumatic interruption in the children's lives would have served just as well to portray the writers' main intent — an insight into the minds of their protagonists and whether maturation results" (p. 283). Although they may experience air raids and food shortages and temporary separation from family, most of the children in these novels do not live with the threat of physical danger or death. They are free to be children "concerned with 'growing up' or 'coming to terms with themselves'" (p. 284).

In contrast, the children in the European novels "...are enmeshed in the events and cannot stand apart from the war's destruction and death" (p. 284). These children are more closely involved with the actual events. They become helpless victims of political tyranny; brutality, evil, and death are part of their daily existence. They do not have the luxury of childhood concerns; most grow up overnight and become wise beyond their years as they take on the burdens of the adult world. Thus, the themes in the European novels are not about personal growth or the search for identity. They carry larger thematic statements about war and political tyranny, and about the impact of adult corruption and evil on children. These novels explore larger issues of good and evil and significant truths about the human condition and questions about war as a means for solving differences.

III. Character Development and Conflict

The central characters in these novels cope with universal human problems that are at the same time specific to the historical context in which they live and the events that mold their lives. They are young people faced with crises, caught in a web of historical forces that alter their lives and, in most cases, threaten their survival.

Friendship

Some of these novels are stories of friendship. *The Devil in Vienna* (Orgel, 1978) is the story of Inge, a Jewish girl, and Liesolotte, the daughter of a Nazi. They have been best friends since the first grade, but by the time they reach age 13 the political climate forces them to continue their friendship in secret. When Hitler takes over Vienna, the Jews live with the constant threat of the concentration camp and death. In this context, any contact between the friends is dangerous.

In *Friedrich*, the friendship between the narrator and Friedrich Schneider begins early in their lives. But Nazi terror comes between them, and it becomes increasingly dangerous to maintain their friendship. At the end of the story, the narrator watches helplessly as Friedrich is denied entrance to an air-raid shelter and is sent out to his death.

Number the Stars is told from the viewpoint of ten-year-old Annemarie Johansen, whose best friend, Ellen Rosen, is Jewish. When the Nazis occupy Denmark and begin to search for hidden Jews, the Johansen family takes Ellen in as Annemarie's sister.

In *Fireweed* (Walsh, 1969), two young people who refuse to join the evacuation remain in London during the blitz of 1940. Bill and Julie meet and survive together amidst the ruins of London. They develop a close relationship but, when Julie is reunited with her wealthy family, she cuts off the relationship, and Bill is emotionally wounded and scarred. As in other British novels of World War II, the lives of the central characters are interrupted and changed by the war, but the destruction they witness is less important for them than their growing relationship. The focus of the story is Bill's emotional response to another person and the pleasures and pain that result from the relationship.

The Machine Gunners (Westall, 1976) is another British novel, in which a group of children form a secret gang and build a hideout for themselves, their "Fortress" and safe haven in a world where not only the Germans but all adults are the enemy. The war serves as a catalyst for the development of a close-knit group of individuals who depend on each other and learn to care about and for each other. The author's focus is not on the war, but on interpersonal relationships and the inner struggles and special needs of individual characters. The members of Chas's gang turn to each other for support when they realize the adults in their world are no longer sources of protection and security. For example, Chas's reflection on his relationship with his father is revealing: "Ever since he was little, Dad meant safety... But could any grown up keep you safe now? They couldn't stop the German bombers. They hadn't saved Poland, or Norway, or France... He looked at his father, and saw a weary, helpless middle-aged man. Dad wasn't any kind of God anymore" (p. 93). Although the war is an especially traumatic event and forces Chas to discover the limitations of parents, this developmental crisis is universal. All children at some point in their lives discover that their parents are not all-powerful and cannot protect them from all the dangers of life. This discovery opens the way for the growth of independence and self-reliance.

Crutches (Hartling, 1986; 1988) is set in post-war Vienna. Thirteen-year-old Thomas, searching for his mother in the ruins of the city, encounters a man on crutches. They develop a deep friendship, and together they face hardship and deprivation and manage to resist all attempts to dehumanize them.

The Eternal Spring of Mr. Ito (Garrigue, 1985) is the story of Sara Warren, who has been sent to live with an aunt and uncle in Canada to escape the bombing in England. She develops a very special friendship with Mr. Ito, a Japanese-Canadian who had fought as a soldier in World War I with Sara's uncle and had saved his life during the war. Now he is her uncle's gardener and Sara appreciates his beautiful work with nature as well as the wisdom he shares with her. These pleasant and sensitive interactions are cut short on December 7, 1941, when the Japanese attack Pearl Harbor. All Japanese citizens, including those born in Canada, are sent to camps in the mountains. Sara visits Mr. Ito and his family, but all her contact with them must be kept a secret. This is another example of a friendship that ignores barriers of age and culture and lines drawn by hate and war.

Inner Conflicts

In many of these novels, characters are developed by revealing their inner conflicts, which have been caused by moral dilemmas and self-knowledge. For example, when the narrator of *Friedrich* participates in a pogrom against a Jewish home for apprentices, he is initially carried away with a new feeling of power as he swings his hammer: "...smashing aside whatever barred my way... I could have sung I was so drunk with the desire to swing my hammer" (p. 92). Later, having found nothing else to satisfy his "lust for destruction," he is ready to leave. "All of a sudden I felt tired and disgusted. On the stairs, I found half a mirror. I looked in it. Then I ran home" (p. 93). When he discovers that Friedrich and his family are also victims of this pogrom, the narrator weeps.

In the story *The Borrowed House,* Janna has spent two years as an active member of the Hitler Youth. She had been taught to believe that Jews are dangerous, evil, and inferior and that the Aryans are the master race. But when she hears the screams and shots in the sealed Jewish quarter and sees a Jewish mother and child beaten by an SS soldier, she questions the injustice she has witnessed and the truth of what she's been taught. She struggles with the contradiction between her observations and what the Hitler Youth organization has instilled in her.

Guido, an orphan in war-torn Naples (*The Little Fishes*), chooses the compassionate, humane course of action throughout his long struggle to survive as a homeless victim of war. As witness and victim of man's inhumanity to man, Guido reflects on the human condition:

> They are strong men, but they have no kindness and they wear themselves out, without ever having enjoyed the beauty of the strength, which is to protect the weak not to threaten them (p. 125).

With a wisdom beyond his 12 years, Guido has developed a system of values that guides him in his endless search for food, shelter, and safety. Thus, for example, he takes on the responsibility of caring for Anna and Mario, two young orphans, sharing with them whatever he can find for himself. His actions throughout their dangerous journey reveal his efforts to sustain his integrity as a human being in spite of extreme conditions of hunger and fear and the ruthless, brutal behavior of those around him. When Anna asks him why he doesn't hate, Guido replies:

> The suffering, it must have a point and if I hate that man who only saw that we were dirty and did not ask himself why we were dirty...then...I would be like him... it is understanding that makes the difference between us and the animals... And when you understand you can feel a kind of happiness even in the worst misery (p. 213).

Throughout his escape-journey in *North to Freedom*, David engages in an ongoing inner dialogue about right and wrong. He struggles to do what he thinks is right. "And it was most important to do what one knew was right, for otherwise the day might come when one could no longer tell the difference between right and wrong, and then one would be like *them*" (p. 53).

In *Code Name Kris*, Jesper knows he must shoot the German Gestapo policemen before they kill him and the other members of the Resistance, but his inner struggle is revealed as he thinks:

> I hated the Germans for turning me into a killer. I knew if it hadn't been for the Germans I would still be a school kid... not willing to crush a spider (p. 87).

Disillusionment

Some characters have distorted notions of war as consisting of deeds of valor, heroism, and glory. Then they discover the grim reality of starvation, suffering, and death, which has nothing to do with their fantasy of heroic soldiers and cheering crowds. *Petros' War* (Zei, 1972) is set in Athens during the Nazi occupation. Petros' fantasies about war are drawn from popular adventure stories, but his dreams of glory and heroism are replaced by realistic experiences with the horror and tragedy of war. He sees the degradation of human beings as they struggle to survive; he sees children and adults die of starvation; he knows about the firing squad and the cruelty of the German soldiers; he knows the fear of being shot. When his Uncle Angelos returns from war in rags, wounded, and covered with lice, Petros' dreams of glory are shattered:

> The glittering medals, the shiny boots, the white horse, the sword flashing like lightning, the victories, and the valorous deeds of heroism that Petros had awaited with the return of his uncle, all swept across his mind and vanished (p. 41).

When fifteen-year-old Jack Raab lies about his age to join the U.S. Air Force, in Harry Mazer's *The Last Mission* (1979), he dreams of destroying Hitler and being a hero. On his last bombing mission over occupied Europe, Jack and his crew are shot down behind enemy lines. Jack is the only survivor; he is taken prisoner by the Germans. When his captors take him through towns, Jack sees for the first time that the bombs he had dropped had hit more than just military targets. These bombs had destroyed whole towns and killed innocent people, including children. He comes face to face with the realities of war — human misery and death and the loss of his best friend.

The setting of *Rain of Fire* (Bauer, 1983) is America after the Second World War. Twelve-year-old Steve is anxious to impress his friends with the heroic deeds of his older brother. Only later does Steve understand that his brother is ashamed of being in an army that dropped the bombs on Hiroshima and Nagasaki.

Hans Richter, the author of *I Was There*, precedes his autobiographical narrative with a statement about his own disillusionment: "…I was not merely an eyewitness. I believed — and I will never believe again."

In *The Borrowed House*, Janna discovers that what she believed to be "truth" is propaganda, a cruel distortion of truth. She discovers that what she believed to be "good" is actually evil.

Loss of Childhood

Central characters in the war novels set in Europe are generally forced to grow up overnight. As victims of war, these children must face horror and pain without protection from adults. They must assume responsibilities usually reserved for adults.

Guido *(The Little Fishes)* is without a home or family and must fend for himself. He is responsible for his own survival, and assumes responsibility for the lives of Anna and Mario as well. As he struggles to survive physically, he is also concerned about his spiritual survival. He gains a degree of human understanding and compassion and wisdom beyond his years.

Misha Edelman *(Shadow of the Wall*, Laird, 1989) lives in the Warsaw ghetto and assumes responsibility for his mother and two sisters. They rely on him for food smuggled in from "outside."

In *Lisä's War* and *Code Name Kris*, the central characters are young people who join the underground resistance after the Nazi occupation of Denmark. Their work carries with it the risk of capture by the Nazis, torture, and death. They show courage and resourcefulness beyond their years. There are moments in each book when the reader is reminded that these are young people who, in another time, would have been focussing their attention on their studies, dates, parties, movies, and parental concerns about staying out too late.

In *Escape from Warsaw*, the Balicki children are alone in Warsaw after both parents are arrested by the Nazis. Thirteen-year-old Ruth gradually assumes the role of mother for her brother and sister as well as Jan, another homeless victim of the war. She also becomes a teacher for many other urchins who beg to become part of the "school" she establishes in the ruins.

David, in *North to Freedom*, has spent nearly all of his twelve years in a concentration camp and has no memory of a childhood. He knows only evil and death, until he begins his journey toward freedom. For the first time he learns about beauty and laughter, the joy of washing in clean water and eating good food and making his own decisions. But it is too late for David to enjoy the innocence of childhood because he has already acquired a knowledge of evil and carries the pain and sorrow of the adult world.

Character Foil and Points of Contrast

In some of the novels, minor characters have attitudes and behavior which are in sharp contrast to those of the central character. These minor characters are used as a foil to highlight the traits and qualities of the principal character.

In *Lisa's War*, Erik is a minor character whose indifference to the threat of the Germans directly contrasts with the intense concern of Lisa and her brother. Throughout the book, Erik refuses to believe that the Nazi invasion of Denmark will have any significant impact on his life. He hides from the truth whereas Lisa confronts it and takes action.

In *I Was There*, the narrator describes his experiences as a member of the Hitler Youth movement with his friends Heinz and Gunther. Gunther, with his strong sense of right and wrong and his intense motivation and fierce loyalty, provides a sharp contrast to his friends. He is not a minor character but serves as a foil to highlight traits of the other boys.

Liesolotte's brother, in *The Devil in Vienna*, is an enthusiastic supporter of Nazi brutality and becomes one of "them." Liesolotte, in contrast, is shocked by the Nazi mentality and vows to maintain her own integrity so as never to become like them (p. 160). In her friend Inge's family, the grandfather is more realistic about the possibility of Nazi occupation, and he obtains a visa to go to America. In contrast, the father refuses to see that they are in danger until it is almost too late.

In *The Borrowed House* it is Hugo, the tutor, whose wisdom and clear-sighted understanding of justice and truth and human nature is in sharp contrast to Janna's confusion and ignorance about the realities of the world in which she lives. Hugo's humane qualities, his selflessness and compassion highlight the qualities of other characters whose behavior is driven by greed, cruelty, worship of power, and self-serving motives.

In *North to Freedom*, the del'Varchi children highlight the vast difference between David and ordinary children who have grown up outside the concentration camp. The grim deprivation of David's twelve years is brought into sharp focus when compared to the lives of these children who have always had their own home, loving parents, and the luxury of being children.

IV. Plot Structure

The authors of these novels use different techniques to tell their stories and build plots. Rebecca Lukens (1990) distinguishes between two types of plots: *progressive plots* with a central climax followed quickly by denouement, and *episodic plots* "in which one incident or short episode is linked to another by common characters or by a unified theme" (pp. 75-76). Some stories combine both types of plots. For example, *Friedrich* consists of a series of separate episodes arranged in chronological order. At the same time there is a central conflict and a final climax. The initial episodes introduce the central characters and the historical context. These early scenes foreshadow subsequent tragic events produced by Hitler's rise to power and his "Final Solution." Anti-Semitism intervenes in brief moments during these opening domestic scenes; by the time the two boys enter school in 1933, the systematic restrictions against the Jews have begun. The number of anti-Jewish incidents, decrees, and regulations mount from one episode to the next, and there is a growing strain between the two families. As the Nazis gain power, the reader sees that anti-Semitic acts are encouraged and applauded, leading to Kristallnacht, the night when Jewish establishments and synagogues are attacked and destroyed. Each successive episode reflects the escalation of the Nazi's war against the Jews and the step-by-step destruction of the Jewish family that lived in the apartment above the narrator.

Touch Wood is another example of a combined episodic and progressive plot. The author uses a diary format for this autobiographical novel and explains her choice in the Preface:

> I chose the diary format as the best way to portray the climate of the times and the escalating terror that I felt. I tried to keep the entry dates as close as I could to the events as they occurred.
>
> Many years have passed since I was a girl in occupied France, bringing inevitable lapses and inaccuracies. But the essence of my emotional memories has been captured, with its tragic, cruel, and tender moments.

The entries begin in 1940 with accounts of episodes in her home, her neighborhood, and school. Like the episodes in *Friedrich*, the diary entries in *Touch Wood* reveal the daily tightening of restrictions against the Jews. On June 16, 1942, she writes:

> I have stopped counting the anti-Jewish decrees that keep pouring in on us.
> We are forbidden to go to neighboring squares and parks, libraries, cafes, restaurants, swimming pools — even movie houses, for goodness' sakes! (p. 103).

The plot is driven by the central conflict: the threat of destruction by the Nazis. There is a gradual progression toward the moment when the three sisters are forced into exile and to hide their Jewish identity. The final climax occurs after the Allies land and the family is reunited; they have survived the war, but too many of their family and friends have not.

The significant difference between *Friedrich* and *Touch Wood* is the viewpoint. *Friedrich* is narrated by a non-Jewish witness; the reader is never given insight into what it felt like to be a Jew in Nazi Germany. *Touch Wood* is narrated by a Jewish girl who shares her "emotional memories" — her thoughts and feelings, her terror and shame, and anger. It is a personal account of her struggle to survive and to maintain her identity and integrity as a human being.

The narrator in *The Devil in Vienna* is also a Jewish girl who shares her thoughts and feelings, along with her observations of the events which interrupt, shape, and threaten her life. She writes in a "book of blank pages" given to her by her grandfather for Chanukah.

Hide and Seek (Vos, 1991) is an autobiographical novel about a young Jewish girl's experience during the Nazi occupation in Holland. It is told in a series of vignettes, narrated from the viewpoint of a young child who tries to make sense of the persecution that invades her secure life. The vignettes are linked together to form a progressive plot that begins before the war, follows the family as they go into hiding, and ends after the war is over. The family is reunited and free of the Nazi threat, but when they come out of hiding they discover that one hundred and five members of their family are gone.

Anne Frank: The Diary of a Young Girl (Frank, 1952) was one of the first books to call attention to the Holocaust as it affected a single individual. Mind-numbing facts and figures are turned into living human experience through this dramatic and intimate first-hand narrative. Anne records the story of her life in hiding as it unfolds. The diary is unfinished, but we know the ending. [Johanna Hurwitz's *Anne Frank: Life in Hiding* (1988) provides additional information about Anne and her family and those who helped them.]

Mischling, Second Degree: My Childhood in Nazi Germany (Koehn, 1977) is written as a memoir covering the years from 1926 to 1945. Specific dates are given throughout the chronology of the author's experiences to connect the story of her life with the historical events that shaped it. What is unusual about this reconstruction of a childhood is the fact that the reader is informed of a secret which has not been revealed to the child-narrator. The reader learns in the Foreword and in Chapter 1 that Ilse is a "Mischling, second degree" under Hitler's racial laws. That is, she had one Jewish grandparent, her father's mother. This status, if discovered, would condemn her to the same fate intended for all Jews. For her own protection, this secret of her heritage is kept from Ilse until after the Nazi defeat. She spends the war years as a member of the Hitler Youth in Berlin and later in various evacuation camps and, finally, hiding with her mother from Russian soldiers. Her story allows us to enter the world of a German schoolgirl who "wears a swastika and the black kerchief of her Jungmaedel classmates" (p. vi).

Flashback is used to tell the story of *Carrie's War* (Bawden, 1973). Carrie returns with her children to the small Welsh mining town where she had been sent to live during the war. She was twelve years old when she and her brother were evacuated out of London with the rest of their classmates. Now thirty years later, she tells her children what happened during her stay in this town. The story she tells has the characteristics of a good mystery with a progressive plot, complex events, well-developed characters, secrecy, deception, and suspense. World War II and the evacuation of British children provide the setting for

Carrie's story, but the focus is on her experiences with the family with whom she and her brother have been assigned to live.

Flashback is also used in the novel, *Gideon* (Aaron, 1982). In this first-person account of his struggle to survive in Poland's Warsaw ghetto during World War II and, later, in Treblinka, the central character goes back in time to provide relevant background about his family and the context in which they lived. The story as a whole is a flashback in the form of a letter written in 1978 to his wife and children. In this letter, the narrator reveals to them his identity as a Jew for the first time and tells what happened to him during the war.

Some authors use the *journey* as the basic structure for their novels. *North to Freedom* is the story of David's journey from a prison camp in Eastern Europe to Denmark. But it is also an inner journey as he gradually develops a sense of himself as an individual and learns to trust other human beings. He learns what it means to live in freedom, and he eventually discovers his own identity. In the final scene David stands in the sunshine in Denmark and says to the woman who opens the door: "'Madam... I am David...' The woman looked into his face and said clearly and distinctly, 'David... my son, David'" (p. 239)..He had journeyed from darkness to light.

Escape from Warsaw is another story of a journey. The Balicki children travel alone from Warsaw, Poland to Switzerland in search of their parents. It is a journey marked by danger and hardship and constant fear. The hope that their parents are still alive keeps them going and helps them survive this treacherous journey.

To Life (Sender, 1988) is the author's own story of her liberation from a Nazi concentration camp, her long search for surviving members of her family, her migration from one displaced persons camp to another, and finally, to freedom, to a home in America. The story opens with her first sight of the Statue of Liberty on February 2, 1950, and then flashes back to May 5, 1945, to "the barbed-wire cage of the Nazi concentration camp in Germany" (p. 2).

One of the most unusual books about the Holocaust is *The Devil's Arithmetic* by Jane Yolen (1988), who uses *time travel* as a basic literary technique to structure its plot. Hannah and her family are celebrating the traditional Passover seder in her grandparents' home. She is embarrassed and uncomfortable about her grandfather's frequent references to his experiences with the Nazis and concentration camps. She does not want to "remember"; she wants to distance herself from the horror of that time. But during the Seder service, Hannah is transported back in time and becomes Chaya in a shtetl in Poland in 1942. As Chaya, Hannah experiences the Holocaust first hand and knows the suffering and the terror and the dehumanization that shaped the lives of its victims. When Chaya enters the oven, Hannah finds herself standing at the open door where she had stood during the Seder to symbolically welcome the prophet Elijah and there, behind her, was the "large table with a white cloth" (p. 161). Hannah returns to the table with a new knowledge of the realities of the past. She learns, along with the reader, the lesson taught by a fictional account of the truth:

"To witness. To remember. These were the only victories of the camps" (p. 169).

V. Genre

The term historical fiction refers to realistic stories which have settings in the past. The question "What is the author's relationship to the historical events in the story?" addresses some of the significant differences in the types of historical fiction written for young children.

Some authors create historical fiction by reconstructing events and lives of the past through careful research of historical texts, documents, records, personal memoirs and letters and, if possible, interviews with those who actually lived through the events of the past. Other authors create fiction based on memories of their own experiences or the experiences of family or friends during a time that has now become history. Others write autobiographical accounts of what actually happened to them and what they lived through as children in that period of history.

Those who write about the distant past rely on extensive research of primary and secondary sources as well as visits to museums and historical locations. Actual events and people can be woven into their stories or the historical facts may be used as background and a guide for creating the social context: how characters live, their clothing, occupation, homes, transportation, language, and so forth. The challenge for authors who write about historical periods which have no connection to their personal experience is to bring a remote period of history to life and to create an authentic portrait of the people and their way of life.

World War II is part of our more recent history, and survivors of the Holocaust remember that tragic period. Many of the historical novels about this war are based on personal experiences or stories told by friends and relatives who survived as witnesses.

Marietta Moskin tells her readers that her novel, *I Am Rosemarie* (1972), is based on her own wartime experiences and those of her friends. Carol Matas created *Lisa's War* (1989) and *Code Name Kris* (1990) based on her research in Denmark and the stories told to her by her husband and his parents as well as people she met in Denmark, including the chief Rabbi of Copenhagen. Lois Lowry, in an "Afterword" to *Number the Stars*, explains that her fictional character Annemarie Johansen is drawn from stories told to her by a friend who was a child in Copenhagen during the German occupation. Both authors mention the German official, G. F. Duckwitz, who warned the Jewish community of Copenhagen about the Germans' plan to trap the Jews in their homes on Rosh Hashanah, the Jewish New Year, in 1943, thus giving them a chance to escape.[2] Lowry was inspired to write this story about the Danish Resistance after she read about a Danish Resistance leader who was captured and executed by the Nazis. A picture of this courageous and determined young man, who was only twenty-one years old when he was killed, convinced her to tell his story and the story of the Danish people.

In his Preface to *Gideon* (Aaron, 1982), the author clarifies his connection to the events in the novel:

> I was with the American troops that opened the gates at Dachau.
> In writing this novel I have relied on conversations I had in May and June of 1945 with survivors of Dachau...

Journals, diaries, reflections, and histories that I have read since 1945, many
written by survivors, have supplemented these conversations (p. vii).

Doris Orgel explains in an "Author's note" about *The Devil in Vienna* that
this novel is based on her own experience as a child in Vienna but the "...char-
acters are fictional... made up of memories, imaginings, and aspects of actual
people." Hans Peter Richter, author of *Friedrich* and *I Was There*, states that these
"...are in fact autobiographical books." He was an eyewitness and reported
what he saw and how he lived.

In her epilogue to *As the Waltz Was Ending*, Emma Butterworth explains that
her husband and children urged her to write an account of her childhood in
Vienna during the war. Barbara Gehrts, the author of *Don't Say a Word* (1975,
1986), decided to tell the story of her childhood in Berlin during the war after
hearing a debate in 1968 at a German university in which a student stated:
"Freedom is merely the absence of force." She was determined to record her
childhood experiences to clarify the difference between freedom and tyranny.

In a Foreword to the American edition of *Hide and Seek* (1991), the author, Ida
Vos, explains to the reader the reason she wrote about her childhood experiences in Holland during the Nazi occupation and her years in hiding: "To let you
feel how terrible it is to be discriminated against, and to let you know how
terrible it was to be a Jewish child in Holland during those years" (p. ix).

At the end of the book *The Endless Steppe* by Esther Hautzig (1968), information about the author reveals that the impetus for this autobiographical account
came from the late Adlai E. Stevenson. He suggested to her in a letter that she
should "write a book about life on the frontier of the Soviet Union during those
trying war days." So she wrote about the five years she and her family lived in
exile in Siberia after their deportation from Vilna, Poland.

In her epilogue to *Alicia, My Story* (1988), a remarkable personal narrative
of survival, resistance, and heroism during the Holocaust, Alicia Appleman-
Jurman writes:

> Through the story of "Alicia" I wish to reach out, not only to survivors like
> myself, but to all people. I hope that it will help strengthen today's youth by
> imparting a better understanding of the true history of my whole lost genera-
> tion. I believe that the book will teach young people what enormous reserves
> of strength they possess within themselves.
>
> I pray that all its readers, Jew and non-Jew alike, may unite in the resolve
> that evil forces may never again be permitted to set one people against another
> (p. 356).

Jeanne Wakatsuki Houston, with her husband, James Houston, wrote
Farewell to Manzanar (1973), which is about the internment of Japanese-Americans during World War II. In the Foreword to this book, Mrs. Houston tells the
reader what it meant to her to write this book about the three and a half years
she and her family spent in Manzanar: "... I began to dredge up memories that
had lain submerged since the forties. I began to make connections I had
previously been afraid to see. It had taken me twenty-five years to reach the
point where I could talk openly about Manzanar... Writing it has been a way of
coming to terms with the impact these years have had on my entire life (pp. ix-x).

Yoshiko Uchida's *The Invisible Thread* (1992) is a first-hand account of her experiences growing up as a second-generation Japanese-American in Berkeley, California, and her family's internment in a Utah concentration camp during World War II.

The historical novels featured in this unit range from those whose authors lived through the historical events in the story to those who did not. The novels can be classified in terms of the author's relationship to these events. Authors of autobiographical novels were intimately involved in the events described in their accounts of wartime childhoods. They had survived to tell their stories from the perspective of adults who had gained enough emotional distance from the actual events to be able to relive their memories as they recorded them on paper.

The Diary of Anne Frank is the only autobiographical account in this collection that was written at the time the events unfolded and by an innocent victim who did not survive to tell the rest of her story as an adult. *Sadako and the Thousand Paper Cranes* (Coerr, 1977) is a biographical account of the brief life of another innocent young victim of war who faced death with remarkable courage. Sadako was exposed to radiation when the atom bomb was dropped on the city of Hiroshima, where she lived with her family. She died of leukemia ten years later. Both Anne and Sadako are unforgettable heroines who give us a child's view of historical events.

Many authors who were not personally involved in the historical events used what they had learned about them to reconstruct believable stories of people who lived through these events. Some authors were more successful than others in creating in their readers a feeling of identity with the central characters.

Although the story of *Gideon* by Chester Aaron is told with vivid detail, the use of first-person and present tense by an author who did not actually live through the events described, was, for some readers, a barrier to identification with the central character. One young reader suggested that the use of third-person viewpoint would have made it seem less artificial or forced as a "memoir" and more like a novel which invites its readers to become involved in the story itself rather than questions about the nature of the author's role in it.

Noel Streatfield drew from memories of her own experiences in the Woman's Voluntary Service when she wrote about three children evacuated from London during World War II in *When the Sirens Wailed* (1976). Although she lived through these historical events, she did so as an adult. This may explain some readers' impressions that the story is told from the viewpoint of an adult rather than the children who are the central characters.

In contrast, authors such as Carol Matas and Lois Lowry, who did not live through the historical events in their stories and do not have childhood memories to use as a basis for their stories, were able to reconstruct the lives of children caught in the web of these events as seen through their eyes as children. Their narratives are about children who witness, experience, and respond to historical events and are told through the words and deeds of these children.

Historical fiction written for young readers generally features central characters who are also young. These young characters engage in the complex process of making sense of the world in which they live and finding their own identity and role within this world. Young readers can relate to these characters, because they, too, are engaged in attempts to make sense of their own world and their role in it.

VI. Themes

Historical novels explore personal truths as well as universal ones. Most of today's children, who once associated war with history, have now lived through their first war. They watched television news coverage of the Gulf War in 1991. They saw bombs fall. They watched as frightened children put on gas masks. They felt the growing anxiety and fear in the adults around them. Some knew the pain of separation from parents and loved ones and the fear that they might not return. For some, life changed significantly. For most, the war raised many questions. Children and adults alike struggled to make sense of this war. Many confronted moral issues and universal truths about the human condition.

The historical novels that allow readers to enter into the lives of children of the past address many of the questions — personal and universal — raised before, during, and after the Gulf War. In homes and classrooms across the country, children were asking: Why do we have wars? Why do people have to fight to solve problems? How do wars get started? When is it *necessary* to fight?

Both fiction and non-fiction selected for this unit provide an excellent background and starting point for productive discussions about the origins of war and the parallels between historical and contemporary conflicts. Basic themes found in many of the historical novels have continued to be relevant up to the present day. For example, the nature and consequences of ancient hatreds and prejudice; the meaning of freedom and tyranny; the impact of war on innocent people; man's inhumanity to man; the consequences of the rise to power of a single leader driven by ruthless ambition; the heroic actions of single individuals or small groups who attempt to counter the evil unleashed by those in power; and the triumph of the human spirit are some of the themes that offer readers an historical perspective as they confront relevant issues in today's world.

The issue of resistance is the central focus in novels such as *Lisa's War; Code Name Kris; Number the Stars; Gideon; Shadow of the Wall; Snow Treasure; Twenty and Ten; Uncle Misha's Partisans; Petro's War; Ceremony of Innocence;* in the stories collected by Meltzer in *Rescue;* and in personal narratives such as *Alicia: My Story* (Appleman-Jurman, 1988). In some novels of the resistance against the enemy, the potential victims of the Nazis were helped to escape and to hide in order to save their lives. The heroic uprising of the remnant of starving Jews in the Warsaw ghetto against the great German army is described in *Gideon, Shadow of the Wall,* and *The Man From the Other Side* (Orlev, 1991). *Gideon* also includes a record of the rebellion of the Jews at the Treblinka Death Camp, where hundreds of thousands of Jews were slaughtered by the Germans. Ultimately, these courageous acts of resistance against those whose mission was the extermination of the Jews allowed a few survivors to escape in order to tell the world what happened in the ghettos and death camps.

Many of the authors who wrote autobiographical accounts of their personal experiences under Nazi occupation felt the need to tell their story to teach subsequent generations about the evil of the Holocaust. The underlying message to young people is to learn, to remember, and to never allow a repetition of this crime against humanity.

Stories of survivors, Jewish and non-Jewish rescuers, and participants in resistance movements reveal the morality and courage of individuals who maintain their humanity and compassion in the midst of evil and brutality and all attempts to dehumanize them. They draw from deep reservoirs of resourcefulness and ingenuity to survive or to help others survive. These inspiring stories celebrate the triumph of the human spirit over evil. Ruth Sender in *To Life* (1988), an account of her life after her liberation from a Nazi concentration camp, uses the term "spiritual resistance" to describe the secret classes and libraries and creativity in the ghetto in spite of "the suffering, the hunger, the fear [they] had to endure" (p. 121).

Almost all the novels portray individuals who act on the basis of a moral choice to make a significant difference in the lives of others. The message communicated to young readers is that they, too, are capable of making moral choices and acting on them as humane and compassionate individuals willing to take a stand against evil.

Anti-war themes are often balanced by a focus on peace and freedom on a personal, social, national, and international level. The novels that tell the stories of Jews under Nazi occupation or of Japanese-Americans in internment camps make it very clear that peace is the context in which freedom can exist.

Sadako and the Thousand Paper Cranes (Coerr, 1977) is the story of Sadako, who lived in Japan from 1943 to 1955. She died on October 25, 1955, as a result of radiation from the atom bomb dropped on Hiroshima by the U.S. Air Force. This biographical narrative is also a plea for world peace. In 1958 a statue of Sadako holding a golden crane was unveiled in the Hiroshima Peace Park. It is a monument to honor the memory of Sadako and all the children who were killed by the atom bomb. On the base of the statue these words are engraved:

> This is our cry,
>
> This is our prayer,
>
> Peace in the world.
>
> (Coerr, p. 64)

Phase Three: From Fiction to Non-Fiction

The scribe from each dialogue group shares key insights and discoveries about self-selected texts during a series of whole-class meetings. Each dialogue group is responsible for creating a chart or poster which will provide a visual display of the results of their comparative analysis of the novels selected as the focus for their dialogue. As each group shares the significant similarities and differences found in their analysis, members of other groups are asked to identify connections with the novels they have discussed and analyzed. Thus, the sharing process changes from a series of reports to a sharing-comparing interchange in which the whole class is invited to become actively involved.

In the course of these whole-group meetings, students identify new questions or areas of special interest generated by the historical fiction they have read. The teacher records these questions and interest areas and invites students to return to the non-fiction to search for answers to their questions or to learn more about a particular topic or individual. For example, students who read about the Warsaw ghetto in historical fiction such as *Gideon* (Aaron) or *Shadow of the Wall* (Laird) may be inspired to read non-fiction accounts of the Warsaw ghetto. Students introduced to the Danish Resistance in *Number the Stars* (Lowry), *Lisa's War* (Matas), and *Code Name Kris* (Matas) may choose to learn more about these heroic attempts to resist the Nazis and to save Jews from death. Thus, in this third phase of this integrated literary-historical unit, historical fiction serves as a context and springboard for further research using non-fiction sources. Some students may choose to read autobiographical accounts or biographies of heroes and heroines, witnesses, survivors, and victims of the Holocaust. Others may choose to read biographical profiles of such people as Mohandas Gandhi, Martin Luther King, Jr., Mother Teresa, and other winners of the Nobel Peace Prize. Some may choose to read *Talking Peace* by former President Jimmy Carter (1993).[3] Students are asked to record the results of their inquiry in their journals or in more formal written reports.

For a final assignment, students are asked to think about what they have learned from the fiction and non-fiction they have read in the context of this unit and to identify what they consider to be the most important message or messages sent by the writers of these texts. Students can work independently or collaborate with classmates on this assignment. Their task is to formulate a brief statement and to share it in the final whole-group session.

Concluding the Integrated Literary-Historical Unit

In the final whole-class session, students share and discuss their statements of basic themes or messages which represent a synthesis of fiction and non-fiction. The statements which highlight anti-war themes and messages of peace provide the focus for the concluding segment of this session. Students who have read biographical profiles of Nobel Peace Prize winners or Mr. Carter's book are invited to share what they have learned to initiate a discussion about ways to promote peace. Each individual student is invited to think seriously about the meaning of the word *peace*, and what he or she can do as an individual or as part of a group to take a step toward the achievement of peace. A knowledge of historical events and an understanding of the realities of war and its impact on human beings provide the foundation from which this first step can be taken. Knowing what did happen allows children to begin to address hypothetical questions such as "what might have been if..." and "what might be if..."

References

Bond, Nancy. (1984). "Conflict in Children's Fiction," in *The Horn Book Magazine*, pp. 297-306.

Egoff, Sheila. (1981). *Thursday's Child: Trends and Patterns in Contemporary Children's Literature*. Chicago, IL: A.L.A.

Lukens, Rebecca. (1990). *A Critical Handbook of Children's Literature*. (4th Edition.).Glenview, IL: Scott, Foresman and Co.

Meltzer, Milton. (1988). *Rescue: The Story of How Gentiles Saved Jews in the Holocaust*. New York: Harper and Row.

Tunnell, Michael and Richard Ammon, editors. (1993). *The Story of Ourselves: Teaching History Through Children's Literature*. Postsmouth, NH: Heinemann.

Bibliography: Historical Fiction and Non-Fiction

I. Historical Fiction: World War II

Aaron, Chester. (1982). *Gideon*. J.B. Philadelphia, PA: Lippincott.

Bauer, Marion. (1983). *Rain of Fire*. Boston: Houghton Mifflin.

Bawden, Nina. (1973). *Carrie's War*. Philadelphia, PA: Lippincott.

Bergman, Tamar. (1991). *Along the Tracks*. Boston: Houghton, Mifflin.

Bergman, Tamar. (1984). *The Boy from Over There*. Translated from the Hebrew by Hillel Halkin. Boston: Houghton-Mifflin. (post-war)

Bishop, Claire. (1964). *Twenty and Ten*. New York: Viking.

Butterworth, Emma Macalik. (1982). *As the Waltz Was Ending*. New York: Scholastic.

Choi, Sook Nyul. (1991). *Year of Impossible Goodbyes*. Boston: Houghton Mifflin.

Coerr, Eleanor. (1977). *Sadako and the Thousand Paper Cranes*. New York: Putnam.

Cooper, Susan. (1970). *Dawn of Fear*. San Diego, CA: Harcourt.

Degens, T. (1974). *Transport 7-41-R*. New York: Viking.

DeJong, Meindert. (1956). *The House of Sixty Fathers*. New York: Harper.

Dillon, Eilis. (1992). *Children of Bach*. New York: Macmillan.

Drucker, Malka, and Michael Halperin. (1993). *Jacob's Rescue: A Holocaust Story*. New York: Bantam.

Fife, Dale. (1981). *Destination Unknown*. New York: E.P. Dutton.

Foreman, Michael. (1990). *War Boy: A Country Childhood*. New York: Arcade.

Forman, James. (1970). *Ceremony of Innocence*. Columbia, MO: Hawthorne Books.

Forman, James. (1976). *The Survivor*. New York: Farrar, Straus & Giroux.

Frank, Anne. (1967). *Anne Frank: Diary of a Young Girl*. New York: Doubleday.

Gallico, Paul. (1940). *The Snow Goose*. New York: Knopf.

Garrigue, Sheila. (1976). *All the Children Were Sent Away*. New York: Bradbury.

Garrigue, Sheila. (1985). *The Eternal Spring of Mr. Ito*. New York: Bradbury Press.

Gehrts, Barbara. (1986, 1975). *Don't Say a Word*. Translated from German by Elizabeth Crawford (1986). New York: Macmillan.

Glassman, Judy. (1991). *The Morning Glory War*. New York: Dutton.

Greene, Bette. (1973). *The Summer of My German Soldier*. New York: Dial.

Hahn, Mary Downing. (1991). *Stepping on the Cracks*. New York: Clarion.

Hamannaka, Sheila. (1990). *The Journey*. New York: Orchard. (picture book)

Hartling, Peter. (1986, 1988). *Crutches*. Translated from the German by Elizabeth Crawford. New York: Lothrop, Lee & Shepard. (post-war)

Haugaard, Erik Christian. (1967). *The Little Fishes*. Boston: Houghton Mifflin.

Hautzig, Esther. (1968). *The Endless Steppe*. New York: Harper & Row.

Heuck, Sigrid. (1988). *The Hideout*. New York: Dutton.

Holm, Anne. (1965). *North to Freedom*. Translated by L.W. Kingsland. San Diego, CA: Harcourt.

Houston, Jeanne Wakatsuki, and James D. Houston. (1973). *Farewell to Manzanar*. Boston: Houghton Mifflin.

Innocenti, Roberto, and Christophe Gallaz. (1985). *Rose Blanche*. Mankato, MN: Creative Education. (picture book)

Irwin, Hadley. (1987). *Kim/Kimi*. New York: McElderry.

Keneally, Thomas. (1992, 1983). *Schindler's List*. New York: Simon & Schuster.

Kerr, Judith. (1972). *When Hitler Stole Pink Rabbit*. Coward McCann.

Kluger, Ruth, and Peggy Mann. (1978). *The Secret Ship*. New York: Doubleday and Co.

Koehn, Ilse. (1977). *Mischling, Second Degree. My Childhood in Nazi Germany*. New York: Greenwillow.

Kogawa, Joy. (1988). *Naomi's Road*. New York: Oxford University Press.

Laird, Christa. (1989). *Shadow of the Wall*. New York: Greenwillow.

Leviton, Sonia. (1993). *Annie's Promise*. New York: Atheneum.

Leviton, Sonia. (1970). *Journey to America*. New York: Mcmillan.

Leviton, Sonia. (1989). *Silver Days*. New York: Atheneum.

Levoy, Myron. (1977). *Alan and Naomi*. New York: Harper & Row.

Lingard, Joan. (1990). *Tug of War*. New York: Dutton.

Little, Jean. (1977). *Listen for the Singing*. New York: Harper Collins.

Lowry, Lois. (1980). *Autumn Street*. New York: Dell.

Lowry, Lois. (1989). *Number the Stars*. Boston: Houghton Mifflin.

McSwigan, Marie. (1942). *Snow Treasure*. New York: E.P. Dutton.

Maruki, Toshi. (1982). *Hiroshima No Pika*. (The Flash of Hiroshima). New York: Lothrop, Lee & Shepard.

Matas, Carol. (1989). *Code Name Kris*. New York: Scribner's.

Matas, Carol. (1993). *Daniel's Story*. New York: Scholastic.

Matas, Carol. (1989). *Lisa's War*. New York: Scribner's.

Mattingly, Christobel. (1986). *The Angel with a Mouth Organ*. New York: Holiday House. (picture book)

Mazer, Harry. (1979). *The Last Mission*. New York: Delacorte.

Mochizuki, Ken. (1993). *Baseball Saved Us*. New York: Lee and Low.

Morimoto, Junko. (1987). *My Hiroshima*. New York: Viking. (picture book)

Morpurgo, Michael. (1990). *Waiting for Anya*. New York: Viking.

Moskin, Marietta. (1972). *I Am Rosemarie*. New York: Delacorte.

Nöstlinger, Christine. (1975). *Fly Away Home*. New York: Watts.

Oppenheim, Shulamith. (1992). *The Lily Cupboard*. New York: HarperCollins. (picture book)

Orgel, Doris. (1978). *The Devil in Vienna*. New York: Dial.

Orlev, Uri. (1984). *The Island on Bird Street*. Translated from Hebrew by Hillel Halkin. Boston: Houghton Mifflin.

Orlev, Uri. (1991). *The Man from the Other Side.* Translated from Hebrew by Hillel Halkin. Boston: Houghton Mifflin.

Ossowski, Leonie. (1985). *Star Without a Sky.* Translated by Ruth Crowley. Minneapolis, MN: Lerner Pub.

Pearson, Kit. (1990). *The Sky is Falling.* New York: Viking.

Ramati, Alexander. (1986). *And the Violins Stopped Playing: A Story of the Gypsy Holocaust.* New York: Franklin Watts.

Reiss, Johanna. (1972). *The Upstairs Room.* Crowell.

Richter, Hans Peter. (1970). *Friedrich.* Translated from the German by Edite Kroll. New York: Holt Rinehart & Winston.

Richter, Hans Peter. (1962). *I Was There.* Orlando: Holt Rinehart & Winston. (Translation, 1972)

Roth-Hano, Renée. (1988). *Touch Wood — A Girlhood in Occupied France.* New York: Four Winds Press.

Rylant, Cynthia. (1993). *I Had Seen Castles.* San Diego, CA: Harcourt Brace.

Sachs, Marilyn. (1973). *A Pocketful of Seeds.* New York: Doubleday.

Savin, Marcia. (1992). *The Moon Bridge.* New York: Scholastic.

Sender, Ruth Minsky. (1988). *To Life.* New York: Macmillan.

Sender, R.M. (1986). *The Cage.* New York: Macmillan.

Serraillier, Ian. (1972, 1959). *Escape from Warsaw.* New York: Scholastic.

Siegal, Aranka. (1985). *Grace in the Wilderness: After the Liberation 1945-1948.* New York: Farrar, Straus & Girou.

Siegal, Aranka. (1981). *Upon the Head of a Goat, A Childhood in Hungary, 1939-1944.* New York: Farrar, Straus & Giroux.

Streatfield, Noel. (1976). *When the Sirens Wailed.* New York: Random House.

Suhl, Yuri. (1975). *On the Other Side of the Gate.* New York: Watts.

Suhl, Yuri. (1973). *Uncle Misha's Partisans.* New York: Four Winds Press.

Treseder, Terry Walton. (1990). *Hear O Israel: A Story of the Warsaw Ghetto.* New York: Macmillan/Atheneum. (picture book)

Uchida, Yoshiko. (1993). *The Bracelet.* New York: Philomel. (picture book)

Uchida, Yoshiko. (1978). *Journey Home.* New York: Atheneum.

Uchida, Yoshiko. (1971, 1984). *Journey to Topaz: A Story of the Japanese-American Evacuation.* Berkeley, CA: Creative Arts.

van Stockum, Hilda. (1975). *The Borrowed House.* New York: Farrar, Straus & Giroux.

Vinke, Herman. (1984). *The Short Life of Sophie Scholl.* New York: Harper & Row.

Vos, Ida. (1991). *Hide and Seek.* Translated from the Dutch by Terese Edelstein and Inez Schmidt. New York: Houghton Mifflin.

Vos, Ida. (1993, 1986). *Anna Is Still Here.* Boston: Houghton Mifflin.

Walsh, Jill Paton. (1969). *Fireweed.* New York: Farrar, Straus & Giroux.

Westall, Robert. (1989). *Blitzcat.* New York: Scholastic.

Westall, Robert. (1991). *Echoes of War.* New York: Farrar, Straus & Giroux.

Westall, Robert. (1991). *The Kingdom by the Sea.* New York: Farrar, Straus & Giroux.

Westall, Robert. (1976). *The Machine Gunners.* New York: Greenwillow.

Yolen, Jane. (1992). *Briar Rose.* New York: Tom Doherty Associates.

Yolen, Jane. (1988). *The Devil's Arithmetic.* New York: Viking.

Zei, Alki. (1972). *Petros' War*. Translated by Edward Fenton. New York: E.P. Dutton.

Zei, Alki. (1968). *Wildcat Under Glass*. New York: Holt.

Zyskind, Sara. (1981). *Stolen Years*. Minneapolis, MN: Lerner.

Zyskind, Sara. (1989). *Struggle*. Minneapolis, MN: Lerner.

II. Non-Fiction: World War II

Abells, C.B. (1983). *The Children We Remember*. New York: Greenwillow Books.

Adler, D.A. (1989). *We Remember the Holocaust*. New York: Holt.

Appleman-Jurman. (1988). *Alicia: My Story*. New York: Bantam (Doubleday).

Armor, John, and Peter Wright. (1988). *Manzanar*. New York: Times Books (Random House).

Arnothy, Christine. (1986). *I Am Fifteen and I Don't Want to Die*. New York: Scholastic.

Atkinson, Linda. (1985). *In Kindling Flame: The Story of Hannah Senesh (1921-44)*. New York: Lothrop, Lee & Shepard.

Auerbacher, Inge. (1993). *I Am a Star: Child of the Holocaust*. New York: Puffin.

Baldwin, Margaret. (1981). *The Boys Who Saved the Children*. New York: Julian Messner.

Bernbaum, Israel. (1985). *My Brother's Keeper: The Holocaust Through the Eyes of an Artist*. New York: Putnam.

Chaiken, Miriam. (1987). *A Nightmare in History: The Holocaust 1933-1945*. New York: Clarion.

Chrisp, Peter. (1991). *Blitzkreig!* The Bookwright Press.

Davis, Daniel. (1982). *Behind Barbed Wire: The Imprisonment of Japanese-Americans During World War II*. New York: Dutton.

Emmerich, Elsbeth. (1992). *My Childhood in Nazi Germany*. Bookwright.

Epstein, Helen. (1979). *Children of the Holocaust*. New York: Putnam.

Finkelstein, N. (1985). *Remember Not to Forget*. New York: Franklin Watts.

Frank, Anne. (1967). *Anne Frank: The Diary of a Young Girl*. New York: Doubleday.

Friedman, Ina R. (1991). *The Other Victims: First Person Stories of Non-Jews Persecuted by the Nazis*. Boston: Houghton Mifflin.

Fry, Varian. (1993). *Assignment: Rescue — An Autobiography*. New York: Scholastic.

Goldston, Robert. (1982). *Sinister Touches: The Secret War Against Hitler*. New York: Dial.

Graff, Stewart. (1978). *The Story of World War II*. New York: E.P. Dutton.

Handler, Andrew. (1993). *Young People Speak: Surviving the Holocaust in Hungary*. New York: Watts.

Harrison, Michael, and Christopher Stuart Clark. (1989). *Peace and War: A Collection of Poems*. New York: Oxford University Press.

Hart, Kitty. (1982). *Return to Auschwitz: The Remarkable Life of a Girl Who Survived the Holocaust*. New York: Atheneum.

Hurwitz, J. (1988). *Anne Frank: Life in Hiding*. Philadelphia, PA: The Jewish Publication Society.

Isaacman, Clara, and Joan A. Grossman. (1984). *Clara's Story*. Philadelphia, PA: Jewish Publication Society.

Landau, Elaine. (1991). *We Survived the Holocaust.* New York: Watts.

Leckie, Robert. (1964). *The Story of World War II.* New York: Random House.

Leitner, Isabella. (1992). *The Big Lie: A True Story.* New York: Scholastic.

Meltzer, Milton. (1976). *Never to Forget: The Jews of the Holocaust.* New York: Harper & Row.

Meltzer, Milton. (1988). *Rescue: The Story of How Gentiles Saved Jews in the Holocaust.* New York: Harper & Row.

Nicholson, Michael, and David Winner. (1989). *Raoul Wallenberg: The Swedish Diplomat Who Saved 100,000 Jews From the Nazi Holocaust Before Mysteriously Disappearing.* Milwaukee, WI: Gareth Stevens.

Rogasky, Barbara. (1988). *Smoke and Ashes: The Story of the Holocaust.* New York: Holiday.

Rossel, Seymour. (1981, 1990). *The Holocaust.* New York: Watts.

Scholl, Inge. (1983). *The White Rose.* Middletown, CT: Wesleyan University Press.

Senesh, Hannah. (1972). *Hannah Senesh, Her Life and Diary.* New York: Schocken.

Speigelman, Art. (1986). *Maus.* New York: Pantheon.

Takashima, Shizuye. (1991). *A Child in Prison Camp.* Plattsburgh, NY: Tundra.

Toll, Nelly S. (1993). *Behind the Secret Window: A Memoir of a Hidden Childhood.* New York: Dial.

Uchida, Yoshiko. (1992). *The Invisible Thread.* New York: Messner.

Verhoeven, Rian, and Ruud van der Rol. (1993). *Anne Frank: Beyond the Diary — A Photographic Remembrance.* New York: Viking.

Vinke, Hermann. (1984). *The Short Life of Sophie Scholl.* New York: Harper & Row.

Vogel, Ilse-Margaret. (1992). *Bad Times, Good Friends: A Personal Memoir.* San Diego, CA: Harcourt Brace Jovanovich.

Wheal, Elizabeth Anne. (1990). *A Dictionary of the Second World War.* New York: Peter Bedrick.

Wiesel, Elie. (1982). *Night.* New York: Bantam.

Foot Notes

1. Rebecca Lukens' (1990) *A Critical Handbook of Children's Literature,* Glenview, IL: Scott, Foresman, is a useful resource for teachers who want to review literary analysis before introducing literary elements and genres to their students.

2. Milton Meltzer's (1988) *Rescue: The Story of How Gentiles Saved Jews in the Holocaust,* New York: Harper and Row, has a segment on Danish Rescuers, including Duckwitz.

3. Jimmy Carter, (1993) *Talking Peace: A Vision for the Next Generation,* New York: Dutton.

ON THEIR OWN

Survival tales have long been popular among middle-grade readers. Struggling to become independent and to develop the competence and confidence to confront and cope with the challenges in their own lives, these young readers identify with fictional characters who are on their own, pitted against a reality in which they must learn to survive without adult help.

Each of the heroes and heroines in popular survival stories such as *Island of the Blue Dolphins* (O'Dell, 1960), *My Side of the Mountain* (George, 1959), *The Cay* (Taylor, 1969), and *Julie of the Wolves* (George, 1972) must learn to survive alone in a physical environment that threatens to destroy them. Nature is antagonist in these narratives. The protagonists must use ingenuity and resourcefulness to protect themselves against the dangers of nature and, at the same time, to make use of its bounty in order to stay alive.

Ivan Southall's *Ash Road* (1965), *Hill's End* (1962), and *To the Wild Sky* (1967) all involve groups of children who are cut off from adult help and must learn to work together as a group to survive in a hostile environment. The children in these novels are portrayed as distinct individuals who change emotionally and socially as a result of their experience together, fighting for survival.

The central characters in these survival stories, whether alone or in a group, are tested in reality situations in which they prove their personal courage and determination and their cognitive and physical competence. They survive physically and psychologically by drawing from inner resources and strengths and developing new ones. The experience is a rite of passage, a transition from childhood to adulthood; the characters change and grow in the course of their emotional journey.

Another group of survival tales includes the tragic stories of victims of war and revolution, children who are on their own and struggling to survive and to escape the enemy. In *North to Freedom* (Holm, 1965), David travels alone from a prison camp in Eastern Europe to Denmark, where he hopes to find his mother. *Escape From Warsaw* (Serraillier, 1972) is another story of flight and quest. The Balicki children travel alone from Warsaw, Poland to Switzerland in search of their parents.

The Wild Children (Holman, 1983), based on actual stories of the "bezprizorni," the wild children of Russia, is the fictional account of a twelve-year-old boy who is left behind when his family is arrested following the Bolshevik Revolution. He is forced to flee from his home and eventually joins one of the many gangs of desperate, homeless children who struggle to stay alive in cellars and caves.

In contrast to these survival novels in which children and youth are separated from adults due to accident, natural disaster, war, or by choice, a new type of realistic fiction for middle-grade readers features children who have been abandoned by their parents or the significant adults in their lives. In some of these novels, children are left on their own because of poverty or mental illness.

In Cynthia Voigt's *Homecoming* (1981), four children are abandoned by their emotionally disturbed mother at a shopping mall. Their father had deserted them years earlier. In *Monkey Island* (Fox, 1991), Clay Garrity lives on the streets of New York after his father and then his mother leave him. Victims of poverty, they are overcome with desperation and hopelessness.

In some novels, children live with an emotionally disturbed parent who is unable to care for them. *The Bears' House* (Sachs, 1971) portrays the harsh reality of five children, deserted by their father and living in a crowded apartment with their emotionally disturbed mother. In *Afternoon of the Elves* (Lisle, 1989), a young girl lives alone with her mentally ill mother. Sara Kate takes care of her mother as well as herself. In *Randall's Wall* (Fenner, 1991), a fifth grader, Randall, lives with his siblings and emotionally disturbed mother in a ramshackle house with no running water. His abusive father is absent most of the time. Randall builds an invisible wall around himself in order to survive the harsh reality of his life.

In a growing number of novels, children are abandoned by mothers who are more concerned with their own well-being than with the welfare of their family. For selfish reasons, they abdicate their traditional roles as nurturers and protectors of children. In *Fish Friday* (Pearson, 1986), the mother leaves her family to study art in New York. In *Patchwork Summer* (Holl, 1987), the mother leaves her family in order "to find herself" and become a writer. In *Julie's Daughter* (Rodowsky, 1985) and *Midnight Hour Encores* (Brooks, 1986), mothers abandon their daughters when they are still infants. All of these children are scarred by the feeling that their mother did not love them or care enough to stay with them.

Children's literature tends to reflect the values and attitudes and trends of the social context out of which it emerges. These realistic novels in which adults relinquish their responsibilities as parents reflect some of the social issues of the 1980s: child neglect and abuse, homelessness, and the breakdown of the family unit. Although desertion by a father is not unusual in realistic fiction for middle-grade children, a mother who abandons her family is only recently appearing as a significant character in contemporary novels for this age group. The growing number of books involving abandonment by a mother published in the

1980s may reflect the changing attitudes of women about their rights and needs as individuals. In these novels, children are often asked to try to understand their mothers as individuals who have personal needs and dreams. Whether the pain of abandonment can be eased by understanding is a question raised in many of these novels.

Middle-grade readers can develop a deeper understanding of human problems and human relationships as they enter into the lives of characters portrayed in realistic fiction. In the process they can learn about themselves as individuals and as social beings.

Some middle-grade students may recognize themselves as they read the survival tales mentioned above and feel reassured that they are not the only ones with emotional burdens and conflicts. Most middle-grade readers will identify with central characters in these novels because of developmental characteristics they share with them. Children in this age group are anxious to become independent and to prove their ability to cope with reality situations without adult help. They want to use their growing cognitive and physical skills to master reality instead of being mastered by it. By entering into a survival story, young readers are able to experience mastery of reality within the safe boundaries of fiction. Through these vicarious experiences as readers, they can discover possibilities for their own growth toward independence.

Realistic fiction also provides young readers with windows into unfamiliar worlds and opportunities to enter into the lives of those whose experiences are unlike their own. Young readers can find out what it means to be "on your own," to be separated from adult help and protection, to be abandoned by one's parents, to live in poverty, and to realize that the significant adults in one's life are unable to provide physical and emotional sustenance.

Introducing the Focus Unit

The Focus Unit described in this chapter features novels about young people who are "on their own." During the first group session, students are asked to share their interpretations of the phrase "on their own" and to suggest titles which could be included in a Focus Unit with this title. Then they are given an overview of four types of survival novels which will be studied in this unit and used to organize the classroom collection into four categories. The teacher and students build the collection together and record the categories and titles on a chart posted near the collection. In some cases a particular title is included in two different categories. The following list is presented here to suggest relevant titles for this unit. Teachers who choose to adapt this unit for their own classrooms can work with their students to put together a collection which will meet the specific needs and interests of these students.

I. **Survival in Natural Settings**
    Adrift (Baillie, 1992)
    Ash Road (Southall, 1965)
    Hatchet (Paulsen, 1987)
    Hills End (Southall, 1962)

The Island of the Blue Dolphins (O'Dell, 1960)
The Island Keeper (Mazer, 1981)
Julie of the Wolves (George, 1972)
My Side of the Mountain (George, 1959)
Snowbound (Mazer, 1973)
To the Wild Sky (Southall, 1967)

II. Survival in Urban Settings

At the Sound of the Beep (Sachs, 1990)
The Beggar's Ride (Nelson, 1992)
Cave Under the City (Mazer, 1986)
The Crossing (Paulsen, 1987)
From the Mixed-Up Files of Mrs. Basil E. Frankweiler (Konigsburg, 1967)
Homecoming (Voigt, 1981)
Lyddie (Paterson, 1991)
Monkey Island (Fox, 1991)
The Planet of Junior Brown (Hamilton, 1971)
Slake's Limbo (Holman, 1974, 1986)
Wildflower Girl (Conlon-McKenna, 1992)

III. Victims of Revolution and War

The Cay (Taylor, 1969)
Crutches (Hartling, 1986)
Escape from Warsaw (Serraillier, 1959, 1972)
Fireweed (Walsh, 1969)
Island on Bird Street (Orlev, 1984)
The Little Fishes (Haugaard, 1967, 1986)
North of Danger (Fife, 1978)
North to Freedom (Holm, 1963)
Sarah Bishop (O'Dell, 1960, 1980)
The Wild Children (Holman, 1983)

IV. Abandonment, Neglect, and Overwhelming Responsibility

Afternoon of the Elves (Lisle, 1989)
Baby (MacLachlan, 1993)
Bears' House (Sachs, 1971, 1987)
Cave Under the City (Mazer, 1986)
The Crossing (Paulsen, 1986)
Daphne's Book (Hahn, 1983)
Fish Friday (Pearson, 1986)
The Girl (Branscum, 1986)
Homecoming (Voigt, 1981)
Journey (MacLachlan, 1991)
Julie's Daughter (Rodowsky, 1985)
Kumquat May, I'll Always Love You (Grant, 1989)
Lyddie (Paterson, 1991)

Mama, Let's Dance (Hermes, 1991)
Midnight Hour Encores (Brooks, 1986)
Monkey Island (Fox, 1991)
Night Swimmers (Byars, 1980)
Patchwork Summer (Holl, 1987)
Randall's Wall (Fenner, 1991)
Two Thousand Pound Goldfish (Byars, 1982)
Where the Lilies Bloom (Cleavers, 1969)
Yesterday's Daughter (Calvert, 1986)

The Classroom Collection and Independent Reading

For the unit described in this chapter, students are expected to select for independent reading at least two novels from two different categories. The nature of the independent reading assignments will vary in different classroom settings. To prepare students for selecting these two novels, the teacher presents a series of brief book talks and invites students who have read one or more of the titles on the list to share something about them. Students are also given time to browse through the collection before making their choices for independent reading.

Questions

A second chart — a list of questions that suggest ideas for oral and written response — is posted next to the list of titles in the collection. Some of the questions on this list are suggested by students during the initial discussion of the meaning of "on their own" and during subsequent discussions about books in the collection. Other questions are formulated by the teacher to call attention to literary elements and authors' craft and to suggest ways to interact with literary texts. Thus, the list of questions is generated out of the combined input of teacher and students, and it evolves during the course of the Focus Unit experience. The teacher draws questions from this posted list to generate or to extend discussion of the novel selected for the shared reading experience and to demonstrate how the list can be used to trigger new ways to think about the novel and new ideas for literary analysis. As students become involved in reading their self-selected novels and begin their running record of response in their literary journals, they are encouraged to make use of this list of questions to expand their own thinking about these novels. (Copies of the list of questions can be provided for each student to keep in his/her journal.) The list of questions developed for the Focus Unit described in this chapter is presented below.

1. FOCUS: What is the nature of the survival in each novel? Why are the central characters on their own?

2. PROTAGONISTS: Describe the protagonists. What techniques do authors use to develop these characters? How do authors reveal emotional and social growth in the central characters?

What are significant turning points in their emotional journeys? Identify changes in outlook and attitude which resulted from the ordeal described in each novel. Discuss authors' use of viewpoint to develop their characters.

3.   CHARACTERS ON THEIR OWN: What special qualities enabled the central characters to survive? What inner resources were discovered and used? What new cognitive and physical skills were developed? What new attitudes, perspectives, and insights helped the central characters cope with the challenges driving the plot of each novel? Find evidence that reflects the development of decision-making skills and logical reasoning as well as self-esteem and self-confidence.

4.   SUPPORT CHARACTERS: Identify characters who support, guide, inspire, and/or protect the protagonists. How do these characters influence the protagonist? What role do they play in shaping the course of events in each narrative?

5.   ANTAGONISTS: Identify characters who are in conflict with the protagonists. What role do they play in shaping character and plot development in each narrative?

6.   SETTING: What role does the setting play in plot and character development? What is the dual nature of natural settings in which central characters struggle to survive? Contrast urban and wilderness survival tales. Identify and discuss the role of small-town or neighborhood settings in shaping the course of events in particular novels.

7.   CONFLICT: What *external conflicts* influence or determine character and plot development? What *internal conflicts* play a significant role in character development and growth? What moral dilemmas confront the central characters? Find evidence of a moral code used by the central characters to guide choices and behavior. Identify characters who have created an inner reality that is in conflict with outer reality. What is the role of denial in generating this type of conflict? Find scenes in the novel that suggest that the character is beginning to move beyond this denial and to accept a painful reality.

8.   PLOT: What techniques does each author use to develop plot? Do you think the plot is driven more by internal conflict or external opposing forces? Support your response with evidence from the text. Identify narratives which are structured as journey or quest tales. Make a diagram of the journey or quest.

9.   SYMBOLS: Identify symbols woven into the narrative. How do these symbols illuminate characters and/or themes?

10. THEME: What are the central themes? What social and moral issues are explored? What significant truths about the human condition are revealed? Discuss the meaning of survival as it is

developed in each novel. Contrast physical and psychological survival. After basic needs are met, what other needs are important? Examine the title, cover illustration, dedication, and authors' notes for clues about the underlying meaning of each novel.

11. GENRE: Identify the genre of each novel. In a novel identified as historical realism, how does the historical context influence character and plot development? What historical events and external conflicts force central characters to struggle for survival without adult help? In a novel identified as contemporary realism, how does this contemporary context influence character and plot development? What issues, events, and trends in contemporary society are reflected in the central conflicts that challenge the characters and drive the plot?

12. COMPARATIVE ANALYSIS: Compare the two novels you selected to read independently and the one selected for the shared reading experience in terms of characters, setting, conflicts and problems, theme, narrative structure, literary techniques, and genre. What significant connections and contrasts do you find?

13. READER AND TEXT: Put yourself in the shoes of a central character. What connections do you find between this fictional character and yourself? What would you have done differently? Why? What did you learn about characters whose experiences, problems, and conflicts are unlike your own? What did you learn about self-reliance, courage, resourcefulness, personal determination, and commitment as you entered into the lives of fictional characters in these survival novels? What did you learn about yourself as you lived through the experiences of these characters?

The Shared Reading Experience

Patricia MacLachlan's slim volume, *Journey* (1991), is selected as the focus for the shared reading experience to introduce one type of survival tale included in the Focus Unit collection. *Journey* is an example of the contemporary novels about abandonment, and it is used to set the stage for a study of survival in diverse contexts that is guided by the questions listed above.

Before opening the book, the teacher invites the students to discuss the title and to suggest possible meanings. Later, after the entire story has been read aloud, they are asked to expand this discussion of the title and to use it to generate an analysis of the meaning of the story [see question 10]. In addition, they are encouraged to think about this word, "journey," as they read the novels they've selected for independent study and to consider its relevance in an analysis of each story.

Beneath the title on the front cover of this book is a picture of an old camera. Again, the students are asked to think about the possible significance of this object featured alone on the cover. A follow-up discussion after the novel has been read aloud allows students to extend their thinking and reinforces the notion that the process of generating meaning as readers begins with the cover of the book.

The title page features a segment of a torn photograph showing a child's arm. This page provides a further clue about the significance of photography and photographs in this novel. And two pages prior to Chapter One, the author offers two quotations which enrich the discussion of the title and the pictures of the camera and the photograph:

> "It is our inward journey that leads us through time — forward or back, seldom in a straight line, most often spiraling." Eudora Welty, *One Writer's Beginnings*
> "Photography is a tool for dealing with things everybody knows about but isn't attending to." Emmet Gowin, in *On Photography* by Susan Sontag.

The page which immediately precedes Chapter One is written in italics and further sets the stage for the story which begins in Chapter One. This introductory page, or prologue, provides significant information about the story. The prologue opens with these lines:

> Mama named me Journey. Journey, as if somehow she wished her restlessness on me. But it was Mama who would be gone the year that I was eleven —

Then the reader is given a glimpse of the scene of Mama's departure. When she tells Journey that she will be back, his grandfather says, "No, son.... She won't be back." Journey's response to these words is to hit his grandfather. Here, the scene ends.

By this time, students have a great deal of information about this story. The title of the book not only refers to an inward journey but to the name of the protagonist and to the journey taken by his mother in response to an inner restlessness. The prologue suggests that the story is told as a first-person account from the viewpoint of Journey [see question 2] and is about his response to being abandoned by his mother, who has left him and his older sister, Cat, with their grandparents [see question 1]. The prologue also suggests the nature of Journey's inner conflict. When his grandfather contradicts the words of his mother and tells him that she won't be back, Journey cannot tolerate this and hits his grandfather. He prefers to hold on to his own idealized image of his mother rather than face the harsh reality his grandfather presents to him. His need to deny this reality is behind the attack on his grandfather which, in turn, foreshadows the conflict between Journey and his grandfather in the story itself [see question 7]. This scene also provides a clue about the setting of the story: "Mama stood in the barn, her suitcase at her feet" [see question 6].

In the first chapter, the author offers a verbal snapshot of each of the four central characters. Grandfather is intent on capturing every detail of their world with Cat's old camera; Cat gives up her camera and her flute and other things associated with her past life, as if she can put it behind her; Grandmother takes the flute and a sweat shirt with "LIDDIE" printed on it, a connection to the daughter who has left her; Journey's anger erupts with, "That's Mama's shirt!" (p. 5). His anger is also captured in his grandfather's first picture of him, at a moment when Journey is preoccupied with thoughts of his father, who had left years earlier. He had been thinking of the picture of their father on Cat's dresser, a picture which tells him nothing about this man he cannot remember.

The second chapter opens with the arrival of a letter from their mother that contains two small packets of money for Cat and Journey but no message and no return address. Cat responds with angry activity in an attempt to escape her disappointment; Journey's response reflects his denial: "She forgot the return address" (p. 9). Grandma reaches out to Journey and tries to help him understand his mother and why she abandoned them. She shares an old family album, with pictures showing her as a young girl Cat's age and his mother at the same age. Grandma says, "The camera knows," as she shows the picture of herself smiling happily and the pictures of his mother: "All around her were people, laughing, talking.... But my mother looked silent and unhearing" (p. 11). Grandma explains what the camera saw: "Your mama always wished to be somewhere else" (p. 12). This picture prompts a memory of an earlier time when Journey had fallen into the brook. It was his grandfather who had picked him up, but he had wanted his mother. "But Mama is far ahead, and she doesn't look back. She is somewhere else" (p. 13).

Some students respond to this family album scene with personal comments; others use it to understand story characters:

> Student one: "I like those old albums. You can sort of see what your parents used to be like."
>
> Student two: "I'm like Journey. I like to see what I was like when I was little. They're my *own* memories.
>
> Student three: "But Journey's grandma wanted him to know his *mom*...when she was young."
>
> Student four: "Yeah. She's trying to get him to see she left because of *herself*, not *him*. Like it's not his fault."

In Chapter Three, Journey takes his first picture while he watches his grandfather holding his friend's baby brother on his knees. A similar scene from his own childhood flashes into Journey's mind, but he has no memory of who was holding him. His sister shows him an old photograph of a boy who looks like Journey. "'Is that a picture of Papa?' I asked Cat" (p. 20). It is a picture of his grandfather.

By this time the students are ready to discuss what they have learned about each character and the author's craft. Questions 2, 4, 7, 9 and 10 can be used to generate discussion about the first three chapters. Students are asked to find evidence in the text of Journey's emotional journey as he searches for clues about his past and his parents. They are asked to find evidence of the author's use of the camera as a literary device in this search for truth. Journey's grandfather says: "And sometimes pictures show us what is really there" (p. 19). The camera captures a reality that Journey wants to deny. The camera is used so frequently throughout the narrative that it functions as a symbol of this search for the truth about his family and himself.

In the fourth chapter, Journey is drawn into his grandfather's fascination with photography, and their relationship improves as he begins to share in the enjoyment of taking pictures. At one point, Journey examines a picture he has taken and comments, "Well, it's not perfect" (p. 29). His grandfather responds, "What is perfect?... Things can be good enough" (p. 29). Finally, Journey is able to ask a question that he must have been carrying inside since his mother left: "Do you think that Mama left because things weren't good enough? Do you think that I wasn't...." (p. 29). His grandfather tells him, "It-is-not-your-fault" (p. 30). Journey may be able to accept this truth, but he is not yet ready to blame his mother. Although Journey does not express his thoughts, it is clear to his grandfather that Journey places the blame on him. When Journey asks to see the pictures of his childhood, his grandfather has to tell him the truth: "Your mama tore them up" (p. 32).

The shock of this knowledge causes Journey to withdraw into himself — until a stray cat enters his life and pulls Journey out of himself and into the family circle. Now it is the cat that is the center of attention as they wait for her to deliver her babies. It is the cat that finds the box of torn pictures hidden under Mama's bed. The family stares at the "bits and pieces of faces and arms and bodies.... A baby's hand" (p. 48). Cat says, "She sure did in our family.... It looks like murder to me" (p. 49). When Journey sees the tears in his sister's eyes, he tells her he will tape the pictures together. His grandfather says of the torn pictures: "It's Journey's past" (p. 50).

This chapter prompts some students to ask questions and make connections to their own experiences:

> Student one: "I don't get why his mom tore up the pictures."
>
> Student two: "Once I tore up a picture of my friend when we split. But then I taped it back when I wasn't so mad."
>
> Student three: "What was she so *mad* about to do that?"

In Chapter Nine, when Journey faces the reality that he cannot put the pictures together, he also knows that his mother will not return. He gives the box to the cat, and it is here that the kittens are born. Journey is fascinated with the way the cat takes care of its babies and asks, "Who taught her...how to be a mother?" (p. 59). When his grandfather replies, "Mothers know," Cat responds with the words Journey was thinking: "Not all of them" (p. 59).

At the end of Chapter Ten, Journey's mother telephones and Journey is able to tell her about the cat: "And the cat is a very good mother.... And she is staying here with me. Forever" (p. 64).

As the story unfolds, students are invited to respond spontaneously at the end of each chapter with their personal experiences as listeners and with comments and questions about the characters; their relationships; the emotional journey of each member of the family; and the author's craft. They discuss the role of the stray cat in Journey's life and why the author introduces the cat into the story. They discuss the significance of the torn pictures and their role in moving Journey toward an acceptance of the harsh reality about his mother. At the end of the tenth chapter, students focus on another turning point in the emotional journey: When his mother calls, Journey's response to her reflects the distance he has travelled since she left him [see question 2].

In Chapter Twelve, during a scene in which Journey and Cat are remembering a shared experience in their childhood, Cat explains why grandfather takes so many family pictures: "Don't you know that grandfather wants to give you back everything that Mama took away? He wants to give you family" (p. 73).

In the final chapter, Thirteen, grandfather sets up a darkroom in the barn and develops some old negatives he has found — the negatives of Mama's pictures. Journey looks at the pictures and sees his past. And what he discovers is a memory captured by the camera. He is a baby sitting on someone's knee. But it was not his papa who held him, as he had wanted to believe. It was his grandfather.

After the story of Journey is read aloud, the students discuss the book as a whole, beginning with a follow-up of the initial discussions focussing on the clues found on the book jacket and the pages prior to the first chapter. The sets of questions about themes and symbols [9 and 10] are used to guide the discussion of the central themes and the way symbols are used to develop themes. For example, the camera can be interpreted as a symbol that develops the theme identified as the search for truth. Journey's search for the truth about his mother and his past guides his emotional journey toward the moment of confronting the truth and a gradual acceptance of the cold reality of abandonment.

The family circle has been broken; but, by the end of the novel, a new family unit has been established, bound together by love and caring.

The questions about support characters [4] call attention to the role of each character who helps the protagonist on his journey. Evidence from the text can be used to highlight particular scenes in which Journey's sister, grandmother, and best friend reach out to help him. However, the grandfather is identified as the central support character; evidence of his supportive role can be found throughout the text.

Some students identify the grandfather as the antagonist in the beginning of the story and revise their judgment as the story unfolds [see question 5]. Others note that Journey sees his grandfather as an antagonist until he gains enough information and insight to discover that his grandfather has always supported him.

The questions about the plot [8] generate discussion that is concluded with the collaborative production of a diagram of the journey of the protagonist.

The set of questions labeled "Reader and Text" [13] are reviewed at the end of this shared reading experience, and students are invited to respond in their literary journals. Those who wish to share these personal responses are given an opportunity to do so in subsequent group sessions, or with a peer partner.

Independent Reading and Writing
and Dialogue Groups

Dialogue groups are established to allow students to share and discuss with classmates one of the novels they have selected to read independently. Each group is made up of about six students who have read titles from one of the four categories listed above. Four sign-up sheets are posted; each student records his/her name and book title under the appropriate category. If more than six students choose a particular category, two dialogue groups are formed.

Once the students have decided which novel they would like to discuss in the context of a dialogue group, they are asked to draw from two of the sets of questions listed above to begin a written analysis of this novel. These written analyses are brought to the dialogue-group sessions to provide a starting point for sharing and discussion. Although a few groups may be made up of students who have chosen to read the same title, most groups are made up of students who have read several different titles within one category. In these latter groups, students begin the dialogue by sharing a brief summary of their book guided by the questions in 1, 2, 6, and 7. The nature of the dialogue in each group depends on the participants and their unique responses as readers and the specific novels they have selected to study. Examples of the types of analyses which can emerge in the dialogue groups established in the context of the Focus Unit, "On Their Own," are presented in the following pages.

Survival in Natural Settings

Students in the dialogue group or groups studying novels featuring survival in natural settings introduce the novel they have selected by describing the nature of the survival situation; what led up to this situation; the central characters and their development; the setting; and the external and/or internal conflicts which drive the plot [see questions 1, 2, 6, and 7]. After presenting these introductory summaries, students share their written analysis of the novel they have selected to study in this group context. Students are encouraged to continue to use the list of questions to stimulate further analysis and a search for connections between these novels. The third set of questions, "Characters On Their Own," is particularly relevant for studying novels featuring survival in natural settings.

My Side of the Mountain by Jean George (1959) is a story of survival by choice. A city boy, Sam Gribley, chooses to spend a winter alone in the Catskill Mountains, where he masters the techniques of survival and learns to live off the land.

Two other novels discussed in this dialogue group, *Julie of the Wolves* (George, 1972) and *The Island Keeper* (Mazer, 1981), feature heroines who choose to leave home because of personal and family problems but find themselves alone in a wilderness setting and must cope with the harsh challenges of winter on their own.

In *Julie of the Wolves*, thirteen-year-old Julie (Miyax is her Eskimo name) manages to survive alone on the Alaskan tundra with the help of a pack of Arctic wolves who come to accept her as a friend as she learns to communicate with them and to love them as brothers.

In *The Island Keeper*, sixteen-year-old Cleo Murphy, mourning the loss of her beloved sister, runs away from a domineering grandmother and an indifferent father, to a deserted island. She is determined to escape her life as an overprotected, coddled child and to prove that she can survive on her own. When she feels physically and psychologically ready to return to her family, a storm destroys her canoe and she must survive a brutal Canadian winter. This is the story of Cleo's personal evolution. She gains a sense of her own identity and self-esteem by being on her own. Students find turning points in Cleo's journey, revealing her insights about her own growth.

In these three stories, the central characters begin their journeys as a matter of choice. In contrast, other novels studied in this dialogue group are about heroes or heroines who are thrust into survival situations due to natural disasters, tragic accidents, or other events beyond their control.

Island of the Blue Dolphins (O'Dell, 1960), based on an actual incident, is the story of Karana, an Indian girl who survived alone on an island off the coast of California for eighteen years. The author uses first-person point of view, which gives readers a sense of immediacy as Karana struggles to survive physically and psychologically. She is forced to decide whether to make weapons or to obey the tribal law that prohibits women from constructing weapons. Later, she makes the decision not to kill the leader of a pack of wild dogs after wounding him. She cares for him and names him Rontu; he becomes her companion and protector.

In Gary Paulsen's novel, *Hatchet* (1987), thirteen-year-old Brian Robeson, deeply hurt and embittered by his parents' divorce, is on his way to visit his father in the Canadian wilderness when the pilot of the small plane (in which he is the only passenger) suffers a fatal heart attack. He manages to crash-land the plane in an isolated lake and then survives fifty-four days on his own in the rugged Canadian wilds, with only a hatchet that had been given to him by his mother. Now he must put aside thoughts of the divorce and turn his attention to survival.

The author tells the story from the viewpoint of the protagonist and invites the reader to enter into Brian's mind as he confronts each new life-threatening challenge and thinks through ways to solve life-and-death problems: creating a shelter, getting food, making a fire, and constructing tools and weapons.

In *Snowbound* (Mazer, 1973), two teenagers are stranded during a blizzard in a desolate area far from the main highway in New York State. Tony Laporte — fifteen years old, handsome, spoiled, and self-centered — decides to leave home. He takes his mother's car without permission and sets out in a severe snowstorm, driving without a license. His intention is to teach his parents a lesson for refusing to give in to one of his demands. Along the way he picks up a hitchhiker, Cindy Reichert, who is preoccupied with her own problems.

Their story is told from the alternating viewpoints of Cindy and Tony. When Tony wrecks the car, they find themselves alone in an isolated area. It is Cindy who first confronts the reality of their plight and realizes that they must act to save themselves. It takes Tony a long time before he is ready to think beyond his own immediate needs and to realize that only through cooperative effort can they survive. For eleven days they manage to stay alive. When their ordeal is finally over, Tony is aware of his own growth as a person. For him, the ordeal is a rite of passage.

Questions about character development and growth, conflict, and plot [questions 2, 3, 7, and 8] are especially useful in analyzing, sharing, and comparing the novels studied in this dialogue group. The connections between external and internal conflicts can be explored in each novel and used as a point of comparison between novels. The journey of each protagonist can be diagramed and used as another point of comparison as students engage in a comparative analysis of all the novels selected as the focus in this dialogue group.

Three survival tales by Ivan Southall, an Australian, feature groups of children who must learn to work together in order to survive in hostile environments. *Hill's End* (1962), *Ash Road* (1965), and *To the Wild Sky* (1967) are about small groups of children cut off from adult help, struggling to survive a natural disaster, a bush fire, and a plane crash, respectively. Individual members in each group grow and mature as they respond to crises, develop the capacity for cooperation, gain an understanding of others and the meaning of interdependence, and discover their own inner strengths and resources.

Ash Road is especially powerful as a survival adventure because three of the boys in the group are responsible for the raging bush fire which destroys lives, homes, and land. The others fight for physical survival while Graham, the boy directly responsible for starting the fire, struggles to survive emotionally.

As each book is discussed in this dialogue group, students look for connections and patterns which can be used to develop larger statements about this group of survival stories. Members of the group consider ways to share their analyses and synthesis with the rest of the class in the concluding whole-group sessions scheduled for this purpose.

For example, these students can use their "journey diagrams" to focus on the emotional, cognitive, and physical growth of the central characters as they battle an antagonistic setting. Another approach is to develop charts that summarize their comparative analysis of these novels in terms of protagonists, support characters, and antagonists; conflict and plot structure; setting; symbols; and themes.

A symbol collage can set the stage for discussing the role of significant objects or animals in the lives of protagonists: Brian's hatchet is the key to his survival in *Hatchet*; Cleo's canoe, in *The Island Keeper*, symbolizes the safety net she builds into her experiment in survival. When the canoe is destroyed, her experience on the island changes from "safe survival" to a matter of life or death. Cindy's tin of cookies, in *Snowbound*, serves as a symbol of a survival need and illuminates character traits of Cindy and Tony: Cindy plans to share the cookies equally and, looking ahead, she rations them so that their supply of food will last longer, but Tony's greed, selfishness, and impatience are highlighted as he steals Cindy's share of the cookies while she is asleep and, unwilling to think beyond himself and the moment, eats them all at once. Rontu, the wild dog Karana tames in *Island of the Blue Dolphins*, symbolizes the companionship needed after basic needs are met.

This symbol collage can be expanded to include pictures of symbols contributed by members of the other dialogue groups. A collection of symbols drawn from novels in all four categories can be used to call attention to the relationship between symbol and theme in these stories.

Survival in Urban Settings

Students in the dialogue group(s) formed to study novels featuring urban survival use questions about characters, setting, and conflict to begin the process of sharing the novels they've selected to read independently and to discuss in a group setting.

Slake's Limbo (Holman, 1974) is the story of thirteen-year-old Aremis Slake, an orphan who escapes from the cruelty and degradation that mark his existence and finds refuge in a cave-like room hidden in New York City's subway system. He makes this underground space his home for 121 days. The questions about setting call attention to the realities of poverty and life on inner-city streets. It is this setting which produced the character Aremis Slake, intimidated and defeated, who sees himself only as a "worthless lump" (p. 5). In the first part of the narrative, Slake behaves like a hunted animal in a hostile world. But once he settles into his hidden cave, Slake begins to take control of his life. He discovers his own inner resources and learns to recognize the positive qualities and good intentions of other human beings. The narrative chronicles Slake's emotional journey toward self-respect and self-confidence. When he finally emerges from his hiding place, he is no longer the beaten creature who had escaped into it.

Monkey Island (Fox, 1991) is the story of eleven-year-old Clay Garrity, who is forced to live on the streets of New York City when his mother disappears from their room in a welfare hotel. Unlike Slake, Clay has memories of a comfortable home and a loving mother and father. But this world falls apart when his father loses his job, falls into a depression, and eventually deserts his family. When his mother, too, disappears, Clay is determined to wait for her and to stay away from the authorities who might separate him from his family.

In his wandering, Clay finds a park where the homeless live in cardboard boxes. Here he meets Calvin and Buddy, two homeless men who befriend Clay and take him into their crate home. They become his family.

Through the eyes of Clay, Buddy, and Calvin, readers see the world of the homeless. They learn about the daily struggle for survival of those who live on the street. Most students have seen homeless people in their own communities or in larger cities they visit. *Monkey Island* offers them a new perspective and an opportunity to learn what it means to be homeless. Like Clay, readers can learn to see the shadows that are other people "trying to find better ways to sleep on stone" (p. 79).

At the Sound of the Beep (Sachs, 1990) has a much lighter tone, but the plight of the homeless is woven into the plot. Matthew and Mathilda Green are twins whose parents are getting a divorce. The twins refuse to accept their parents' plan to separate them. They decide to run away and end up in Golden Gate Park, where they meet homeless people who live in the park at night. The twins are drawn into their lives, and the park becomes their temporary home.

Although they learn some of the skills necessary for survival in an urban setting and what it means to be homeless, they are merely witnesses, not victims. They are part of this world as a matter of choice and only on a temporary basis. They have a safety net; they know they can choose to leave whenever they are ready, a luxury not available to those who are truly homeless. The author of this novel separates the chapters by inserting news items about the plight of the homeless and the attitudes and beliefs of people interviewed by reporters about the homeless. Important social and moral issues can be discussed by the students in connection with their analysis of *Monkey Island* and *Slake's Limbo*.

The Planet of Junior Brown (Hamilton, 1971) is a story of homeless children struggling to survive in the inner-city. The three central characters are outcasts who live on the fringe of society. Two are African-American eighth-grade boys: Junior Brown, a talented musician who weighs 300 pounds, is being suffocated by an overprotective, neurotic mother; Buddy Clark is an intelligent, homeless boy who has lived on his own since he was nine. He is a leader in a complex network of secret underground shelters, called "planets," for homeless street children. In this subculture, he is one of the "Tomorrow Billys" who assumes responsibility for these children, working to feed and clothe them, and teaching them how to survive physically and to become strong, moral, and caring individuals. The third central character is Mr. Pool, the school janitor. When Buddy takes Junior and Mr. Pool to his underground community, Mr. Pool recognizes that this "planet" is a humane and compassionate world of human beings who are learning to integrate freedom and responsibility.

The questions about theme [10] call attention to the meaning of survival as it is explored in this story: Buddy Clark makes it clear that survival is more than just staying alive. It means staying human as well. To this end, Buddy teaches his group of homeless children about self-respect, love, and caring about others.

The Planet of Junior Brown can be compared with other stories of group survival. For example, the three novels by Ivan Southall mentioned earlier all focus on groups of children who learn the meaning of interdependence and how to work together to survive. In *The Beggars' Ride* (Nelson, 1992), a small group of homeless children struggle to survive on the streets of Atlantic City. Their leader is a boy named Cowboy, who, like Buddy, has earned the trust of these homeless children whose painful histories have taught them to distrust society.

Homecoming (Voigt, 1981) — which is also included in the list of novels about abandonment, neglect, and overwhelming responsibility — is the story of four children whose father had left them long ago and who have now been abandoned by their emotionally ill mother. Thirteen-year-old Dicey Tillerman assumes the role of parent and is determined to take care of her younger siblings and to find them a home. Without enough money to travel by bus, they walk down the length of the Connecticut coastline, along Route 1. Dicey takes on the responsibility of finding food and shelter and keeping her family together by avoiding the authorities who would separate them.

Students who create a diagram of the Tillerman's journey can include the people who help or hinder them along the way. Key events, adventures, challenges, and problems that marked their journey can also be included on the diagram. Students can use this graphic representation of the Tillerman's quest for a home and roots as a context for responding to the questions listed under "Characters On Their Own;" "Support Characters;" "Antagonists;" and "Conflict."

An incident in the first part of the journey reflects the moral code that guides Dicey's behavior and expectations for her siblings. When James steals money from two college students who befriend them, Dicey is ashamed and furious.

James responds to her anger with: "You didn't yell at Sammy...." Dicey wants him to understand the moral standards he should follow. "Sammy's six! And Sammy didn't take money, he took food. And Sammy didn't take it from someone who'd helped us. Even you can see the difference" (p. 105).

The Crossing (Paulsen, 1987) is about Manuel Bustos, a fourteen-year-old Mexican orphan fighting to survive alone on the streets of Juáres. He lives in a cardboard box; fear and hunger are constant companions. He must fight bigger boys for every coin or bit of food he is able to find, and he is the prey of men who would sell him. He has only one hope for survival. His goal is to cross through the shallows of the Rio Grande, past the searchlights and border patrol to get to Texas.

The questions about antagonists and support characters focus attention on the street bullies who threaten his life and on Sergeant Robert Locke, who gives him a chance to live by providing him with the means of escape, money for the crossing.

The moral code that guides Manny's behavior is revealed the first time he sees Sergeant Locke in a back alley where the American soldier is "throwing up all the liquor he had spent good money on" (p. 47). When Manny decides to take the man's wallet, he thinks to himself, "It is not stealing — he will only spend it on something to throw up anyway" (p. 48).

The set of questions about plot can be used to focus on the parallel plot structure, in which the story of Sergeant Locke is enclosed within the story of Manny Bustos. The two stories are told through alternating points of view. Locke is a Vietnam veteran and Army prefect stationed across the border. He is haunted by thoughts of friends he could not help and seeks escape from nightmares of the Vietnam War. To drown out the cries of his dead friends, he gets drunk in the bars of Juárez. When he is not getting drunk, he is his other self, the military man. He is the "man in the mirror who stands ramrod straight" (p. 14).

The two stories come together when Manny and Locke meet and form a relationship. In the final scene, Locke loses his life in a violent encounter with the street bullies who are after Manny. Before he dies, Locke is able to help Manny, in contrast to his inability to help his friends in battle.

The Crossing is a moving story of physical and psychological survival. It also portrays immigration, legal and illegal, from the viewpoint of a young boy for whom immigration is a matter of life and death. In discussing the central themes of this novel, students can focus on economic, social, and political problems that drive immigrants to leave their homelands, as well as the economic, social, and political problems which are viewed by some as the products of immigration in the United States today.

Lyddie (Paterson, 1991) is an historical novel set in New England in the 19th century. Lyddie Worthen is on her own at age 13. Forced to leave their debt-ridden Vermont farm, Lyddie's family can no longer stay together. When Lyddie hears about the mill jobs in Lowell, Massachusetts, she decides to work in a textile mill for real wages, determined to earn enough money to reunite the family and to pay the debt on the farm.

This novel portrays Lyddie's life as a mill girl in America's first factory town. The reader is drawn into the life she endures in the deafening noise of the factory, where she works at a loom for hours without a break, in constant fear of catching a hand or her hair in the machinery. Lyddie works from dawn to dusk, six days a week, in dust- and lint-filled air that causes fevers and coughs; she works in spite of health risks and the sexual harassment by the overseer.

The author lists at the end of the book a number of sources which she used in writing this historical novel and which readers can use to learn more about the Lowell textile mills and about the Lowell mill girls from their own diaries and from biographies. Like many of the mill girls depicted in these biographies, Lyddie is a fiercely independent, motivated, and courageous young woman. She teaches herself to read and eventually reaches out for an education. In a discussion of the genre of this novel, students consider the role of the historical context in plot and character development. Lyddie's experience as a mill girl in the early days of the factory system has a profound effect on the direction of her life.

The cover of *Wildflower Girl* (Conlon-McKenna, 1992) identifies this as another historical novel: the picture on the cover is a city scene with horse-drawn carriages, women in long dresses, and men in top hats. The reader soon discovers that the young girl in the foreground has just arrived in Boston after a long and perilous sea voyage from her home in Ireland. It is the mid-nineteenth century; thirteen-year-old Peggy O'Driscoll, orphaned after the Great Famine, sees no future for herself in Ireland. Longing for a better life, Peggy sets out alone for America and opportunity. She gets a job as a maid and begins a new life in the big city of Boston — on her own.

Survival of Victims of Revolution and War

Students in the dialogue group(s) formed to study novels about the victims of revolution and war begin their discussion by focussing on the nature of historical fiction as a literary genre. Each student introduces the novel he/she has selected to share with this group by providing relevant information about the historical context that shapes plot and character development and by identifying the external conflicts that force central characters to survive on their own.

Sarah Bishop (O'Dell, 1960, 1980) takes place during the American Revolution and is based on the experiences of the real Sarah Bishop who "came to the colonies [from England] shortly before the American Revolution and with her family settled on Long Island" (p. viii). O'Dell's story is a fictionalized biography of a young girl caught in the middle of the conflict between the rebels and the redcoats during the Revolution. Her father, a British loyalist, dies after being tarred and feathered by Patriot sympathizers. Her brother starves to death on a British prison ship. After the battle for Brooklyn Heights, Sarah flees from the British, the hatred, and the killing, into the Connecticut wilderness. Like the protagonists in other stories of wilderness survival, Sarah is fiercely independent and resourceful in her fight for physical survival. However, unlike protagonists in stories such as *My Side of the Mountain*, Sarah's challenge is compounded by her fear of a hostile and violent human environment.

The Wild Children (Holman, 1983) is set in Russia during the period following the Bolshevik Revolution. In her "Acknowledgments" preceding the first page of the story, the author writes: "This book is fiction, but it is based on carefully examined facts." Her research was prompted by a reference to "the wild children of Russia" made by the late anthropologist, Margaret Mead. These were the children left homeless because their parents were dead or imprisoned after the Revolution. Gangs of "bezprizorni" — wild children — banded together in packs in order to survive on their own without adults. Holman dedicates her book to a New York City cabdriver named Igor, "whose father was a bezprizorni and who talked to me without the meter running. He was proof that some of the wild children made it."

This story is told from the viewpoint of Alex, a twelve-year-old boy who is left behind when his family is arrested by the secret police. He escapes to Moscow and joins a gang of homeless children. The unspoken rule that binds them together is that they must help each other. Like the homeless children living on the streets of New York City portrayed in *The Planet of Junior Brown*, these bands of homeless children, on the streets of Moscow decades earlier, create their own family units and survive through caring and loyalty and an understanding of their need for each other.

The ultimate antagonist in this story is the society which created these bands of "wild children" in the first place. In the day-to-day struggle for survival, individual antagonists are ever-present in the lives of these children in the form of police, other adult authorities, and competing bands of homeless waifs fighting starvation and the cold.

One of the questions about central themes calls for an examination of the title for clues about the underlying meaning of the novel. Although "wild children" is used as the generic term for all the homeless children in Russia during this period in its history, the band of children portrayed in this novel are not uncivilized, unruly, or uncontrolled, as the word "wild" suggests. The laws by which they govern themselves are rational and humane. They live for each other. As innocent victims of a tragic moment in history, these young people exemplify the triumph of the human spirit in the midst of degradation and deprivation.

Many of the novels studied in this dialogue group are set in World War II. *North of Danger* (Fife, 1978) takes place on a remote island belonging to Norway. Twelve-year-old Arne is living with the Paulson family while his father is away on a scientific mission. When British rescue ships come to evacuate the towns-people before the Nazi invasion, Arne stays behind. He knows he must warn his father not to return to the town, where he would be captured by the Nazis. In order to reach his father, he must travel over 200 miles of frozen wasteland on skis.

The Cay (Taylor, 1969) is about the impact of World War II on an American child. The novel opens with the line: "Like silent, hungry sharks that swim in the darkness of the sea, the German submarines arrived in the middle of the night" (p. 9). This lead sentence sets the stage for the story told in first person by eleven-year-old Phillip, who has moved with his parents from Virginia to the island of Curacao. His mother decides to return with Phillip to Virginia, but their freighter is torpedoed by a German submarine, and Phillip finds himself isolated on a small Caribbean island with a West Indian man named Timothy. A blow on the head during the shipwreck has left Phillip blind and dependent on Timothy for his survival. Phillip gradually overcomes his racial prejudice and learns to respect Timothy for his wisdom and dignity and to appreciate his selflessness and capacity for love. Timothy forces Phillip to become independent in preparation for the time when he might have to survive on his own. Phillip's resistance, hostility, and prejudice disappear as they begin to work together and develop a close friendship. During a hurricane, Timothy shelters Phillip with his own body, sacrificing his life to save Phillip. Phillip is able to survive alone on the island because of Timothy's legacy, the careful training in survival he had given him.

This novel is not only about island survival during wartime. It is also about overcoming racial prejudice. The author's dedication illuminates this theme: "To Dr. King's dream, which can only come true if the very young know and understand." Overcoming prejudice depends, in large part, on understanding and seeing people as individual human beings instead of as stereotypes.

Theodore Taylor's *Timothy of the Cay* (1993) offers both a prequel and a sequel to *The Cay* for those students who want to learn more about Timothy's early years and about Phillip after his return to civilization.

Crutches (Hartling, 1986) is set in post-war Vienna. Thomas, a twelve-year-old boy, is searching for his mother amidst the ruins of a war-torn city. He meets a man on crutches, another survivor, and they develop a deep friendship as they join the hundreds of refugees searching for relatives and a place to call home. The reader is drawn into their desperate quest, in which physical survival is never separated from the survival of human dignity and love and humane values.

Escape From Warsaw (Serraillier, 1959, 1972) is the story of thirteen-year-old Ruth Balicki, her eleven-year-old brother Edek, and their three-year-old sister Bronia, who are alone and homeless after their father and then their mother are arrested and their house is blown up by Nazi Storm Troopers. They set out on a long and dangerous journey from Warsaw, Poland to Switzerland in search of their parents.

A diagram or map of their journey would include places where they stopped along the way; the people they met, both friends and foes; and events which represented turning points that brought them closer to their goal or that held them back.

The original title of this novel was "The Silver Sword" (1959). It refers to a tiny silver paper knife in the shape of a sword that has a dragon breathing fire engraved on its brass hilt and which had belonged to the children's mother. It plays an important role throughout the narrative and serves as a symbol of hope and the link between the children and their parents.

Guido, a twelve-year-old orphan who is a beggar on the ruined streets of Naples in 1943, tells the story of his struggle to survive the hunger, loneliness, and degradation caused by the war in the novel, *The Little Fishes* (Haugaard, 1967). Guido sees himself as two selves: one self searching for food, the other self searching for the meaning of the suffering and an understanding of human nature. Throughout the book, readers find thought-provoking statements that can serve as springboards for discussion within the context of the dialogue group. For example: "Everything leaves a little scar: both the good and the bad; and when you grow up, then the scars are the story of your life" (p. 115).

Guido assumes responsibility for two young orphans, Anna and Mario. These three homeless children travel on their own from Naples to Cassino, in search of a home. It is the journey of all the "little fishes" — the innocent victims of war who have no families, no adults to protect them.

These children become old before their time, and the wisdom they acquire from their knowledge of hunger, fear, and cruelty belies their age. But their words remind the reader that these victims are still children, young in years, old in wisdom. As eleven-year-old Anna kneels beside her little brother, Mario, who is dying, a monk says, "God wills." Anna turns to him in rage: "God wills it! God is a man. But Our Lady will not allow it for she is a woman... It is God who rules the world and He will not listen to Our Lady; and that is why we have war. He has locked Our Lady in her room in heaven and that is why our prayers cannot reach Her" (pp. 188-189).

This childish utterance of wisdom, coming from the depths of Anna's suffering, has profound implications and provides a stimulus for serious dialogue about the author's message.

The Island on Bird Street (Orlev, 1984) is the story of an eleven-year-old Jewish boy, Alex, who is on his own in a deserted Polish ghetto during World War II. Alex creates an ingenious hiding place in the ruins of a bombed-out building and like the hero of his favorite book, *Robinson Crusoe,* he learns to survive on his own isolated island and manages to escape detection by German soldiers.

North to Freedom (Holm, 1963, 1965) is the story of David, a twelve-year-old boy who is given a chance to escape from the prison camp in eastern Europe where he has spent most of his life. He sets out alone on his escape-journey across the European continent to Denmark, with the fear of capture and death a constant companion. It is an emotional journey during which he learns about the beauty of nature and about normal human experiences, and what it means to live in freedom. He gradually begins to trust people and to reach out to them in friendship.

In this dialogue group, the search for connections between these historical novels begins with a focus on the historical context and the external conflicts which plunged the central characters into life-threatening situations and forced them to fight for survival on their own. Students identify and compare antagonists in the form of natural forces and physical deprivation, which are compounded by threats from the police or military or other authorities representing the power structure during wartime. They identify and compare the relationships between the author and his/her story. Is it based on personal experience or on extensive research about the people and events portrayed in the story? Is it a fictionalized biography of an actual individual or is it a narrative that weaves together the stories of many individuals whose lives are shaped by historical events? How does this relationship between the author, the story, and historical events affect reader response?

Central themes are given special attention in the comparative analyses. What do these novels say about the nature of human relationships? About human interdependence? The role of hope and the will to survive? The triumph of the human spirit in the midst of deprivation, degradation, pain, and death? This analysis of central themes in these historical novels provides the starting point for a discussion of the differences between survival tales of victims of revolution and war and survival of characters in the second novel selected for independent reading: The sudden loss of childhood experienced by victims of war versus the transition from childhood to adulthood in the "rites of passage" experiences of contemporary characters; physical and/or psychological scars carried by the survivors in these novels; and the differences related to the insights and wisdom and knowledge acquired by these survivors.

These comparative analyses are a significant part of the literary study in each dialogue group and serve as preparation for the sharing-comparing sessions in which the survival tales in all four categories are discussed by the whole class in the final sessions of this Focus Unit..

Abandonment, Neglect, and Overwhelming Responsibility

The nature of the characters' survival in the group of novels studied in this dialogue group is, for the most part, significantly different from the survival experiences featured in the novels listed in the three other categories. Their focus is more on the struggle for emotional survival than on the challenges of physical survival. However, there are a number of stories in which coping with abandonment is compounded by the struggle for physical survival and/or overwhelming responsibility.

The discussion in this dialogue group might well begin with *The Crossing,* because the situation of the central character is the most desperate and life-threatening. Abandoned at birth, Manny has no memories of a mother or a home. On the streets of Juárez, Mexico, every waking hour is spent fighting for survival. In Juárez, Manny knows there is no safety net for him.

The characters in *Homecoming* and *Monkey Island* have also been abandoned and struggle to find food and shelter. But there is a safety net for them. They have memories of parents and a home, and they carry a dream of finding a home and family where they will belong. Clay, in *Monkey Island,* dreams of a reunion with his parents; the Tillerman children, in *Homecoming,* dream of finding relatives who will give them a home and love. In America there is an official safety net created by the social service network for helping homeless and abandoned children. Clay and the Tillermans choose not to make use of these services. The determination to keep the abandonment a secret is an important factor that drives the plot in a number of the novels in this category and is a significant focus for discussion in the dialogue group. Such a discussion requires students to try to understand the thinking process, the fears, and the dreams of these characters as they make the decision to avoid the "authorities." Students can explore the reasons behind the decision and the consequences, as well as the alternative choices available and the possible consequences. The questions listed under "Reader Response" [13] can be used to guide this discussion about novels such as *Monkey Island; Homecoming; Where the Lilies Bloom* (Cleaver, 1969); *Afternoon of the Elves* (Lisle, 1989); *Daphne's Book* (Hahn, 1983); *Mama, Let's Dance* (Hermes, 1991); *Kumquat May, I'll Always Love You* (Grant, 1986); *The Bears' House* (Sachs, 1971); *Cave Under the City,* (Mazer, 1986); and *Randall's Wall* (Fenner, 1991).

The central characters in the novels in this category respond in different ways to abandonment. Generally, each character is troubled with conflicting emotions. In *Homecoming.* Dicey is angry because her mother has left her with the enormous responsibility of taking care of her siblings. At the same time she feels a fierce determination to find them a home.

At one point during their long journey, Dicey is overwhelmed with a sense of despair. It is at this low point in their journey that Dicey begins to grasp what happened to her mother: "Was this how Momma felt? Was this why Momma ran away? Because she couldn't think of anything more to do and couldn't stand any more to try to take care of her children?" (p. 80). But Dicey has more emotional strength and resourcefulness than her mother had and is able to pull herself out of her despair to think of solutions to their problems.

In *Monkey Island*, Clay reaches a similar insight about his parents' desertion: "Ma has said his father couldn't bear it. Now she had gone. Had she too not been able to bear it? It was because everything had fallen away — Daddy, the apartment, things like a television set, a refrigerator, a telephone, a place of one's own, a private place among millions of people" (p. 49).

In *Mama, Let's Dance* (Hermes, 1991), as in the two previous titles, a woman is abandoned by her husband, and unable — either financially or emotionally — to care for her three children on her own, she eventually abandons them. Eleven-year-old Mary Belle is left in charge of the household and seven-year-old Callie; sixteen-year-old Ariel is the breadwinner. They survive on their own, keeping their situation a secret so the authorities will not separate them and send them to foster homes. This is Mary Belle's story. Her night dreams are filled with longing for her mother. "But that was only in my night dreams. In my day dreams, I pictured her dead" (p. 4). Mary Belle struggles with the overwhelming responsibilities thrust upon her — taking care of her younger sister, the shopping, the meals, the laundry, the accounts. She has to put her own interests and needs on hold.

Livvy was fifteen years old when her mother wandered off, leaving her alone in the big family house, in the novel *Kumquat May, I'll Always Love You* (Grant, 1986). When the story opens, Livvy has been alone for two years, waiting for her mother's return. Livvy has decided to keep her situation a secret so that her mother will not get into trouble with the law for abandoning her child and so that she, Livvy, will not be forced to live with relatives she abhors. Deep down, Livvy feels that her mother did love her only daughter (p. 9). She looks at the heart necklace sent by her mother "...a fragile, shining chain connecting Mother and me" (p. 77). Then these thoughts take over: "A door closed deep inside me. Lost in my heart, a tiny child was weeping" (p. 77).

Afternoon of the Elves (Lisle, 1989) is the story of nine-year-old Hillary and eleven-year-old Sara Kate, a social outcast who lives behind Hillary in a dilapidated house. Sara Kate lives alone with her mother, who is mentally ill. She nurses her invalid mother and assumes responsibility for all household matters, struggling to survive even when there are no checks from her absent father. This part of her life she keeps hidden. Sara Kate manages to escape into a fantasy world she has created in her backyard, a miniature elf village. When she draws Hillary into the magic of this tiny village, they "put together a sort of friendship" (p. 32). Sara Kate uses the elves to tell Hillary about herself, who she really is. But she does not reveal her other life, her life in the house.

This story is told from Hillary's viewpoint; the reader learns about Sara Kate through Hillary. But there is much that Hillary doesn't know about Sara Kate, who so fiercely defends the secrecy of her private life inside the house. Probably the most powerful and poignant moment in the narrative is when Hillary violates this privacy and enters the house out of concern for her friend. Hillary catches a glimpse of Sara Kate sitting in a rocking chair holding her mother. This unforgettable picture tells the reader more about Sara Kate's other life than a thousand words possibly could.

The Bears' House (Sachs, 1971) is about nine-year-old Fran Ellen who lives with her four siblings and their emotionally disturbed mother in a small apartment. They tell lies to the social worker so they will not be placed in foster care. Fran Ellen escapes the frightening and confusing reality of her life by withdrawing into a fantasy world, a doll house inhabited by the Bear family.

Twelve-year-old Daphne, in *Daphne's Book* (Hahn, 1983), is another social outcast. She takes care of her younger sister, Hope, and their grandmother, who has Alzheimer's disease. Their parents are dead, and their grandmother is not well enough to assume responsibility for them. They are often without food or electricity, but Daphne refuses to reveal their plight for fear they will be sent to an orphanage. When Daphne's English teacher assigns partners to work on the seventh grade Write-a-book contest, Daphne is paired with Jessica. Jessica and Daphne become reluctant partners and eventually friends as they work together on the book — collaborating as author and artist — and entering into the magic of the miniature world they are creating for their book. Their story is told from the viewpoint of Jessica and, as in *Afternoon of the Elves,* the reader learns about Daphne through her relationship with Jessica.

Randall's Wall (Fenner, 1990) is the story of another social outcast whose father is absent most of the time and whose mother is too physically and emotionally ill to care for her children. They have no running water, and it is nearly impossible to keep themselves and their clothes clean. Randall's peers will not go near him. To defend himself against the cruel reality of his life, Randall builds an invisible wall around himself so that he can withdraw into his dreams. By the end of the book, Randall's plight is revealed, and he and his family are given the help they need. The safety net is in place.

In *Patchwork Summer* (Holl, 1987), thirteen-year-old Randi McBride is in charge of running the household and caring for her five-year-old sister Meggie. Her mother had run away a year ago "to find herself" and to become a writer. Her father is too preoccupied with his own concerns to care for or about his children. Randi manages to assume the role of housekeeper and to be a real mother to Meggie, who is shattered by her mother's abandonment. Randi seethes with bitter feelings and resentment, and is determined to do such a good job in her mother's place that she will prove that her mother is not needed.

When her mother suddenly returns a year later and acts as if nothing had happened, Randi is filled with rage that her mother is so unaware of and indifferent to the pain she had caused her husband and children. Later, Randi reaches beyond her resentment to try to understand her mother's perspective. She sees that both her grandmother and her father have never seen her mother as a person in her own right, and they have refused to take her writing seriously. However, the mother's words in the final scene — "I knew my leaving would be a shock at first, but I didn't think it would hurt that much" (p. 112) —

prompted one reader to comment: "I can't believe she said that! She's not really a believable character, and the ending doesn't even seem real."

The Two-Thousand-Pound Goldfish (Byars, 1982) is told from the viewpoint of eight-year-old Warren, whose mother left when he was five. She had always been deeply involved in political movements, but when she moved from peaceful to violent protests, she had to leave home. She was wanted by the FBI. Living with his grandmother and Weezie, his older sister, Warren longs for his mother. He carries an idealized image of her and the dream that she will return. His sister tries to get him to face the truth about their mother, a woman who was more interested in her own life than in her children. But he wants so desperately to have a mother who loves him that he refuses to accept the picture Weezie portrays.

Toward the end of the novel, Warren, like Journey, is able to move beyond this denial to confront the harsh reality that his mother would never be a part of his life. This is the turning point for Warren, as it was for Journey. He emerges from his day dreams to get on with his life. "I will not waste family and friends, he said to himself — they are hard to come by" (p. 149).

In a number of novels studied in this dialogue group, the mother walks away from her infant, letting others care for her child.

Midnight Hour Encores (Brooks, 1986) is a first-person narrative written by the protagonist, Sibilance T. Spooner, who was abandoned by her mother on the day of her birth. It is her father who nurtures her and gives her the love and support she needs to become a self-sufficient individual. Sib is sixteen years old when she asks, for the first time, to meet her mother. On their journey from Washington, D.C. to San Francisco for this encounter, her father tries to re-create for her what it was like in the Sixties, what her mother was like, and the details about her own history as a child growing up with her father. He wants her to try to understand her mother's abandonment. At the end of the narrative, Sib is confronted with a choice — to live with her mother or to stay with her father. Her final decision, revealed in the dramatic conclusion of this novel, reflects the insight she has gained during the journey to San Francisco.

Yesterday's Daughter (Calvert, 1986) also begins when the protagonist is sixteen years old and about to meet her mother for the first time. Leenie O'Brien was deserted by her mother when she was an infant and left with her grandparents. Leenie is filled with anger and resentment, and does not want to let her mother into her life. However, she eventually learns to feel compassion for her mother, who was only seventeen years old when she gave birth to Leenie.

Julie's Daughter (Rodowsky, 1985) is the story of Slug October, who was only three weeks old when her mother, Julie, left her in a red wagon at the bus depot and disappeared. Since then, she has lived with her grandmother, Gussie, but has always dreamed of the day her mother would return. Now, Slug is seventeen years old and meets her mother for the first time at Gussie's funeral. The story is told in three voices, in chapters alternating between three viewpoints and three generations: Slug's, Julie's, and that of an elderly neighbor.

In *Baby* (MacLachlan, 1993), Sophie is almost a year old when her mother leaves her in a basket at the island home of twelve-year-old Larkin and her family at the end of the tourist season. Unlike the other novels studied in this dialogue group, this story is told from the viewpoint of the people who take

Sophie into their lives and hearts, knowing that some day her real mother will return for her child and they will have to cope with the loss.

Fish Friday (Pearson, 1986) is the story of fourteen-year-old Jamie and her younger brother, Inky, whose mother has left her children and husband to study art in New York City. Jamie struggles to cope with her mother's desertion and the new responsibilities she must assume. Unlike some of the other stories about mothers abandoning their families for selfish reasons, Jamie's mother does not return to her husband and children by the end of this novel.

This is also the case in *The Girl* (Branscum, 1986), probably the most powerful and disturbing of all the novels in this category. When their father dies, five young children are taken by their mother to their grandparents' poor sharecropper's farm in Arkansas. The grandparents agree to keep the children because of the welfare checks they bring in and because eventually the three older children do most of the backbreaking work on the farm. Grandma is physically and psychologically abusive — especially toward the girl, who is never named. Uncle Les, Grandma's favorite child, who uses most of the welfare payments meant for the children, is an additional threat; he abuses the girl sexually. The children support and comfort each other as they struggle to survive in this hostile, oppressive environment and dream of the day their mother will come and take them away.

This story of almost unrelieved hardship and tension is told from the viewpoints of the three older children: the girl, who is eleven years old; Lee, who is twelve; and Gene, who is fourteen. Gene had promised his Daddy that he would take care of the others, and he has kept this promise all during the seven years since their mother abandoned them.

This novel is primarily a portrait of the girl, who talks only to her siblings and who lives in a secret world inside herself. The secret that is central to her inner life is that she can read and reads everything she can find.

When a letter finally comes from their mother, the children are filled with hope. But when she arrives at the farm, she only stays for a few hours. She leaves without them. "They stood in the yard watching the blue car turn around and head down the narrow dirt road. Suddenly the girl seemed to explode. She broke from the others running, running after the car.... She ran, but mother never looked back" (p. 113). The book closes as she is held and comforted by her siblings.

A discussion of this story can begin with speculation about the author's reason for omitting the girl's name throughout the novel. This sets the stage for an analysis of "the girl" as the central character and the literary techniques used by the author to produce this portrait of a young girl who is abandoned by her mother and forced to live in a hostile environment where she must struggle to stand up to those who try to crush her spirit.

The stark realism of this novel forces readers to confront the issue of abandonment in contemporary society, the fact that adults may choose to abdicate their traditional roles as protectors and nurturers of children. Stories of abandoned, abused, and neglected children appear in the newspaper regularly, but students who have entered into the world of *The Girl* can read these brief articles with a new perspective and understanding.

The comparative analysis of this group of novels featuring abandonment, neglect, and overwhelming responsibility begins with a focus on the ways different protagonists respond to their situations and the types of coping mechanisms they use to handle their pain. Some protagonists respond to abandonment with anger and resentment; others respond with denial and the creation of an ideal image of the absent parent. For some protagonists, the emotional journey involves learning to let go of anger and resentment and gaining enough insight and understanding to accept the parent as an individual in order to get on with their lives. For others, the emotional journey means developing the inner strength to confront the truth about the absent parent and the reality of their own lives.

Another pattern found in this group of novels is the coping mechanism with which protagonists escape from the harsh reality and pain of their lives into a fantasy world. For some, this fantasy life contributes to their psychological survival. Often, the fantasy life has a temporary value and then becomes an obstacle to emotional growth.

Another pattern emerges in stories in which the traditional family no longer exists: the children create new family units which provide mutual support and love. These units are often built around a moral code and expectations of cooperation and loyalty. Generally these stories are about physical as well as psychological survival. Children without adults must find the strength and inner resources to cope with the challenges of survival as they take responsibility for their own lives. Some children choose independence over rescue by outsiders; some avoid authorities who might split up their family unit.

In most of the novels in this category, the theme of hope is developed as a central factor in survival. These novels offer portraits of human resilience and eloquent examples of the triumph of the human spirit in the midst of hardship and loss.

Independent Writing: Character Portraits

Time for the dialogue group meetings is built into the class schedule. Students are also given time during the school day for writing in their journals and reading the two assigned novels. Some of this independent reading and writing can be completed as part of their homework.

For a final writing assignment, the students are asked to produce three character portraits: one portrait will feature a protagonist in one of the novels they have selected for independent reading; one portrait will feature an antagonist; the third portrait features a support character. Each portrait will reveal the character through a careful analysis guided by the questions used throughout this literature unit. Whenever explicit information is not available in the text, implicit information can be used in the analysis as long as textual evidence is included to support these inferences. For example, a character's inner thoughts, motives, goals, and feelings can be inferred from behavior described in the text. Students can incorporate personal opinions, reactions, assumptions, and beliefs in their analyses if they identify these as subjective statements. Students who write about the same character are given an opportunity to share their finished portraits with each other. Those who enjoy artistic expression are invited to create visual portraits to complement their verbal portraits.

This writing project serves to reinforce what has been learned about literary analysis in the process of studying this group of novels. This project also provides the teacher with a way to evaluate each student in terms of the quality of his/her understanding of character development in realistic novels.

Synthesis

During the final sessions of this Focus Unit, the whole class comes together to share and compare the novels selected for independent reading. A scribe from each dialogue group is invited to review the central themes, patterns, insights, and discoveries which emerged from the comparative analysis of the novels studied in his/her group. Graphic representations such as charts or diagrams can be used to illuminate these presentations. These reports from the dialogue groups, combined with a brief review of the earlier discussion of *Journey*, set the stage for the concluding discussion of this collection as a whole. To contribute to this discussion, each student can draw from his/her first-hand experience with three novels, as well as from a knowledge of a number of the other novels shared by classmates. The goal is to find connections between novels in different categories and to create a synthesis out of the diverse literary selections studied in this Focus Unit experience. That is, students search for fundamental truths about human nature and the human experience which can be found within these stories of survival and children on their own.

Bibliography: On Their Own

Baillie, Allan.(1992). *Adrift*. New York: Viking.

Branscum, Robbie. (1986). *The Girl*. New York: Harper and Row.

Brooks, Bruce. (1986). *Midnight Hour Encores*. New York: Harper and Row.

Byars, Betsy. (1980). *The Night Swimmers*. New York: Delacorte Press.

Byars, Betsy. (1982). *The Two-Thousand-Pound Goldfish*. New York: Scholastic, Inc.

Calvert, Patricia. (1986). *Yesterday's Daughter*. New York: Charles Scribner's Sons.

Cleaver, Vera, and Bill Cleaver. (1969). *Where the Lilies Bloom*. Philadelphia: PA: J.B. Lippincott.

Conlon-McKenna, Marita. (1992). *Wildflower Girl*. New York: Holiday House.

Fenner, Carol. (1991). *Randall's Wall*. New York: McElderry.

Fife, Dale. (1978). *North of Danger*. New York: E.P. Dutton.

Fox, Paula. (1991). *Monkey Island*. New York: Orchard Books.

George, Jean. (1972). *Julie of the Wolves*. New York: Harper and Row.

George, Jean. (1959). *My Side of the Mountain*. New York: E.P. Dutton.

Grant, Cynthia D. (1986). *Kumquat May, I'll Always Love You*. New York: Atheneum.

Hahn, Mary Downing. (1983). *Daphne's Book*. New York: Clarion Books.

Hamilton, Virginia. (1971). *The Planet of Junior Brown*. New York: Macmillan.

Hartling, Peter. (1986, 1988). *Crutches*. New York: Lothrop, Lee & Shepard.

Haugaard, Erik. (1967, 1986). *The Little Fishes*. Boston: Houghton Mifflin.

Hermes, Patricia. (1991). *Mama Let's Dance*. Boston: Little, Brown.

Holl, Kristi D. (1987). *Patchwork Summer*. New York: Atheneum.

Holm, Anne. (1965, 1963). *North to Freedom*. San Diego, CA: Harcourt Brace Jovanovich.

Holman, Felice. (1986, 1974). *Slake's Limbo*. New York: Charles Scribner's Sons.

Holman, Felice. (1983). *The Wild Children*. New York: Charles Scribner's Sons.

Konigsburg, E.L. (1967). *From the Mixed-up Files of Mrs. Basil E. Frankweiler*. New York: Atheneum.

Lisle, Janet. (1989). *Afternoon of the Elves*. New York: Orchard/Watts.

MacLachlan, Patricia. (1991). *Journey*. New York: Delacorte.

MacLachlan, Patricia. (1993). *Baby*. New York: Delacorte.

Mazer, Harry. (1986). *Cave Under the City*. New York: Thomas Crowell.

Mazer, Harry. (1981). *The Island Keeper*. New York: Delacorte Press.

Mazer, Harry. (1973). *Snowbound: A Story of Raw Survival*. New York: Delacorte Press.

Nelson, Theresa. (1992). *The Beggars' Ride*. New York: Orchard Books.

O'Dell, Scott. (1960). *Island of the Blue Dolphins*. Boston: Houghton Mifflin.

O'Dell, Scott. (1980). *Sarah Bishop*. Boston: Houghton Mifflin.

Orlev, Uri. (1984). *The Island on Bird Street*. Boston: Houghton Mifflin.

Paterson, Katherine. (1991). *Lyddie*. New York: Lodestar (Dutton).

Paulsen, Gary. (1987). *The Crossing*. New York: Dell.

Paulsen, Gary. (1987). *Hatchet*. New York: Bradbury Press.

Pearson, Gayle. (1986). *Fish Friday*. New York: Macmillan.

Rodowsky, Colby. (1985). *Julie's Daughter*. New York: Farrar, Straus & Giroux.

Sachs, Marilyn. (1990). *At the Sound of the Beep*. New York: Dutton.

Sachs, Marilyn. (1987, 1971). *The Bears' House*. New York: Dutton.

Serraillier, Ian. (1959). *Escape from Warsaw (The Silver Sword)*. New York: Scholastic, Inc.

Southall, Ivan. (1965). *Ash Road*. New York: Greenwillow Books.

Southall, Ivan. (1962). *Hill's End*. New York: Macmillan.

Southall, Ivan. (1967). *To the Wild Sky*. St. Martin's Press.

Taylor, Theodore. (1993). *Timothy of the Cay*. San Diego, CA: Harcourt Brace.

Taylor, Theodore. (1969). *The Cay*. New York: Doubleday.

Voigt, Cynthia. (1981). *Homecoming*. New York: Atheneum.

Walsh, Jill Paton. (1969). *Fireweed*. New York: Farrar, Straus & Giroux.

9

BETWEEN TWO WORLDS

Many students in our nation's schools are caught between two worlds. Children who are immigrants or children of immigrants know what it means to be caught between the mainstream culture and their own ethnic culture. They face a common dilemma: how to assimilate into the mainstream culture while maintaining their ethnic identity. The focus of this chapter is on contemporary and historical fiction and biographical and autobiographical accounts of young people whose racial and cultural heritage places them outside the mainstream of society. For middle grade students who see themselves reflected in these stories, this Focus Unit has the potential for building self-esteem and self-knowledge. For their peers who are part of the mainstream culture, this unit has the potential to expand their perspective and their understanding of the traditions, values, life styles, and histories of diverse ethnic groups. A central goal of this unit is to offer literary experiences that will serve as a context for addressing issues of acculturation, loss of identity, and separation from one's roots, as well as the costs of prejudice, discrimination, and ethnic illiteracy to members of our multicultural society.

The books selected for this Focus Unit portray real people instead of stereotypes. They tell their own stories, and middle-grade readers are invited to walk in their shoes, to view the world through their eyes. Readers will have opportunities to enter into the lives of individuals whose experiences and heritage are unlike their own.

Like the other Focus Units presented in this book, this one focusses on craft as well as content. Students' experiences with the fiction and non-fiction selected for this unit include opportunities to examine literary elements and techniques used by writers to tell the stories of individuals who are caught between two worlds.

Introducing the Focus Unit

The teacher introduces the unit, "Between Two Worlds," by calling attention to the collection of books on display in the classroom and holding up several specific titles to generate discussion:

Between Two Worlds: A Story About Pearl Buck, by Barbara Mitchell
In the Year of the Boar and Jackie Robinson, by Bette Bao Lord
Kim/Kimi, by Hadley Irwin
Thank You, Dr. Martin Luther King, Jr!, by Eleanora Tate
Zeely, by Virginia Hamilton

Students are asked to examine the titles and covers of each of these books to find clues about their content and a common theme. Those familiar with Pearl Buck as an American writer who had been brought up in China will recognize that the two worlds mentioned in the title of this biography are China and America. An examination of the covers of *Zeely* and *Thank You, Dr. Martin Luther King, Jr!* reveals that behind the African-American children are two women who appear to reflect their African heritage. These cover illustrations suggest that these novels are also about two worlds. The two forms of the name used for the title, *Kim/Kimi,* suggest that this will be another story of two worlds. Many students are familiar with the book, *In the Year of the Boar and Jackie Robinson,* and can explain that this is the story of a Chinese girl who comes to America. Again, the title reflects these two worlds.

After sharing their thoughts about the possible content and themes of these five books, students are asked to respond to these two questions:

1.   **What do you think is meant by the phrase, "between two worlds"?**
2.   **What kinds of conflicts or problems could drive the plots in each of the novels?**

Responses to the second question are recorded on a chart near the collection of books selected for this unit. As the books are read aloud or independently during the course of the Focus Unit experience, this chart is consulted to confirm or revise these predictions about possible conflicts. Other conflicts identified during the course of reading the fiction and non-fiction in the Focus Unit collection are added to this list.

Connecting Autobiography and Fiction

The Star Fisher, by Laurence Yep (1991), is selected as the first book to be read aloud to the class in a series of shared reading sessions. Students are asked to choose from the collection another book by Laurence Yep to read independently, in addition to the one being read aloud. Thus, they can choose to read his autobiography, *The Lost Garden* (1991), or one of his realistic novels: *Dragonwings* (1975); *Child of the Owl* (1977); or *Sea Glass* (1979). Students are also invited to read some of the tales included in Yep's two collections of folklore, *The Rainbow People* (1989) and *Tongues of Jade* (1991), or the stories and poems in *American Dragons:*

Twenty-five Asian-American Voices (Yep, 1993), or the illustrated edition of the Chinese folktale, *The Shell Woman and the King,* retold by Yep (1993). Students are expected to record in their literary journals a summary and analysis of the book they've selected to read independently, as well as connections between this book and *The Star Fisher.*

A list of questions is posted near the Focus Unit collection. The teacher introduces several questions during the shared reading sessions and invites students to develop additional questions as they engage in oral and written response to shared and self-selected texts during the course of the Focus Unit experience. Thus, the list expands as teachers and students collaborate in an ongoing process of literary response, analysis, reflection, interpretation, and comparing and contrasting diverse texts. Meanings, insights, and connections generated through this collaborative effort are translated into questions and recorded on the list.

The list below is made up of a series of key questions (in bold italic) and several related questions which are added by students during the course of the Focus Unit experience to extend or elaborate these key questions. The list of questions is used as a source of suggestions for studying single texts in terms of craft and content and for exploring connections between two or more texts and between readers and texts. Both teacher and students draw from this list to generate oral dialogue in small and large groups and written responses in literary journals and for more formal writing assignments during this unit.

The Questions

1. *What is the genre of this book?* How does the genre influence your response as a reader? What is the relationship between the author and the events? Find connections between a biography or autobiography of an author and his/her fiction. Identify a novel which is based on the author's personal experience or on family stories. How does an awareness of these connections shape your experience as a reader of this novel?

2. *What external conflicts drive the plot?* How do factors such as racial tension, prejudice, discrimination, language barriers, and poverty shape the experience of the central characters and affect their self-esteem, behavior, and interpersonal relationships?

3. *What internal conflicts are central to character development and growth?* Find scenes in the text which reveal the inner struggles of the central characters. How do they attempt to resolve their inner conflicts? What are the connections between the external and internal conflicts?

4. *Find evidence in the text of conflicts between the majority culture and the cultural heritage of the central characters.* How do the characters respond to these conflicts? To what extent do the characters assimilate into the mainstream culture? To what extent do they maintain or lose their cultural identity? Which characters are able to resolve this conflict? What is the nature of their

struggle for personal balance? Identify characters who discover or regain a lost cultural identity. Use evidence from the texts to support your responses.

5. *Discuss the problems and conflicts associated with "living between two worlds."* Identify the types of issues or problems confronted by recent immigrants to America and those faced by American-born children of immigrants. Discuss the tensions between generations resulting from differences in perspectives, experiences, attitudes, memories, and dreams.

6. *How does the author reveal emotional and social growth in the central characters?* What are significant turning points in their growth? Find evidence in the texts of growth of self-esteem and self-confidence and strengthening of cultural identity.

7. *Find evidence in the text which supports the notion that cultural heritage is a significant problem for some characters and a source of pride for others.*

8. *What is the role of folklore in plot, character, and theme development?*

9. *Identify characters who support, guide, inspire, or protect the protagonist.* What role do these individuals play in the development of character and plot? What is the role of family and/or community in the development of the protagonist?

10. *Identify antagonists.* Discuss their role in the development of character and plot.

11. *Identify stereotypes used to define individual characters.* What is the role of stereotypes in shaping the self-concepts, behavior, and interpersonal relationships of the central characters? Find evidence in the texts which reflects the use of stereotypes against the white majority as well as against ethnic or racial minorities. Discuss the types of barriers which are created by the use of stereotypes.

12. *What techniques are used by writers of fiction to address the issue of stereotypes?* Find evidence in a text that suggests the author is using the novel to attempt to change attitudes and beliefs which form the basis of stereotypes.

13. *Find connections between past events as portrayed in historical fiction and current events.* What significant social, political, and legal changes have occurred since the historical period presented in a given historical novel? What problems and conflicts continue to be an integral part of contemporary society?

14. *Compare two or more novels selected for this Focus Unit.* Find connections between problems and conflicts of central characters. Explore the role of setting in the development of plot and character in these novels. Compare them in terms of genre and the author's relationship to the fictional people and events. Look for

thematic connections. What significant truths about the human experience in general and the challenges of acculturation, in particular, are explored in these novels?

15. *Examine the title and cover illustration of each book in the collection.* What new meanings or interpretations do you discover as you re-examine covers of books you have already read and analyzed? Drawing from your experience with these books, what can you say about books in the collection you have not read?

16. *What connections can you find between the experiences, challenges, and conflicts in the lives of the fictional characters you have met in these novels and experiences, challenges, and conflicts in your own life?* Can you identify with any of the central characters in terms of feelings of isolation, being left out or rejected? Feelings of being misunderstood or treated unfairly? Feelings of longing to be accepted, to belong, to fit in, to be like everyone else? Feelings of confusion and insecurity in new situations in which you do not know appropriate behavior or dress? Discuss your personal connections with these characters.

The Shared Reading Experience: *The Star Fisher*

According to the "Author's Preface," this novel is based on Laurence Yep's own family history, beginning with his grandmother who reached America at the age of sixteen and who later journeyed with her husband and three children (including the author's mother, Joan) to Clarksburg, West Virginia. *The Star Fisher* is the story of fifteen-year-old Joan Lee who moves with her family from Ohio to West Virginia in 1927. They hope to set up a laundry business in Clarksburg and to build a better life for themselves. However, the Lees are the first Chinese-Americans to settle in Clarksburg, and they are confronted with insults and isolation from the moment they arrive. Although Joan's parents speak only Chinese, she and her brother and sister were born in America and speak English.

A scene on the second page of the novel reveals the tension often experienced between immigrant parents and their American-born children: ten-year-old Bobby asks a question in English and his mother responds in Chinese, "Speak in your own language" (p. 4). Joan, the narrator, translates for her mother "...the way I usually did." Bobby answers in Chinese, "Mama, people stare when we use Chinese." "Let them stare," Mama said. "I don't want you to forget your Chinese." This scene is an example of the textual evidence which can be used to support responses to question 5. This scene reflects the mother's need to maintain her Chinese identity and the need of the American-born children to assimilate into the mainstream culture. This scene also reveals another common pattern found in immigrant families: the children serve as translators for their parents. This can be an unwanted burden for the children as well as for parents who find it difficult to be forced to depend on their children for help in all social interactions with members of the majority culture.

The nature of the external conflict that drives the plot is foreshadowed in the first chapter [see question 2]. The first verbal attack comes from a man in old coveralls who stares at the Lee family as they arrive on the railroad platform in Clarksburg. "'Darn monkeys,' he said, staring at us" (p. 7). At the end of this first chapter, the narrator reveals her initial response to the social climate they encounter in Clarksburg: "As people passed in the street, they stared at us but did not say anything. More and more, I began to feel as if that man on the platform had been right: in this town, we were like monkeys in a zoo" (p. 12).

The man on the platform proves to be the antagonist as the story unfolds [see question 10]. In the third chapter, he paints the words "GO HOOM" on the Lee's white fence (pp. 32-33).

In the second chapter another important character is introduced. Miss Lucy is the owner of the building the Lees rent for their business and their home. She plays a key role in their acculturation, and she supports and protects them against racial hostility and discrimination [see question 9]. Miss Lucy is an old and respected citizen of Clarksburg, but she is more generous and open-minded than most of the residents. During the Civil War she had stood up against slavery and now she is standing up against racism. She helps to break down the barriers between the white community and the Lee family. Miss Lucy represents the enlightened and generous side of human nature whereas Sidney, the antagonist, represents the mean-spirited, dark side of human nature.

In this second chapter, Miss Lucy invites Joan and her younger sister, Emily, to tea. Joan had learned about this American custom from the novels she read, but she had never been to a tea. In this unfamiliar setting, Joan shares what it is like to be between two worlds:

> Even though we had been born here and could name all the presidents and the capitals of the states, there were so many little things that we didn't know — like place settings. In some ways, we were often like actors who were thrust on stage without a script, so that we had to improvise. And too often, up in Ohio, our ignorance had gotten us laughed at; and no one likes to feel like a fool (p. 19).

This scene offers the reader a new perspective about the daily crises faced by those who live between two worlds [see question 5]. The reader begins to understand that almost every social situation represents a challenge for those struggling to discover appropriate behaviors and to avoid humiliation.

In the third chapter, Miss Lucy, a former teacher, offers to teach Mrs. Lee how to cook. Although the offer is well-meant, Mr. Lee is insulted. "No.... If anyone will teach my family, it will be me. I'm the teacher" (p. 28). In China, Mr. Lee was a scholar; he has a very definite idea of what a teacher should be, based on "four thousand years of tradition and learning" (p. 30). Mr. Lee reveals the conflict between this Western culture and his own: "The idea of that woman calling herself a teacher! What does she know? How can you write great poetry, great novels, great thoughts in that gobble-gobble talk of the Americans?" (p. 30). Mrs. Lee responds with suspicion to this offer from a stranger. Only in a later chapter does she explain to Miss Lucy that in China, only someone in one's family would offer to help another person (p. 102). The tensions and conflicts caused by deep differences in cultural traditions are brought to the surface by

Miss Lucy's neighborly offer and provide the reader with some insight into the barriers to communication that reach beyond language barriers [see question 4].

In Chapter Four, Joan comforts her younger sister with a traditional Chinese folktale about the star fisher that becomes incorporated into the structure of the novel [see question 8]. "The Star Fisher" is a transformation tale in which a farmer discovers three young women wearing cloaks of golden feathers. When they remove their cloaks to dance in the moonlight, the farmer steals one of the cloaks, thus preventing one of the women from changing into a golden king-fisher, as her sisters are able to do the moment they put on their cloaks and raise their arms. The farmer hides the woman's cloak and pressures her to marry him. She no longer sings or dances; she searches for her cloak. A daughter is born. One evening, her mother's sisters appear and drop a golden feather on the child's arm, marking her with a drop of blood as one of them. Although her father is delighted with his daughter, the villagers avoid her. "'I don't belong here,' she had once complained to her mother. 'Neither of us does,' her mother had sighed" (p. 44). At the end of the tale, she finds the magical cloak and is able to return to the night sky with her daughter. Both of them are golden kingfishers "…swimming through the night and gathering the glittering stars" (p. 41).

Throughout the novel, Joan uses this folktale as a metaphor for her own experience and her mother's. In Chapter Six, she faces racial hostility at school and is diminished by the experience: "I sat down by myself, feeling ugly and stupid and lonely" (p. 60). Feeling cut off from the others, she thinks of the story: "I suppose when the star fisher's daughter had gone for a walk in their village, the neighbors had smirked in just the same way. Moving through the hallways, I felt as if I were marked by a drop of blood from a falling feather" (p. 63). At another point in this chapter, Joan identifies with the star fisher's daughter as one caught between two worlds. Both are treated as aliens in the land where they were born; both know very little about the land of their parents (p. 64).

In Chapter Seven, tension in the Lee family builds as they confront the possibility that their business might fail. When Joan asks why there are no customers, her mother answers, "The people walk by as if we're invisible. Or they just point and laugh" (p. 71). Joan had the same experience at school: "No one acknowledged my existence as I made my way to the principal's office" (p. 54). The stress caused by these daily humiliations, the isolation, and the threat of financial failure strains the relationship between Joan and her mother. Mrs. Lee takes out her own frustration and fear on her elder daughter. In response, Joan feels anger toward her mother and anger at herself for these negative feelings about her mother. This internal conflict is a product of the external conflict [see question 3].

Bernice is a significant character who is introduced in Chapter Six. She is the only girl to reach out to Joan on her first day at school. Bernice, too, is a social isolate even though she had lived in this town for ten years. In Chapter Nine, Joan discovers the reason that Bernice is shunned by her classmates; she is shocked to learn that Bernice's family is in the theater. "Theater people were…well…not very respectable either in China or in America" (p. 89). But Joan is able to transcend her own prejudice because she sees Bernice as an individual. By getting to know Bernice, Joan is able to replace an old stereotype with a new perspective and understanding. In fact, she realizes that Bernice, too, is of "star fisher stock" (p. 92).

This chapter explores the role of stereotypes and prejudice in shaping self-concepts, behavior, and experiences of central characters [see question 11]. At the end of the chapter, Joan reflects on what she has learned from her encounter with Bernice and her family:

> It's funny how there are levels and levels of prejudice in the world. The red-faced man hated us for being Chinese; but he would hate someone like Bernice as well for being the child of theatrical folks — just as Mama would herself (p. 94).

In Chapter Ten, Joan's mother tries to mend the break in their relationship. Mrs. Lee is finally able to admit her fear and shares with Joan some of her own history and how the revolution in China in 1911 had changed their lives forever. "And suddenly I realized that there wasn't another Chinese woman for probably a hundred miles or more. All Mama had was me and Emily, and we were half-alien to her. In her own way, Mama must have felt as cut off as the star fisher" (p. 99).

For the first time, Joan begins to look at her mother as an individual and to feel empathy for her. This is a significant step in her own growth and in building a more mature and understanding relationship with her mother [see question 6]. The insights she has gained from her encounter with Bernice and this experience with her mother enable Joan to try to help her mother form a friendship with Miss Lucy. "If I had learned one thing from my visit to Bernice, it was not to let a lot of silly prejudices blindfold you. It was important to meet with the person and not the notion" (p. 101).

Through his narrator, Laurence Yep makes important thematic statements about prejudice and stereotypes and the process of removing barriers between human beings [see question 12]. Yep invites his readers to learn about prejudice through Joan's experience as a victim as well as a witness. She shares with the reader what it feels like to be the target of racial attacks and social isolation. Joan also witnesses the prejudice against Bernice because she is the child of theater people. As witness, Joan has a new perspective and gains new insights about the nature and costs of prejudice. Toward the end of the book, the reader sees her move from insight to action as she attempts to use her new understanding to remove barriers for her mother and for Bernice.

Laurence Yep creates realistic and well-developed characters instead of stereotypes. Each member of the Lee family is presented as a unique individual with distinguishing characteristics. They are richly drawn as complex human beings with strengths and weaknesses, virtues and faults. The reader learns enough about the Lee family and about Bernice to understand how their personal histories have shaped their inner lives and their personalities. Novelists such as Laurence Yep play an important role in countering stereotypes of ethnic minorities through their realistic portraits of human beings who are members of an ethnic minority.

Through his narrator, Yep also makes a statement about the conflicts of acculturation addressed in question 4. At the end of the book Joan begins to understand what it means to be a Chinese-American and to assimilate to the mainstream culture without losing her own cultural identity: "We may talk and dress and act like Americans, but in our hearts we'll always be Chinese" (p. 146).

An examination of the title and cover illustration after the novel has been read yields more comprehension than the examination prior to reading it [see question 15]. The reader can understand why the author chose "The Star Fisher" as his title. This folktale is woven into the story Joan Lee tells about her family, and the star fisher serves as a symbol of the theme of acculturation or being caught between two worlds. The two girls portrayed on the cover are Joan and Bernice; both of these characters are of "star fisher stock." In the background of the cover illustration, one sees the school that the Lees have converted into a business and a home in their quest for a better life. The words painted on the neat white picket fence, "GO HOOM," provide a stark reminder of the prejudice against foreigners and the racial hostility which are deeply rooted in a community and can erupt as soon as a target appears. There is a special irony in these words since Joan is American-born. America is her home. The body language of the two girls suggests that Joan is reaching out to Bernice in friendship. It is Joan who struggles to understand the nature of prejudice in order to break down the barriers which prevent open encounters between human beings.

The Star Fisher is an historical novel that is based on the story of the author's family. Students are asked to identify details in the novel that provide an authentic picture of an historical period and how this historical context shapes the narrative [see question 1]. They are also invited to comment on how the knowledge of the author's relationship to the events in the novel affected their responses as readers.

Although the events described in this novel occurred in the past, and important social, political, and legal changes mark the years since 1927, human nature tends to remain relatively stable. Students are asked to identify some of these changes and evidence of progress since the historical period that is the setting for this novel. They are also asked to discuss problems that continue to be a challenge for contemporary society [see question 13]. This type of discussion is especially important and relevant because there are so many students in our nation's schools who are caught between two worlds and who have first-hand knowledge of immigration.

The Author and His Work:
Independent Reading and Dialogue Groups

While *The Star Fisher* is being read aloud and discussed in the shared reading sessions, the students are reading independently one of the other books by Laurence Yep included in the collection for this unit. In addition, they are expected to record in their literary journals a summary and analysis of this book and connections between it and *The Star Fisher*. Students who have selected the same title meet in dialogue groups to discuss the book and to collaborate on a report to the class about it. They select relevant questions from the list to help them organize their responses to the book and to write an analysis. Each group decides the format for this presentation.

After *The Star Fisher* is read aloud and discussed, the students who decided to read Yep's autobiography, *The Lost Garden* (1991), report to the class first in order to provide some background about Yep and set the stage for exploring the relationship between the author and his work. The first set of questions [see question 1] is especially relevant for an analysis of this book.

In *The Lost Garden*, Yep describes his experience growing up as a Chinese-American in San Francisco. He shares what it was like to be caught between two worlds. As a child, Yep was not proud of his ethnic heritage. He writes: "In my neighborhood I had grown up thinking that I was as American as all the other children. In the 1950s, few people wanted to be strange and different — let alone foreign" (p. 42). "I didn't want to be Chinese.... It took me years to realize that I was Chinese whether I wanted to be or not" (p. 43).

When his father bought a small grocery store outside of San Francisco, Yep had to leave his friends in Chinatown. In his new neighborhood he felt "like an outsider" as an Asian (p. 38). He also felt like an outsider in his own family. "Comparing myself to my athletic father, mother, and brother, I often felt like a changeling, wondering how I wound up being born into this family. I felt not only inadequate but incomplete" (p. 12).

Yep writes about his attempts to understand his own identity. He began to keep a file of stories about his family. It took him years to fully appreciate his grandmother's remarkable journey from China to Ohio to West Virginia to Chinatown. *The Star Fisher* tells the story of this courageous and strong woman, Marie Lee, who traveled to West Virginia with her husband and children to open up a laundry business.

His grandmother was also the source for a central character, Paw-Paw, in *Child of the Owl*. "When I finally decided to confront my own 'Chineseness,' I wanted to do so in the company of my grandmother — if only in my imagination. I began to write about a Chinese-American girl who has to live with her grandmother (Paw-Paw) in Chinatown. For the first time in her life, the girl has to confront being Chinese" (p. 110).

Other members of his family became characters in his novels: "My father, the kitemaker, became Windrider in *Dragonwings*" (p. 92). Yep's Uncle Francis was the source for the character of Uncle Quail in *Sea Glass*. The central character, Craig, is much like Yep himself. He draws from his own childhood experiences to create this character and the two worlds that shape his life. Like Craig, Yep had traveled between his own neighborhood and Chinatown.

In his search for his identity, Yep found that the Oz books helped him think about his own experience:

> In the Oz books, you usually have some child taken out of his or her every day world and taken to a new land where he or she must learn new customs and adjust to new people.... The children took in the situation and adapted.... They dealt with the real mysteries of life — like finding yourself and your place in the world. And that was something I tried to do every day I got on and off the bus (p. 77).

In *The Star Fisher*, Joan finds her own story to help her think about her identity as a Chinese-American and her between-world dilemma [see question 8].

After these students share with the class what they have learned about Laurence Yep from this autobiography, the students who have read and discussed *Dragonwings* share their analysis in a class meeting.

Dragonwings (1975) is an historical novel which portrays the Chinese community in San Francisco's Chinatown. The story is told through the eyes of a young boy, Moon Shadow, who sails from China to America in 1903 to join his father, Windrider, who lives in Chinatown and works in a laundry. For the Chinese immigrants who lived in the United States in the early part of the twentieth century, Chinatown provided a way to maintain their Chinese cultural heritage and offered protection against the racial hostility, discrimination, and violence of the "white demons."

When Moon Shadow moves out of Chinatown with his father in 1904 to live in the demon section in a house owned by a "demoness," he feels frightened and unprotected. Like the Lee family in *The Star Fisher* they are alone in an alien land. However, Moon Shadow and his father are not far from Chinatown, whereas in the case of Mrs. Lee there was not a single Chinese woman for a hundred miles.

The landlady in *Dragonwings* is Miss Whitlaw, who, like Miss Lucy in *The Star Fisher*, is an independent, open-minded woman, willing to accept Chinese tenants in spite of the rampant racial hostility against foreigners at that time. Like Miss Lucy, Miss Whitlaw offers support and protection, and she plays a significant role in the process of acculturation. The kitchen scene in which Moon Shadow is offered milk and cookies for the first time (pp. 102-104) has much in common with Joan and Emily Lee's first tea in Miss Lucy's kitchen in *The Star Fisher* [see questions 9 and 14].

Miss Whitlaw was the first demoness Moon Shadow had actually met. "I had expected her to be ten feet tall with blue skin and to have a face covered with warts and ear lobes that hung all the way down to her knees...." (p. 101). This stereotype of white women that he had built up reflects the reality that the creation of stereotypes is a two-way street. The Tang men used the derogatory term, "demon," to refer to any member of the white community [see question 11]. But Moon Shadow and his father have the opportunity to "meet the person [instead of] the notion," as Joan states in *The Star Fisher* on page 101. They are able to move beyond the prejudices and stereotypes which produce barriers between people and to come to know Miss Whitlaw as a wise and generous individual.

Like the story of "The Star Fisher," the story of Windrider's name and the Dragon King is woven into the novel [see question 8]. The story is the basis for his belief that in a former life he was a winged dragon who was given the name Windrider because "he was something of a show-off when it came to flying" (p. 38). The story is the source of his ambition to build and fly an airplane. It is this ambition which drives the plot that reaches a climax the day Windrider takes Dragonwings, his airplane, up to a hill in Oakland for its first flight.

In his autobiography, Yep explains that the character of Windrider is based on his father, the kitemaker. In his "Afterword" to *Dragonwings*, the author shares with his readers that he was also inspired by the newspaper accounts of the Chinese flier Fung Joe Guey, who flew in the hills of Oakland on September 22, 1909 (p. 247). This young Chinese immigrant had improved upon the original design of the Wright brothers and had built his own wireless sets and telephones.

In the last paragraph of his "Afterword," Yep states that "...it has been my aim to counter various stereotypes as presented in the media... I wanted to show that Chinese-Americans are human beings upon whom America has had a unique effect" (pp. 247-248) [see question 12].

Child of the Owl (1977), the focus of the third report presented to the class, is the story of Casey, a twelve-year-old Chinese-American girl who has been brought up by her father as an American. He has become a compulsive gambler and takes Casey with him as he travels from one deal to the next, always running away from his debts. When her father lands in the hospital, Casey is sent to live with her maternal grandmother Paw-Paw, in San Francisco's Chinatown. In contrast to Moon Shadow, who moves out of Chinatown into an alien world, Casey moves into Chinatown knowing nothing of her Chinese heritage or the Chinese language. She feels like an outsider in the Chinese school; to her, Chinatown is like a foreign land with strange foods and eating utensils, strange customs and beliefs [see question 4]. But Paw-Paw helps her adjust to this new Chinese-American culture. She learns about her cultural heritage, about her mother, her true Chinese name, and the story of the family's owl charm. As Casey learns the language and customs of Chinatown and develops friendships with the people there, she begins to feel at home.

Paw-Paw, like Miss Lucy and Miss Whitlaw, plays an important role in the process of acculturation [see question 9]. However, in this novel, Paw-Paw helps Casey find her roots and serves as a model of the traditional values which are deeply rooted in her cultural heritage.

Casey discovers her cultural identity in Chinatown as well as in the folktales and myths handed down for generations from her ancestors. Again, an ancient tale forms the centerpiece of *Child of the Owl* [see question 8]. Like the star fisher tale, this is a transformation tale in which a young man takes the feather dress of an Owl Spirit who dances in the moonlight with her brothers and sisters. The young man and the owl woman marry. He hides the dress so that she cannot change back into an owl. The Owl Spirit wife comes to enjoy life upon the ground with her husband and his family. They have seven sons and she enjoys caring for them. But after twenty years she feels a longing to return to her life as an owl and, with the help of her youngest son, discovers where her husband has hidden the feather dress. Unlike the star fisher tale, the owl-wife's husband "gave her the dress of his own free will" (p. 80). She puts on the dress and again takes the form of an owl. Before flying away into the jungle, the owl drops an owl charm at the feet of her youngest son.

When Paw-Paw tells this story to Casey, she explains: "We're all children of the Owl Spirit...." (p. 57). She shows Casey a little jade owl charm hanging from a golden chain. After she hears this story, Casey uses it to think about her own between-world dilemma: "And if I pretended I was an owl, I suddenly had a way of talking about my feelings because I felt like someone who'd been trapped inside the wrong body and among the wrong people" (pp. 81-82).

Paw-Paw also tells Casey some of the stories behind the statues of the Eight Immortals they see in souvenir shops. One of the statues is called the Listener. In *Dragonwings*, when Moon Shadow first meets Miss Whitlaw, he thinks of the Listener: "She had a smile like the Listener, She Who Hears Prayers, who refused release from the cycle of lives until all her brothers and sisters too could be freed from sin" (p. 101) [see question 14]. In *Child of the Owl*, Casey recognizes in a store window a statue of the Listener, "the one who refused to enter Heaven until everyone else was saved" (p. 168). Casey is drawn to the fine, white porcelain statue because of its smile: "It was a smile of longing, a smile of sadness, a knowing smile, a patient smile. It must have been the way the Owl Spirit smiled. I leaned closer to look at her better and saw my reflection on the window.... And the smile of the statue...was the smile on my own face" (p. 169).

Casey gradually learns how to deal with her between-world dilemma. She understands that her cultural heritage is part of her, but the way she relates to the ancient myths is not the same as her ancestors' connection to them: "I realized then that you don't have to believe in the stories. You don't even have to believe in the gods they're about; but you ought to know these stories and the gods and also know your ancestors once believed in them and tried to model their lives after certain good spirits" (p. 114). Toward the end of the novel, Casey tries to explain to her father how important her knowledge of the past is to her and how much she appreciates the traditional values. She says to him, "I'm a child of the owl...[the owl story] tells me who I am" (p. 203) [see question 6].

In his Afterword, Yep explains that the owl story presented in Chapter Two is "...based upon stories of filial devotion once popular among the Chinese and upon Chinese folklore concerning owls and other animals" (p. 217).

Sea Glass (1979) is presented in the last group report to the class. This contemporary novel, based on Yep's own experiences as an adolescent, is about Craig Chin, a Chinese-American boy caught in a between-world dilemma [see question 1]. When his father takes a job as manager of a grocery store, Craig and his family move out of San Francisco's Chinatown. Craig struggles to find a place for himself in this new world of "Western people." His father had warned him: "A Chinese has to try twice as hard as any 'Western person'.... They'll only accept you as an American if you can be twice as good as them. Otherwise, you're the stupid chink who isn't going anyplace" (p. 4). His dad wants him to be a star athlete, but Craig cannot achieve his father's ideal — to become the All-American athlete as he had been. Craig also has difficulty at school, where his classmates call him a fat Chinese 'Buddha Man,' and in his neighborhood, where the old Chinese view him as one of the "white demons."

His cousins try to prove to their peers that they are American and do not want to associate themselves with Chinese people, their language, or their cultural heritage [see question 7]. But Craig thinks of himself as Chinese and speaks Chinese. Although he is American-born, his peers see him as a foreigner. He feels he does not fit in anywhere.

It is his reclusive Uncle Quail who helps Craig find a place for himself as a unique individual. Like Paw-Paw, Uncle Quail shares stories about their family and Craig learns to understand his own father. Uncle Quail tells him about the Chinese who came to America and built the railroads, and who worked on the farms and in the factories. He helps Craig discover the beauty of the sea world as well as the beauty in differences and variety. Eventually, Criag feels more comfortable about being Chinese and is ready to assert himself as an individual [see question 6].

During one of Craig's visits with his Uncle, he hears the story of the Dragon Mother. She was a "person who saw the world" (p. 65). She saw a dragon's egg, but her friends laughed and said it was just a rock. But she cares for it until finally one day it hatches into a dragon, a very important dragon. So humans and dragons give her the name, Dragon Mother. In this novel she is the metaphor for the ability to see beneath the surface of people and the natural world. In the final scene of the book, Craig is at the beach with his Uncle Quail and a classmate when he catches a glimpse of something glistening at the water's edge. When he finally holds it in his hand, his friend asks what it is. "I don't know. But it's no dragon's egg" (p. 212). Uncle Quail calls it 'sea glass' and explains: "Someone must have broken a Coke bottle a long time ago on a rock at a beach, and then some of the pieces must have gotten picked up by the sea. The tide washed the glass and polished the edges so that they're smooth and round now and not sharp" (p. 212). His friend says it is just a piece of junk, but Craig sees its beauty and decides to save it [see question 15].

The study of Laurence Yep and his work includes one class session led by students who had chosen to read some of the folktales collected by Yep in *The Rainbow People* (1989) and *Tongues of Jade* (1991) or his retelling of *The Shell Woman and the King* (1993). *The Rainbow People* is a collection of twenty Chinese folktales brought to this country by early immigrants from China. In his Introduction to this volume, Yep comments that "...the stories offered consolation and more often hope. But beyond that, the stories also expressed the loneliness, anger, fear, and love that were part of the Chinese-American experience" (p. x).

Independent Reading and Dialogue Groups: Phase Two

The books selected for this Focus Unit are organized in terms of different groups represented in the Collection: Native Americans, African-Americans, Asian Pacific-Americans, Puerto Ricans, and refugees. Students are asked to select a second book to read independently and to form small dialogue groups to engage in collaborative analysis of books by the same author, books featuring a specific racial or ethnic group, or books linked by a common theme. The dialogue groups use the analysis of the Yep books as a model for studying these books. Again, students are invited to use the list of questions as they write in their literary journals and talk in their dialogue groups about the "between-world condition" for diverse racial and ethnic groups portrayed in these literary texts.

Yoshiko Uchida

The autobiography and novels of this Japanese-American writer are the focus of one of these dialogue groups. In *The Invisible Thread* (1991), Uchida relates her experiences growing up as a Nisei or second-generation Japanese-American in Berkeley, California and her family's internment in a Utah concentration camp during World War II. Many of her comments in this autobiography reflect her between-world condition:

It was as though a long invisible thread would always bind Mama and Papa to the country they had left behind. And that thread seemed to wind just as surely around Keiko and me as well (p. 5).

A lot more of me was Japanese than I realized, whether I liked it or not.... Mama and Papa had passed on to me so much of their own Japanese spirit and soul (p. 13).

As for me, it was my white baby doll and my Patsy doll that I loved, even though they didn't look like me. I suppose it was because I always thought of myself as being an American (p. 18).

Yoshiko Uchida began to write stories as a young girl. She wrote a seven-chapter book about a white girl in a white world. It didn't occur to her to write about a Japanese-American child: "...the books I was reading at the time were only about white children and were written by white authors. The best world, it seemed to me then, was the white American world" (p. 32).

When she went to Japan to visit her grandmother, she knew she looked like everyone else but she also knew she was really a foreigner in Japan. "Deep down inside...I was thoroughly American...But...in America, too, I was perceived as a foreigner" (p. 52).

At school, she felt insecure and inferior. In high school she was excluded from the social world of the white students. But when she entered the University of California, she joined a community of Japanese-Americans. She had finally found a world where she was totally accepted.

When she was a senior at the University, Japan bombed Pearl Harbor, and she and her family were sent to a concentration camp.

Her experiences as a young girl growing up in California are woven into a trilogy for middle-grade readers: *A Jar of Dreams* (1981); *The Best Bad Thing* (1983); and *The Happiest Ending* (1985). The first of the trilogy, *A Jar of Dreams*, introduces eleven-year-old Rinko who grows up in a Japanese-American family in California during the Depression. The racial hostility and violence directed toward their family is the external conflict that drives the plot. The internal conflict involves Rinko's struggle to gain acceptance in the white community while maintaining pride in her Japanese heritage.

The novel opens with these lines: "I never thought one small lady from Japan could make such a big difference in my life, but she did. I'm talking about my Aunt Waka, who came to visit us the summer a lot of things changed in our house, including me" (p. 3). Like Paw-Paw and Uncle Quail in the novels by Laurence Yep, Aunt Waka has a strong sense of self and is proud of her heritage. Her inner strength and commitment to the traditional values rooted in her cultural heritage help Rinko build a sense of pride and self-esteem.

Uchida expresses the inner struggles she had experienced as a girl through the character of Rinko. For example, Rinko describes what it feels like when her classmates talk among themselves as if she is not there:

And that makes me feel like a big nothing. Some days I feel so left out, I hate my black hair and my Japanese face. I hate having a name like Rinko Tsujimura...I wish I could be like everybody else (p. 6).

If you feel like a big nothing and don't like who you are, naturally you don't speak up in a loud, firm voice. You don't talk to other people either, unless they talk to you first (p. 41).

Mrs. Sugarman, a neighbor, is another key character in this novel. Like Miss Lucy and Miss Whitlaw in the Yep novels, she is an open-minded, generous white woman who befriends and supports Rinko and her family. Mrs. Sugarman transcends the racial prejudice and discrimination which have plagued Rinko's family since her father first arrived in America in 1918. When Mrs. Sugarman reaches out to meet people, she sees human beings, not stereotypes. She develops a very close relationship with Rinko's family, and Rinko sees her as one of her best friends.

In contrast, Wilbur Starr, is filled with hatred and expresses it whenever he sees Rinko. When he calls her a "Jap" it fills her with anger and shame. But when he tries to destroy their home laundry business and kills the family's dog, Rinko's father and uncle confront Wilbur Starr and stand up to him with courage and determination. As the antagonist, Wilbur Starr represents the external conflict that drives the plot in this novel.

The Best Bad Thing and *The Happiest Ending* continue the story of Rinko and her family in California in the 1930s. Two other novels by Uchida, *Journey to Topaz* (1971) and *Journey Home* (1978), reflect the author's experiences as a prisoner behind barbed wire during World War II and after her release from the concentration camp.

Journey to Topaz is the story of an eleven-year-old Japanese-American girl, Yuki, and her family, who live in Berkeley, California. They are preparing for Christmas when Pearl Harbor is bombed and they are among the 120,000 persons of Japanese ancestry who are suddenly uprooted from their homes and evacuated from the West Coast. Yuki and her family are eventually shipped to a bleak desert concentration camp called Topaz. In the sequel, *Journey Home,* Yuki and her parents are released from Topaz near the end of World War II. But when they gain their freedom and try to start a new life, they meet prejudice and violence. Both stories recall a tragic episode in our nation's history, when a terrible injustice was done to thousands of innocent people, many of whom were United States citizens and, like Yuki, had even been born in this country.

According to Uchida's autobiography, she returned to Japan in 1952 to collect folktales for *The Magic Listening Cap* (1955) and *The Sea of Gold and Other Tales From Japan* (1965). She had begun to appreciate the beauty and richness of Japan's life and art and had gained a sense of pride in her cultural heritage. She writes: "Now it was time for me to pass on this sense of pride and self-esteem to the third generation of Japanese-Americans — the Sansei — and to give them the kinds of books I'd never had as a child" (p. 131). The books she wrote for them included collections of traditional folktales to give them a sense of their literary heritage and a series of novels to give them a sense of their own history. *Samurai of Gold Hill* (1972) is a narrative based on the historical account of one of the first groups of Japanese immigrants to settle in California. The Rinko trilogy portrays Japanese immigrant families in the 1930s. The novels about Yuki relate the Japanese-American experience during World War II. In a note from the author included in *The Sea of Gold,* she explains another purpose for her writing: "I want to dispel the stereotypic image held by many non-Asians about the Japanese-Americans and write about them as real people (p. 137)."

After students in the dialogue group that has been studying the work of Yoshiko Uchida have had a chance to analyze her novels and find connections between her own life and the lives of her central characters, they can begin to look for connections between her novels and those written by Laurence Yep and begin to identify significant differences as well as common patterns and themes. Individual students may also choose to do special independent projects using Uchida's collections of Japanese folktales as the basis for story telling or illustration or a study of the cultural elements in particular tales. Folklore reflects the culture in which it emerges and is sometimes called "the mirror of a people." Thus, these collections of the literary heritage of Japan serve as an excellent resource for the study of Japanese culture.

Autobiographical Fiction: Chinese-Americans and Americans in China

Students who chose to read *In The Year of the Boar and Jackie Robinson* (Lord, 1984) or *Homesick: My Own Story* (Fritz, 1982) form another dialogue group. The first book was written by Bette Bao Lord, a Chinese-American and an author of adult fiction. It is based on her own experiences as a young immigrant to America. *In the Year of the Boar and Jackie Robinson* is about Shirley Temple Wong, who sails with her mother from China to Brooklyn in 1947 to join Shirley's father, who has been working in America. Shirley has no friends until a classmate introduces her to baseball. Playing right field gives her a sense of power and of being part of the American way of life. Baseball opens a door for Shirley in the process of acculturation. Her hero is Jackie Robinson, who, like Shirley, managed to break down some of the barriers constructed by racial and ethnic prejudice.

But the story of Shirley Temple Wong is not just a story of assimilation; it is a story about the struggle to maintain a balance between two cultures. Before Shirley enters the American school, her mother says to her: "Remember, my daughter, you may be the only Chinese these Americans will ever meet. Do your best. Be extra good. Upon your shoulders rests the reputation of all Chinese" (p. 43). When Shirley begins to speak more English than Chinese, her mother insists that she must remember her own language. "You must not forget you are still Chinese" (p. 119).

However, as the family becomes involved in their new life in America, they find it increasingly difficult to maintain their cultural identity. Toward the end of the book, grandfather sends moon cakes from China and reminds them about the Mid-Autumn Festival. They suddenly realize they had almost forgotten to celebrate the fullest moon of the year as the Wong Clan had done for centuries. To bring them closer to their relatives in China and to their cultural heritage, Shirley tells a story that her grandfather used to tell about the "filial daughter and the loving bride" (p. 152).

When Shirley learns that her mother is pregnant, she is determined to take care of her new brother, to teach him both English and Chinese and about

American ways and life in China, and to tell him the stories that grandfather told.

On the back cover flap, the author comments on her own immigrant experience: "Many feel that loss of one's native culture is the price one must pay for becoming an American. I do not feel this way. I think we hyphenated Americans are doubly blessed. We can choose the best of both."

The second book discussed in this dialogue group, *Homesick: My Own Story*, was written by Jean Fritz, the author of many books for children. This is Jean Fritz's story of her childhood in China. She defines it as "fiction" because she did not pay close attention to sequence and details.

Fritz was born in China and lived there for twelve years until 1927. Letters from American relatives made her feel American and homesick for this country she had never seen. She attends a British school in China where she is often called a "foreign devil" by her classmates. Although she had close ties to Chinese friends and loved the Yangtze River, Fritz felt she belonged on the other side of the world: "The trouble with living on the wrong side of the world was that I didn't feel like a *real* American" (p. 10). When she returned with her family to the United States, other children teased her with the chant, "Chink Chink Chinaman...." But she stood up to their insults and eventually adjusted to this new culture which was her own.

A third book which this dialogue group can include in their study is *Between Two Worlds: A Story About Pearl Buck* (Mitchell, 1988). It is a biography of a woman who was awarded both the Pulitzer and Nobel prizes for literature.

Pearl Buck's parents were American missionaries and they brought her to China in 1892 shortly after her birth. Like Jean Fritz, she was frequently taunted with the words, "little foreign devil." When she was nine years old she returned to the United States for a year and was delighted to discover "children who looked like her!" (p. 18). By the time she came back to China a year later, she was aware of a between-world dilemma. "America had given her her identity, but China had nurtured her. Pearl felt as though she had a foot in each world, and she did not know how to bring her two worlds together" (p. 20). However, after college Pearl "knew how she would bring her two worlds together. She would do it through her writing. She would be a novelist...telling the story of the China she knew to the Western world" (p. 30). Over the years she used her stories to speak out against prejudice and to bring about understanding between East and West.

Contemporary Realism: Fiction and Non-Fiction about Refugees

The focus of another dialogue group is a group of novels by or about children or youth who came to the United States as refugees. *Onion Tears* (Kidd, 1989) is narrated by a young Vietnamese girl, Nam-Huong, who has escaped from Vietnam but is grieving over the loss of her family and her homeland. Her new home is in Australia, where she has been taken in by a woman she calls Auntie. Her adjustment is slow and painful; she is haunted by the horrors she faced in Vietnam and the long days and nights on the small boat with hundreds of frightened people. She relives the moment of her grandfather's death: "all my tears are locked away inside me — locked away in a secret place...." (p. 53).

At school she is withdrawn and quiet and does not respond to the taunts and cruel jokes of the children. But inside she feels a longing to be like the other children, to run and play, and eat sandwiches at lunchtime instead of the "cha gio" and the other ethnic foods Auntie prepares for her. "And I didn't like being Nam-Huong. I wished I weren't Nam-Huong. I want to be like Tessa and play soccer with the boys and climb trees and ride a bike with no hands...." (p. 15).

Eventually, with the help of Auntie and Miss Lily, her teacher, Nam-Huong learns to trust the people around her and allows herself to express the grief she has bottled up inside her for so long. She cries for her family and her little yellow canary. "My tears poured out like monsoon rains" (p. 55). And she is able to tell Miss Lily about her family, the boat, the refugee camp, her sorrow: "And my words poured out from their secret place" (p. 55).

Now she is ready to be herself at school, to laugh and play, and the other children begin to accept her as one of them. But as she learns to accept her new country as her home, she holds onto memories of her family and her native land.

Hello, My Name Is Scrambled Eggs (Gilson, 1985) is the story of Harvey Trumble, a seventh grader whose parents host a family of Vietnamese refugees until they can settle in their own home. Harvey attempts to Americanize Tuan, a boy his own age. He gives him the name Tom, and as their friendship grows so does Tom/Tuan's knowledge of the English language and the "American way of life." But Tuan is caught between two worlds. His grandmother is disturbed when she sees him in American clothes, and his father is upset because Tuan must translate everything for him because he is the only one in their family who can speak English. Tuan explains to Harvey: "In Vietnam, son not tell father what to do" (p. 138). Tuan knows he *must* learn English to help his family survive, but his father and grandmother think he is *too* American. Tuan says, "I must be American. I must not be American. I do not know what to do" (p. 138). By the end of the novel, Tuan is beginning to come to terms with this dilemma by becoming an active participant in the American way of life but at the same time maintaining his identity as a Vietnamese with a rich cultural heritage. He expresses it this way: "I am not Tom. I decide. I will be American. I will. But my name is Tuan Nguyen" (p. 147).

Children of the River (Crew, 1989) is the story of Sundara, who had escaped with her aunt and uncle from the Khmer Rouge Army when she was thirteen years old. The story begins when she is seventeen years old and struggling to fit in at her Oregon high school *and* to be a good Cambodian girl at home. Her aunt sees her as too American, but at school she is viewed as an outsider. Her aunt expects her to wait for the family to arrange her marriage to a Cambodian boy, but she is drawn to an American boy. She is torn by her love for this boy and her loyalty to her family. And deep down she is grieving for her lost family and the life she had to leave behind.

Letters from Rifka, by Karen Hesse (1992), is based on a true story from the author's family. Rifka is a young Jewish girl who writes about her family's flight from Russia in September, 1919, and about being left behind in Belgium when the rest of her family emigrates to America, being detained at Ellis Island, and finally receiving permission to enter the United States in October, 1920.

Another story of family flight is Frances Temple's *Grab Hands and Run* (1993). Twelve-year-old Felipe, his mother, and younger sister leave their home in El Salvador and set out on a difficult and dangerous journey to Canada.

This dialogue group that has been focussing on refugees reads selections from two no-fiction sources: *Into a Strange Land: Unaccompanied Refugee Youth in America* (Ashabranner, 1987), a collection of individual stories of young Southeast Asian refugees, and *New Kids on the Block: Oral Histories of Immigrant Teens* (Bode, 1989), stories of young people from eleven different countries. They describe the emotional experiences of fleeing from their homelands and adjusting to a new way of life in a new world. Most of them discuss the way they handle the between-world dilemma. For example, Emilio, a Filipino, explains: "When I walk in my house, it's both countries. I speak both languages at home: Visavan, the language we talk on my island, and English.... The living room and formal dining room have Japanese and Filipino furniture. The family room and kitchen are 100 percent American. In my bedroom on the walls, I have posters of fast cars and music groups" (p. 54). Abdul, from Afghanistan, says he has learned to dress and behave like an American kid, but he studies his native language at a special religious school. He is a Muslim and practices his religion. "I don't want to change my culture and forget my language" (p. 27).

Nicholasa Mohr: Puerto Ricans in New York

Another dialogue group is formed to discuss the work of Nicholasa Mohr, who was born in New York City's "El Barrio." *Felita* (1979) is the story of a Puerto Rican family in New York. The external conflict that drives the plot is the racial hostility that confronts the family when they move into a white community. Violence directed at them forces the family to return to their old neighborhood. In the sequel, *Going Home* (1986), Felita is eleven years old when she visits relatives in Puerto Rico for the first time and faces discrimination for being a "Nuyorican". She feels like an outsider in her grandmother's own village. "At home I get called a 'Spick' and here I'm a Nuyorican" (p. 122). The hostility of her peers forces her to think about her identity and to explore her cultural heritage, which she has always taken for granted.

Felita joins a youth group at the church, and works with them on a play about the Tainos, the original inhabitants of Puerto Rico. This historical presentation of Taino culture from 1490-1517 reinforces her pride in her heritage.

This dialogue group also discusses selected short stories about Puerto Ricans in New York City from two collections by Mohr: *El Bronx Remembered* (1989) and *In Nueva York* (1991).

Native Americans

Cultural conflict among Native Americans is the focus of two novels selected for independent reading by another dialogue group: *The Shadow Brothers* (Cannon, 1990) and *Indian Summer* (Girion, 1990). According to Donnarae MacCann, these books have been given positive reviews by Amerind critics (1992). MacCann's review of contemporary fiction about Native Americans reveals that "...books with a white bias vastly outnumber those expressing a

Native American perspective" (p. 140). *Through Indian Eyes: The Native Experience in Books for Children* (Slapin and Seale, 1992), an excellent resource for teachers and students, includes guidelines for selecting literature that provides authentic, non-racist, undistorted portraits of Native Americans to replace literature that demeans and stereotypes them.

The Shadow Brothers (Cannon, 1990) is the story of a Native American teenager, Henry Yazzie, who had come to live with the Jenkins, a Mormon family in Utah, when he was seven years old. Henry's father, a tribal police officer on a Navaho reservation, had sent him to live with the Jenkins family so he could get a good education. Marcus Jenkins tells the story of his close relationship with Henry, his Navaho foster brother. He has always let Henry be the leader in this relationship; he didn't seem to mind standing in his shadow. The story opens when the boys are sixteen. Henry is the only Native American in an otherwise all-white high school. Now for the first time since the boys were seven, their relationship is changing. Henry is dating a beautiful girl in their class, and Marcus is feeling left out. For the first time, Marcus must confront the fact that he has been living in Henry's shadow and has not fully developed his own inner resources. At the same time, Henry is becoming increasingly thoughtful about his Navaho heritage and his family on the reservation.

When Frank, another Native American boy, is enrolled in the school and does not show up for classes or track practice, Henry tries to explain: "It's sort of hard to say, but...some Native Americans have a different sense of time than we do — than *Anglos* do" (p. 43). At this moment Henry realizes that he has begun to see himself as one of the Anglos, and Marcus thinks, "He fits in so well here that I hardly even notice he's Navaho any more" (p. 44). Frank calls Henry an apple: "Red on the outside. White on the inside. Apple" (p. 84).

When Henry decides to go back to the reservation, he explains to Marcus that his grandfather wants to teach him things: "He wants me to understand how Navahos like him — traditional Navahos — see the world" (p. 158). Henry reveals to Marcus that he had been homesick for a long time. "Then I stopped being homesick and some time after that I stopped feeling different. One day I even realized that I felt — I felt white inside" (p. 159). He goes on to explain that when Frank came..."he reminded me that I'm not white no matter how much I pretend to be, and he made me realize that I'm not Navaho either. I'm not Anglo. I'm not Navaho. I'm nothing" (p. 160).

At the conclusion of the story, Henry returns to the reservation to find out what it means to be Navaho. "I want to know who I am" (p. 163).

Indian Summer (Girion, 1990) provides an interesting contrast. In this story, Joni McCord, from suburban New Jersey, lives for a month on an Iroquois reservation where her father serves as the pediatrician. The McCord family lives with the Birdsong family; Joni shares Sarah Birdsong's room. The story is told from the viewpoint of Joni as well as Sarah and begins before they actually meet. The letters exchanged prior to the McCord's arrival foreshadow the deep resentments, prejudices, and misconceptions that will strain their relationship.

Joni does not want to be away from her friends the summer before sixth grade. Sarah does not want to spend a month with white people who "...don't understand reservation life or our history" (p. 15). Sarah knows that her father is also upset, when he says, "why don't we have our own Indian boys coming back here as doctors?" (p. 22). Sarah's grandmother, Maw Maw, extends hospitality to the McCords, and Sarah knows that she, too, is expected to be polite to them.

Sarah and Joni make half-hearted attempts to be friends, but the tension between them builds because of past experiences and prejudices. Almost anything Joni does or says causes Sarah's anger to erupt. Joni is harassed by Sarah's friends who try to get her to leave their world and return to her own. When Joni gets a taste of the cruel and degrading treatment of the Indians by white people living outside the reservation, she "began to realize that Sarah treated her *on* the reservation the way people treated Sarah *off* the reservation" (p. 133).

Joni also learns that Sarah's parents are separated. Her father wants to remain on the reservation and preserve their culture. Her mother lives in Washington, D.C., making and selling jewelry. She wanted to be out in the world. Joni feels sympathy for Sarah: "It was like Sarah was stuck between two worlds. She was proud that she was an Iroquois and she knew all about her heritage and culture...and...language...But living on the reservation meant she was cut off from her mom" (p. 122).

As everyone on the reservation prepares for the annual Iroquois powwow, tensions between the two girls build. But in the final scene in the novel, the beauty of the ancient friendship dances and wisdom shared by Maw Maw give Joni the courage to enter the line of dancers. At first all the dancers stop and stare at her, an intruder. But it is Sarah who reaches out to Joni in friendship — and they dance together.

On the back flap of the book, the author writes that "To research the book, I visited reservations of the Iroquois Confederacy — Tonowanda, Tuscarora, and Cattaraugus — where I met with residents, adults and children. I listened to storytellers, learned the history of individual families and tribes, and tried to absorb the feelings of the Native Americans who live on reservations."

Folklore is woven into both of these novels that portray Native American characters. A number of collections of Native American poetry and folklore are included in the Focus Unit collection so that members of this group can enjoy this vital part of Native American culture:

Dancing Tepees: Poems of American Indian Youth, by Virginia Driving Hawk Sneve (1989).

Tonweya and the Eagles and Other Lakota Indian Tales, by Rosebud Yellow Robe (1979).

Iroquois Stories: Heroes and Heroines, Monsters and Magic, by Joseph Bruchac (1985).

The Sound of Flutes and Other Indian Legends Told by Lame Deer, Jenny Leading Cloud, Leonard Crow Dog and Others, by Richard Erodes (1976).

The Earth is Sore: Native Americans on Nature, adapted and illustrated by Aline Amon (1981).

Keepers of the Animals, by Michael J. Caduto and Joseph Bruchae (1991).

The African-American Perspective

The books selected by the dialogue group that focusses on the experience of African-Americans represent a relatively new trend in the field of children's literature. In her book, *Shadow and Substance: Afro-American Experience in Contemporary Children's Fiction* (1982), Rudine Sims reports the results of an examination of realistic fiction about African-Americans for young people (preschool through grade eight) published between 1965 and 1979. In a discussion of her findings, she introduces the term "culturally conscious fiction" to identify a group of books which appeared during this period. Culturally conscious books reflect "the social and cultural traditions associated with growing up black in the United States... Their primary intent is to speak to Afro-American children about themselves and their lives...At minimum this means that the major characters are Afro-Americans, the story is told from their perspective, the setting is an Afro-American community or home, and the text includes some means of identifying the characters as black — physical descriptions, language, cultural traditions, and so forth" (Sims, p. 49). In this book, Sims reviews the results of studies of children's trade books which document that, historically, the image of African-Americans in children's books has been a negative one. Surveys of children's books published prior to the 1970s reveal that most books about non-whites were written by white authors for white readers, and these books include numerous examples of negative stereotypes and demeaning images of African-Americans as well as white supremist attitudes. The culturally conscious books discussed by Sims offer more authentic images of African-Americans and are written by "Black writers...[who] can illuminate for Black and white readers both the uniqueness and the universality of the experience of growing up Afro-American" (p. 13).

Virginia Hamilton wrote one of the first of these culturally conscious novels, *Zeely* (1967). The central character is Geeder, an imaginative eleven-year-old, who discovers in her uncle's shed a magazine picture of a Watutsi queen. Geeder is enchanted by the beauty and dignity of this woman of royalty. She is struck by the resemblance she sees between this queen and a local woman named Zeely; Geeder convinces herself that Zeely is somehow related to this Watutsi queen.

In this contemporary novel, Hamilton portrays a warm and loving African-American extended family and weaves into their lives the songs of escaping slaves and prisoners as well as a depiction of the Watutsis as regal, proud people with a complex culture. As Geeder gains a sense of herself as an individual, she is inspired by the grace and dignity of Zeely and draws strength from both her African-American and her African heritage.

In Eloise Greenfield's *Sister* (1974), a young African-American girl, Doretha, records her story in the memory book given to her by her father before he died. This is Doretha's story of her struggle to cope with hard times and to develop her own identity and a positive self-concept. She gains strength from her grandfather's stories of her ancestors, who were proud, independent people in spite of their experience as slaves. She also develops a sense of pride and self-confidence when she joins an African school held after school to develop skills in academic subjects and to learn the history of her people.

The Shimmershine Queens (Yarbrough, 1989) is the story of Angie, a fifth grade African-American girl who suffers from the pain of her parents' separation and her mother's bouts of depression. Her classmates taunt her about her dark skin and kinky hair. Her low self-esteem and feelings of inferiority and hopelessness threaten to overwhelm her. It is her elderly cousin Seatta who offers Angie a new perspective about herself and her African heritage. Cousin Seatta tells her about the African people, their culture and beauty and their capture by white slave traders. She tells Angie stories of the slave children who yearned to be able to learn and how they finally managed to get an education against all odds.

Angie is also inspired by the new dance and drama teacher who comes to her school and helps Angie and her classmates to take pride in their African heritage. She guides them in the production of a class play about children who lived in West Africa, but it is Angie who inspires her classmates to come together in a cooperative effort to make this play a success.

Their class play is based on a story that ends with a reference to the flight of slaves "over the fields…going home to Africa" (p. 97). The story, "The People Could Fly," can be found in a collection of Black folktales by that name told by Virginia Hamilton (1985). This story enriches the discussion of Yarbrough's novel in this dialogue group.

Thank You, Dr. Martin Luther King, Jr.! (Tate, 1990) is another story of a young African-American girl who suffers from low self-esteem. Mary Elouise is ashamed of her dark skin and hair; she hates to be reminded about slavery and her African roots and Dr. Martin Luther King, Jr.; she prefers white dolls to the black ones her grandmother buys for her; she longs to be the friend of a classmate with long blond hair; and she definitely does not want to be the narrator of the Black History part in the school play.

Mary Elouise's life changes when two African-American storytellers come to her school with wonderful stories about Africa. They help her develop a new perspective about her heritage and her own identity. Her grandmother, Big Momma, helps her with her lines in the school play by giving her the background necessary to understand the words she is to recite about Black Americans. By the time Mary Elouise stands up on stage in front of an audience, she has developed a sense of self-worth and pride in her heritage and narrates the Black History segment with genuine feeling.

In *Maizon at Blue Hill* (Woodson, 1992), the central character is an African-American girl from Brooklyn who wins a scholarship to a boarding school in Connecticut where there are only four other African-American students. Blue Hill is a beautiful school and provides the academic challenge and support Maizon's grandmother had wanted for her. But Maizon does not feel that she belongs in this school for white girls. She feels remote from the white students, and she feels uncomfortable with the black students. Three of these black students have separated themselves socially from the white students. They express contempt for the other African-American student who hangs out with the white girls and refer to her with words such as "oreo," "assimilated," and "disconnected." One of them comments: "It's like she doesn't want to face the fact that she's black" (p. 57). For the first time Maizon is forced to confront issues such as racism and elitism and where she can fit in as a gifted black girl. she realizes that at this point in her life she must choose between two worlds: this school for white girls, with its excellent academic opportunities, or her black neighborhood in Brooklyn, with her own family, friends, and culture.

These culturally conscious novels provide realistic portrayals of African-Americans and their roots. Some readers will find their own experiences reflected in these stories, as well as a sense of their own history and heritage. Literature has the power to affect readers' attitudes about themselves and others and to serve as a positive source for change: to undo negative stereotypes and to help develop understanding and appreciation of cultural differences.

History and folklore are woven into most of the novels studied in this dialogue group. Students are encouraged to read non-fiction sources to increase their knowledge of African-American history and of significant African-Americans. For example, Virginia Hamilton's *Many Thousand Gone: African Americans from Slavery to Freedom* (1993) traces the history of slavery in America by telling the stories of those individuals who were a part of this history. Students are also invited to read folktales found in collections such as *Black Folktales* by Julius Lester (1969), *The People Could Fly: American Black Folktales* by Virginia Hamilton (1985), and *The Adventures of High John the Conqueror* by Steve Sanfield (1989).

Searching for One's Roots

The dialogue group formed to study *Kim/Kimi* by Hadley Irwin (1981), *Her Own Song* by Ellen Howard (1988), and *Drifting Snow: An Arctic Search* (Houston, 1992) focusses on the nature of the "quest" or "journey" tale as a particular type of narrative and the use of this narrative structure to tell the stories of central characters who respond to a deep need to search for their own roots and their true identity.

Kim Andrews is a thoroughly Americanized sixteen-year-old who lives in an all-white Iowa community with her Irish-American mother, stepfather, and half-brother. But she was born Kimi Yogushi. Her Japanese-American father died before she was born. Kim sets out alone on a journey to find out about her Japanese father. "I'm half and half...Irish-American on the inside and Japanese-American on the outside" (p. 19). Now she wants to learn about the part that's missing. Her search takes her to California to find her father's family. In Sacramento she is befriended by a Japanese-American family that provides her with a great deal of information about her own history as a Japanese-American. She is taken to a Japanese neighborhood where she feels as if she's in a foreign country. She can't speak the language or use chopsticks. During the course of her search she is shocked to learn of the existence of Japanese-American prison camps during World War II. She discovers that her father and his family had been imprisoned in a concentration camp named Lake Tule.

Kim is taken to Lake Tule by Mrs. Enomoto, a woman who had spent four years in the camp. She tells Kim: "As far as most Americans were concerned, camps didn't exist" (p. 134). She explains that this camp is part of the heritage of all Japanese-Americans. "This camp erased a part of my life! ...People must know that in erasing these camps they have destroyed our history. For forty years we have carried this awful anger" (pp. 138-139).

After a tireless search, Kim locates her father's family and, for the first time, she meets her Japanese grandmother and aunt. By the end of her journey Kim has found out about herself as a Japanese-American who has both a history and a family. She has learned about the other half and realizes that *"Me* was Kimi Yogushi Andrews. From now on I would be Kimi Y. Andrews" (p. 192).

Her Own Song is about eleven-year-old Mellie, an adopted child living in Seattle in 1908. At this time white people did not associate with Chinese, but when her classmates taunt the Chinese laundryman she feels very uncomfortable. When Mellie finds her adoption papers hidden in a locked drawer, she discovers that she had been "abandoned" by her birth-mother. Mellie's quest to unlock the secret of her origins takes her to Chinatown, an exotic and mysterious world for an eleven-year-old white girl. She learns that her American birth-mother sold her to a Chinese couple who loved and cared for her for four years until the police tracked them down in Chinatown and forcibly took the child to an orphanage. Later she was adopted by a white couple who never told her about her first adoptive mother, her Chinese mother, Lan-Heung, who died shortly after her child was taken from her.

When Mellie discovers her own history, she understands the content of her dreams and flashes of memory, and she is anxious to learn more about this culture which was her world for four years. She is proud of her Chinese connections, and she feels a powerful bond to both families: her white family and her Chinese family. At the end of the story, she brings these two families together, thus bringing together the two worlds of her heritage.

The central character in James Houston's *Drifting Snow* is a young teenager, Elizabeth Queen, who returns to the Arctic to search for her family and to learn about her own Eskimo culture and language. As a very small child, Elizabeth had been taken south and away from her Inuit-Eskimo parents in the Canadian Arctic in order to save her life, because she was afflicted with tuberculosis. Because her identification papers were lost, Elizabeth had grown up in a Canadian boarding school with no knowledge of her parents' names, where she had lived, or even her exact age. Now, as a teenager, she is determined to find her roots and her identity.

Dialogue Group Reports and Synthesis

Each dialogue group shares with the rest of the class what they have read and discussed. They identify the specific questions on the list that they found to be most relevant in guiding their analysis and report on key connections, insights, discoveries, and themes which emerged during their discussions. They also recommend titles they think their classmates will enjoy reading on their own.

At the conclusion of each group presentation, new entries are recorded on the chart with the list of conflicts and problems associated with being "between two worlds" that was started during the introductory group session and posted near the Focus Unit collection. A second chart is placed next to this one to record responses to question 12 about techniques authors use to address significant issues and to send messages. The information and ideas on these two charts are used in the concluding session as a framework for moving from analysis of single texts or sets of texts toward synthesis. By this time, students are ready to look at the literature in this unit as a whole and to think about what these authors say about acculturation; between-world dilemmas; racial and ethnic tensions; prejudice, stereotypes, and discrimination; and the search for human dignity and personal identity. Students are asked to identify the views and attitudes held by various writers regarding these issues and to share their own experiences, views, and attitudes.

Students are asked to identify the kinds of barriers that separate human beings, how these barriers are established by groups and individuals on both sides, and how they affect the process of acculturation for ethnic and racial minorities. The next logical question is: What can be done to break down these barriers and to improve understanding and respect between diverse groups and individuals? In this way, students work toward synthesis of the major issues and problems presented in these novels and then consider possible solutions and preventative measures.

Finally, students are asked to look inside themselves and to think what they can do *as individuals* to transcend prejudice and work toward breaking down barriers they have constructed in their own worlds. They will find excellent role models among the characters who live in the pages of these books: fictional characters and real people who had the courage and determination to move from understanding and insight to action.

References

MacCann, Donnarae. (1992). "Native Americans in Books for the Young," in *Teaching Multicultural Literature in Grades K-8.* Edited by Violet Harris. Norwood, MA: Christopher-Gordon.

Sims, Rudine. (1982). *Shadow and Substance: Afro-American Experience in Contemporary Children's Fiction.* Urbana, IL: NCTE.

Slapin, Beverly, and Doris Seale, editors. (1992). *Through Indian Eyes: The Native Experience in Books for Children.* Philadelphia, PA: New Society Publishers.

Bibliography: Between Two Worlds

I. Novels

Cannon, A.E. (1990). *The Shadow Brothers.* New York: Delacorte Press.

Crew, Linda. (1989). *Children of the River.* New York: Delacorte Press.

Fritz, Jean. (1982). *Homesick: My Own Story.* New York: Putnam.

Gilson, Jamie. (1985). *Hello, My Name Is Scrambled Eggs.* New York: Morrow.

Girion, Barbara. (1990). *Indian Summer.* New York: Scholastic.

Greenfield, Eloise. (1974). *Sister.* Crowell.

Hamilton, Virginia. (1967). *Zeely.* New York: Macmillan.

Hesse, Karen. (1992). *Letters from Rifka.* New York: Henry Holt.

Houston, James. (1992). *Drifting Snow: An Arctic Search.* New York: Macmillan.

Howard, Ellen. (1988). *Her Own Song.* New York: Atheneum.

Irwin, Hadley. (1987). *Kim/Kimi.* New York: Macmillan.

Kidd, Diana. (1989). *Onion Tears*. New York: Orchard Books.

Larsen, Alice. (1993). *If It Hadn't Been For Yoon Jun*. Boston: Houghton Mifflin.

Lord, Bette Bao. (1984). *In the Year of the Boar and Jackie Robinson*. New York: Harper and Row.

Mohr, Nicholasa. (1979). *Felita*. New York: Dial.

Mohr, Nicholasa. (1986). *Going Home*. New York: Dial.

Perkins, Mitali. (1993). *The Sunita Experiment*. Boston: Joy St. Books (Little Brown).

Tate, Eleanora. (1990). *Thank You, Dr. Martin Luther King, Jr.!* New York: Watts.

Temple, Frances. (1993). *Grab Hands and Run*. New York: Orchard.

Uchida, Yoshiko. (1983). *The Best Bad Thing*. New York: Atheneum.

Uchida, Yoshiko. (1985). *The Happiest Ending*. New York: Atheneum.

Uchida, Yoshiko. (1981). *A Jar of Dreams*. New York: Atheneum.

Uchida, Yoshiko. (1978). *Journey Home*. New York: Atheneum.

Uchida, Yoshiko. (1971). *Journey to Topaz*. New York: Scribner's.

Uchida, Yoshiko. (1972). *Samurai of Gold Hill*. New York: Scribner's.

Watkins, Yoko Kawashima. (1986). *So Far from the Bamboo Grove*. New York: Lothrop, Lee & Shepard.

Woodson, Jacqueline. (1992). *Maizon at Blue Hill*. New York: Delacorte.

Yarbrough, Camille. (1989). *The Shimmershine Queens*. New York: Putnam.

Yep, Laurence. (1977). *Child of the Owl*. New York: Harper and Row.

Yep, Laurence. (1975). *Dragonwings*. New York: Harper and Row.

Yep, Laurence. (1979). *Sea Glass*. New York: Harper and Row.

Yep, Laurence. (1991). *The Star Fisher*. New York: Morrow.

II. Autobiographies and Biographies

Ashabranner, Brent, and Melissa Ashabranner. (1987). *Into a Strange Land: Unaccompanied Refugee Youth in America*. Dodd Mead and Co.

Ashabranner, Brent. (1993). *Still a Nation of Immigrants*. New York: Cobblehill.

Ashabranner, Brent. (1984). *To Live in Two Worlds: American Indian Youth Today*. Dodd Mead and Co.

Bode, Janet. (1989). *New Kids on the Block: Oral Histories of Immigrant Teens*. New York: Watts.

Hamilton, Virginia. (1993). *Many Thousand Gone - African Americans from Slavery to Freedom*. New York: Alfred A. Knopf.

Howlett, Bud. (1993). *I'm New Here*. Boston: Houghton Mifflin.

Ling, Amy. (1990). *Between Worlds: Women Writers of Chinese Ancestry*. Tarrytown, NY: Pergamon Press.

Mitchell, Barbara. (1988). *Between Two Worlds: A Story About Pearl Buck*. Minneapolis, MN: Carolrhoda.

Mohr, Nicholasa. (1993). *All for the Better: A Story of El Barrio*. Milwaukee, WI: Raintree.

Uchida, Yoshika. (1991). *The Invisible Thread*. New York: Julian Messner.

Yep, Laurence. (1991). *The Lost Garden*. New York: Julian Messner.

III. *Folklore, Poetry, and Short Stories*

Adoff, Arnold, ed. (1973). *The Poetry of Black America: Anthology of the 20th Century*. New York: Harper and Row.

Amon, Aline, adaptor and illustrator. (1981). *The Earth is Sore: Native Americans on Nature*. New York: Atheneum.

Bierhorst, John, ed. (1976). *Black Rainbow: Legends of the Incas and Myths of Ancient Peru*. New York: Farrar, Straus & Giroux.

Bruchac, Joseph. (1985). *Iroquois Stories: Heroes and Heroines, Monsters and Magic*. Freedom, CA: The Crossing Press.

Caduto, Michael J., and Joseph Bruchac. (1991). *Keepers of the Animals: Native American Stories and Wildlife Activities for Children*. Golden, CO: Fulcrum Publishing.

Erdoes, Richard. (1976). *The Sound of Flutes and Other Indian Legends Told by Lame Deer, Jenny Leading Cloud, Leonard Crow Dog, and Others*. New York: Pantheon.

Garland, Sherry. (1993). *The Lotus Seed*. San Diego, CA: Harcourt Brace Jovanovich. (picture book)

Hamilton, Virginia, reteller. (1985). *The People Could Fly: American Black Folktales*. New York: Knopf.

Highwater, Jamake. (1984). *Legend Days*. New York: Harper and Row.

Hirschfelder, Arlene, and Beverly Singer. (1992). *Rising Voices: Writings of Young Native Americans*. New York: Charles Scribner's Sons.

Jagendorf, M.A. and R.S. Boggs. (1960). *The King of the Mountains: A Treasury of Latin American Folk Stories*. Vanguard.

Lester, Julius. (1969). *Black Folk Tales*. New York: Grove Press.

Mohr, Nicholasa. (revised edition, 1989). *El Bronx Remembered*. Houston, TX: Arte Publico Press.

Mohr, Nicholasa. (revised edition, 1991). *In Nueva York*. Houston, TX: Arte Publico Press.

Sadler, Catherine Edwards, reteller. (1985). *Heaven's Reward: Fairy Tales from China*. New York: Atheneum.

Sadler, Catherine Edwards, reteller. (1982). *Treasure Mountain: Folktales from Southern China*. New York: Atheneum.

Sanfield, Steve. (1989). *The Adventures of High John the Conqueror*. New York: Watts.

Sanfield, Steve. (1986). *A Natural Man: The True Story of John Henry*. Boston: David Godine.

Sneve, Virginia Driving Hawk, selector. (1989). *Dancing Tepees: Poems of American Indian Youth*. New York: Holiday House.

Uchida, Yoshiko. (1949). *The Dancing Kettle and Other Japanese Folk Tales*. San Diego, CA: Harcourt Brace.

Uchida, Yoshiko. (1955). *The Magic Listening Cap: More Japanese Tales from Japan*. San Diego, CA: Harcourt, Brace.

Uchida, Yoshiko. (1965). *The Sea of Gold and Other Tales of Japan*. Brookfield, VT: Gregg Press.

Yee, Paul. (1990). *Tales from Gold Mountain: Stories of the Chinese in the New World*. New York: Macmillan.

Yellow Robe, Rosebud. (1979). *Tonweya and the Eagles and Other Lakota Indian Tales*. New York: Dial.

Yep, Laurence, comp. (1993). *American Dragons: Twenty-Five Asian American Voices*. New York: HarperCollins.

Yep, Laurence. (1989). *The Rainbow People*. New York: Harper and Row.

Yep, Laurence, reteller. (1993). *The Shell Woman and the King - A Chinese Folktale* (with paintings by Yang Ming-Yi). New York: Dial. (picture book)

Yep, Laurence. (1991). *Tongues of Jade*. New York: Harper Collins.

APPENDIX
RESOURCES FOR TEACHERS

About Children's Literature

Bettelheim, Bruno. (1976). *The Uses of Enchantment: Meaning and Importance of Fairy Tales*. New York: Knopf.

Bulfinch, Thomas. (1958). *Age of Fable: Or, Stories of Gods and Heroes*. Bowie, MD: Heritage.

Butler, Francelia, and Richard Rotert, eds. (1986). *Triumphs of the Spirit in Children's Literature*. Hamden, CT: Library Professional Publications.

Campbell, Joseph. (1968). *The Hero With a Thousand Faces*. Princeton, NJ: Princeton University Press.

Carpenter, Humphrey, and Mari Prichard. (1984). *The Oxford Companion to Children's Literature*. New York: Oxford University Press.

Egoff, Sheila. (1981). *Thursday's Child: Trends and Patterns in Contemporary Children's Literature*. Chicago, IL: ALA.

Frye, Northrup. (1964). *The Educated Imagination*. Bloomington, IN: Indiana University Press.

Harris, Violet, editor. (1992). *Teaching Multicultural Literature in Grades K-8*. Norwood, MA: Christopher-Gordon.

Harrison, Barbara, and Gregory Maguire, eds. (1987). *Innocence and Experience: Essays and Conversations about Children's Literature*. New York: Lothrop, Lee & Shepard.

Hearne, Betsy, editor. (1993). *The Zena Sutherland Lectures, 1983-1992*. New York: Clarion Books.

Hunter, Mollie. (1976). *Talent is Not Enough*. New York: Harper and Row.

LeGuin, Ursula. (1979). *The Language of the Night: Essays on Fantasy and Science Fiction*. New York: Putnam.

Lukens, Rebecca. (1990). *A Critical Handbook of Children's Literature*, 4th edition. Scott, Glenview, IL: Foresman.

Paterson, Katherine. (1981). *Gates of Excellence: On Reading and Writing Books for Children*. New York: Elsevier/Nelson.

Paterson, Katherine. (1988). *The Spying Heart: More Thoughts on Reading and Writing Books for Children*. New York: Dutton/Lodestar.

Propp, Vladimir. (1968). *Morphology of the Folktale.* Austin, TX: University of Texas Press.

Sims, Rudine. (1983). *Shadow and Substance: Afro-American Experience in Contemporary Children's Fiction.* Urbana, IL: NCTE.

Slapin, Beverly, and Doris Seale. (1992). *Through Indian Eyes: The Native Experience in Books for Children.* Philadelphia, PA: New Society Publishers.

Smith, Lillian. (1967). *The Unreluctant Years.* New York: Viking.

Thompson, Stith. (1977). *The Folktale.* Berkeley, CA: University of California Press.

Thompson, Stith. (1955-1958). *Motif Index of Folk-Literature* (six volumes). Bloomington, IN: Indiana University Press.

Yolen, Jane. (1981). *Touch Magic: Fantasy, Faerie and Folklore in the Literature of Childhood.* New York: Philomel.

Zipes, Jack. (1983). *Fairy Tales and the Art of Subversion.* Portsmouth, NH: Heinemann.

Periodicals

The Booklist. ALA, Chicago, IL.

Book Links. American Library Association, Chicago, IL.

Book Review Digest. H.W. Wilson Co., New York, N.Y.

The Bulletin of the Center for Children's Books. University of Chicago Press, Chicago, IL.

Children's Literature in Education. Agathon Press, New York, N.Y.

English Journal. NCTE, Urbana, IL.

Horn Book Magazine. Horn Book, Inc., Boston, MA.

Interracial Books for Children Bulletin. Council on Interracial Books for Children, New York, N.Y.

Language Arts. NCTE, Urbana, IL.

The Lion and the Unicorn. Johns Hopkins University Press, Baltimore, MD.

The New Advocate. Christopher-Gordon, Norwood, MA.

Phaedrus: An International Annual of Children's Literature Research. Farleigh Dickinson University, Madison, NJ.

School Library Journal. R.R. Bowker, Philadelphia, PA.

Wilson Library Bulletin. The H.W. Wilson Co., New York, N.Y.

Literary Experiences in the Classroom: Reading-Dialogue-Writing

Andrasick, Kathleen D. (1990). *Opening Texts: Using Writing to Teach Literature,* Portsmouth, NH: Heinemann.

Atwell, Nancie. (1989). *Coming to Know: Writing to Learn in the Intermediate Grades.* Portsmouth, NH: Heinemann.

Atwell, Nancie. (1987). *In the Middle: Writing, Reading, and Learning with Adolescents.* Portsmouth, NH: Boynton/Cook/Heinemann.

Bauer, Marion Dane. (1992). *What's Your Story? A Young Person's Guide to Writing Fiction.* New York: Clarion.

Benedict, Susan, and Lenore Carlisle, eds. (1992). *Beyond Words: Picture Books for Older Readers and Writers.* Portsmouth, NH: Heinemann.

Blatt, Gloria, ed. (1993). *Once Upon A Folktale: Capturing the Folklore Process with Children.* New York: Teachers College Press.

Bosma, Bette. (1987). *Fairy Tales, Fables, Legends, and Myths: Using Folk Literature in Your Classroom.* New York: Teachers College Press.

Calkins, Lucy McCormick. (1986). *The Art of Teaching Writing.* Portsmouth, NH: Heinemann.

Fulwiler, Toby, ed. (1987). *The Journal Book.* Portsmouth, NH: Heinemann.

Gallo, Donald, ed. (1992). *Authors' Insights: Turning Teenagers into Readers and Writers.* Portsmouth, NH: Boynton/Cook.

Graves, Donald. (1989). *Experiment with Fiction.* Portsmouth, NH: Heinemann.

Graves, Donald. (1989). *Investigate Nonfiction.* Portsmouth, NH: Heinemann.

Hansen, Jane. (1987). *When Writers Read.* Portsmouth, NH: Heinemann.

Harste, Jerome, Kathy Short, and Carolyn Burke. (1988). *Creating Classrooms for Authors: The Reading-Writing Connection.* Portsmouth, NH: Heinemann.

Harwayne, Shelley. (1992). *Lasting Impressions: Weaving Literature into the Writing Workshop.* Portsmouth, NH: Heinemann.

Holland, Kathleen, Rachel Hungerford, and Shirley Ernst, eds. (1993). *Journeying: Children Responding to Literature.* Portsmouth, NH: Heinemann.

Huck, Charlotte, Susan Hepler, and Janet Hickman. (1993). *Children's Literature in the Elementary School,* 5th edition. San Diego, CA: Harcourt Brace Jovanovich.

Jensen, Julie, and Nancy Roser, editors. (1993). *Adventuring With Books: A Booklist for Pre-K-Grade 6* (10th editition). Urbana, IL: NCTE.

Langer, Judith, ed. (1992). *Literature Instruction: A Focus on Student Response.* Urbana, IL: NCTE.

Langer, Judith, and M. Trika Smith-Burke, eds. (1982). *Reader Meets Author/ Bridging the Gap — A Psycholinguistic and Sociolinguistic Perspective.* IRA.

Monseau, Virginia, and Gary Salvner, eds. (1992). *Reading Their World: The Young Adult Novel in the Classroom.* Portsmouth, NH: Boynton/Cook.

Moss, Joy. (1990). *Focus on Literature: A Context for Literacy Learning.* Katonah, NY: Richard C. Owen.

Moss, Joy F. (1984). *Focus Units in Literature: A Handbook for Elementary School Teachers.* Urbana, IL: NCTE.

Nelms, Ben F. (1988). *Literature in the Classroom: Readers, Texts, and Contexts.* Urbana, IL: NCTE.

Norton, Donna. (1992). *The Impact of Literature-Based Reading.* Columbus, OH: Merrill.

Rudman, Masha Kabakow, editor. (1992). *Children's Literature: Resource for the Classroom,* 2nd edition. Norwood, MA: Christopher-Gordon.

Shanahan, Timothy, ed. (1990). *Reading and Writing Together: New Perspectives for the Classroom.* Norwood, MA: Christopher-Gordon.

Sloan, Glenna Davis. (1991). *The Child As Critic: Teaching Literature in Elementary and Middle Schools.* New York: Teachers College Press.

Temple, Charles, and Patrick Collins, eds. (1992). *Stories and Readers: New Perspectives on Literature in the Elementary Classroom.* Norwood, MA: Christopher-Gordon.

Tunnell, Michael, and Richard Ammon, eds. (1993). *The Story of Ourselves: Teaching History Through Children's Literature.* Portsmouth, NH: Heinemann.

Webb, C. Anne, editor. (1993). *Your Reading: A Booklist for Junior High and Middle School* (9th edition). Urbana, IL: NCTE.

Wilde, Jack. (1993). *A Door Opens: Writing in Fifth Grade.* Portsmouth, NH: Heinemann.

Wood, Karen, ed. (1992). *Exploring Literature in the Classroom: Content and Methods.* Norwood, MA: Christopher-Gordon.

Zarnowski, Myra. (1990). *Learning About Biographies: A Reading-and-Writing Approach for Children.* URBANA, IL: NCTE and NCSS.

ABOUT THE AUTHOR

JOY F. MOSS

As a child I was introduced to a rich literary heritage, and as a parent, grandparent, and teacher I have had the opportunity to share this legacy with the next generation.

After several years as a classroom teacher, I became the language arts specialist for the elementary division of a private school in Rochester, New York. In this position as a cross-grade teacher, I introduced a literature program into the school curriculum twenty years ago and have been teaching literature to children ever since. The literary-literacy experiences I have developed for and with my students have served as the basis for my professional writing over the years.

In addition to my work with children, I have been actively involved as a teacher educator. Since 1970 I have taught courses at the University of Rochester Graduate School of Education where I have an appointment as Adjunct Associate Professor. During this time I have also lectured and consulted at schools in the Rochester area, conducted a variety of inservice courses and workshops, and have presented at numerous local and regional conferences. In my work as teacher educator, I have focussed on the connections between literature and literacy learning and the translation of research and theory into classroom practice.

I was co-founder of the first Teacher Center in the Rochester area and, from 1973-1979, I was the Director of the Community Teacher Center which served the educational community in and around Rochester prior to the establishment of teacher centers in individual school districts.

My ultimate goal, as a teacher of young learners and of students of learning, is to bring literature, directly and indirectly, into the lives of children. To this end, I have been exploring ways to create literary experiences in the classroom, to build a literary context for literacy learning, and to promote both children's growth as readers and writers and a love of literature which will last a lifetime. I have drawn from my twenty years of exploration in theory and practice to write numerous articles for professional journals and three books, *Focus Units in Literature* (NCTE, 1984), *Focus on Literature* (Richard Owen, Publishers, 1990), and this one, *Using Literature in the Middle Grades.*

I did my undergraduate work at Wellesley College in Massachusetts and my graduate work at the University of Rochester. My husband, Dr. Arthur J. Moss, and I live in Rochester, NY. Our three children are all married and involved in their chosen professions. Our four grandchildren love books.

INDEX

Author Index

Title Index